Merry Chris~

with all my love

— Mom

NAPOLEON
MAN OF WAR, MAN OF PEACE

By the same author

Delacroix
Napoleon and his Artists

NAPOLEON

MAN OF WAR
MAN OF PEACE

TIMOTHY WILSON-SMITH

CARROLL & GRAF PUBLISHERS
New York

For Pam
In memory of HWS and ME

Carroll & Graf Publishers
An imprint of Avalon Publishing Group, Inc.
161 William Street
NY 10038-2607
www.carrollandgraf.com

First published in the UK by Constable,
an imprint of Constable & Robinson Ltd 2002

First Carroll & Graf edition 2002

ISBN 0-7867-1089-6

Printed and bound in the EU

CONTENTS

ILLUSTRATIONS

——⟫●⟪——

Napoleon as First Consul (*Ingres*)
Le Sacre (*David*)
Napoleon in his Study (*David*)
The Plumb-Pudding in Danger (*Gillray*)
Napoleon with Las Cases' son
Napoleon's tomb as Les Invalides

ACKNOWLEDGEMENTS

The writing of this book was helped by the facilities of libraries in Eton College and at Cambridge University and by use of the internet, often for the purpose of finding books. The book is cast in the shape that it has as a result of the constructive suggestions of my agent Laura Longrigg and of Ben Glazebrook at Constable & Robinson. All mistakes and omissions in it are my fault.

It is dedicated to my wife, who was taught *au couvent* that Napoleon was first among Frenchmen, and to the memory of two men. One, my father, Sir Henry Wilson-Smith, first took me to Paris and from his knowledge of the workings of the Third and Fourth Republics as a British civil servant was the first person to tell me that civil servants run France. The other, Marcel Eve, *pilote de la Compagnie du canal de Suez*, my wife's *grand-père*, lived to enjoy the sense of purpose that returned to France with the creation of the Fifth Republic. The two never met, but I trust that in the heavenly Champs-Elysées they enjoy an entente cordiale.

CHRONOLOGY

DATES	MILITARY AND POLITICAL EVENTS	WORKS OF ART AND LITERATURE
1789	14 July: Fall of the Bastille 6 October: Louis XVI to Paris	
1790	Reorganization of France into departments Civil Constitution of the Clergy	
1792	August: fall of the monarchy Proclamation of the republic Battles of Valmy and Jemappes	
1793	Louis XVI (Capet) executed Napoleon takes part in the recapture of Toulon	
1794	Fall of Robespierre Napoleon in prison	
1795	Napoleon's 'whiff of grapeshot' helps stabilize Directory	

1796	Napoleon married Joséphine (Rose) de Beauharnais First Italian campaign	Gros, *Bonaparte at Arcole*
1797	First Italian campaign	
1798	Napoleon in Egypt	Institute of Egypt
1799	Napoleon in Egypt Brumaire coup d'état: Napoleon First Consul	Discovery of Rosetta stone
1800	Establishment of prefectorial system Second Italian campaign: Battle of Marengo	
1801	Treaty of Lunéville with Austria	David's *Bonaparte crossing the St Bernard*
1802	Peace of Amiens with Britain Concordat with the Papacy Napoleon First Consul for Life	Denon, *Voyage dans la Basse et la Haute Egypte*
1803		Creation of the Napoleonic Institute
1804	Napoleon Emperor	
1805	Battles of Trafalgar and Austerlitz	
1806	Battle of Jena-Auerstädt	Gillray, *The Plumb-Pudding In Danger* Ingres, *Napoleon on His Throne* Arc de Triomphe commissioned
1807	Battles of Eylau and Friedland Treaty of Tilsit	David, *Le Sacre de Joséphine* Boilly, *A Game of Billiards*
1808		Gros, *Battle of Eylau*
1809	Battle of Wagram	Publication of *Description de l'Egypte* begins

1810	Marriage of Napoleon and Archduchess Marie-Louise	
1811	Birth of Napoleon (II), King of Rome	
1812	Russian campaign	David, *Napoleon in His Study* Géricault, *Charging Chasseur*
1813	Battle of Leipzig	
1814	Campaign of France	Géricault, *The Wounded Cuirassier*
	Napoleon surrenders at Fontainebleau First Bourbon Restoration	David, *Leonidas at Thermopylae* Chateaubriand, *De Buonaparte, Des Bourbons*
	Preliminary meeting in London Start of Congress of Vienna	Lawrence, *Blücher*
1815	Imperial Constitution restored with Acte Additionnel Battle of Waterloo Second Bourbon Restoration End of Congress of Vienna	
1816	Napoleon at Longwood (until 1821)	
1818	Congress of Aix-la-Chapelle	
1821	Death of Napoleon	
1822	Suicide of Castlereagh Congress of Aix-la-Chapelle	Vernet, *The Tomb of Napoleon*
1823		Las Cases, *Le Mémorial de Ste-Hélène* (further editions 1824, 1830–32, 1835 and 1840)
1824	Charles X king	Champollion, *Précis du système hiéroglyphe*

1828		Publication of first complete edition of *Description de l'Egypte*
1830	July Revolution: Louis-Philippe King of the French	
1831	Louis-Napoleon in anti-papal rising; death of his elder brother	
1832	Death of Napoleon II	
1836	Failed coup of Louis-Napoleon	Arc de Triomphe finished
1839	Start of Syrian crisis	Louis-Napoleon, *Les Idées Napoléoniennes*
1840	Funeral of Napoleon Failed coup of Louis-Napoleon: trial, imprisonment	
1842		Visconti started work on Invalides crypt for Tomb of Napoleon
1846	Escape of Louis-Napoleon	
1848	February Revolution: Second Republic December: Louis-Napoleon President	
1851	2 December: coup d'état Plebiscite	
1852	2 December: Second Empire Plebiscite	

PREFACE

—⟶∘⟵—

Every year yet more new books are written on Napoleon and some old ones reprinted, and for some readers there is no need to study any other subject. The life of Napoleon affected almost every country in Europe, at least indirectly, as in the case of Norway, Sweden and Finland. His battles have been enough to keep military historians, professional and amateur, pleasantly occupied for many years. His doings were recorded in thousands of collections of letters and memoirs as well as millions of official documents. The ideal expert on Napoleon will be polyglot in linguistic skills and protean in the ability to take on different shapes as innumerable kinds of historian.

Luckily, the subject of Napoleon is not circumscribed by the limitations of those who write about him, whether imaginatively, like Leo Tolstoy or with precise erudition like a scholar educated in the quantitative methods of the Annales school in France. It seems to be a general rule that in every generation there will be new popular histories and biographies – recently in England there have appeared well-researched and readable works by Alastair Horne and Frank McLynn – alongside the steady production of the systematic articles that are held to justify a life devoted to learning. In universities, the time of the French Revolution, dated from 1787 or 1789 and to 1794 or 1799, remains more familiar than the longer period from 1799 to 1814 or 1815, when Napoleon ruled, in much the same way as the focus on the so-called English revolution illumines the decade before the death of Charles I rather than the decade after, when Cromwell became monarch of the British Isles. Violent change holds more attractions for mild-mannered professors than an age when there was a move to stability, but then, just as the firm hand of Cromwell seemed hard to royalists, Anglicans, Scots and above all the Irish, so Napoleon's peace within France meant devastating war for large areas of the Continent outside France and a battle lasting almost fifteen years at sea with England, occasionally by ships of the line and, more frequently, by merchant vessels, blockading boats and commerce raiders.

Clearly, the figure of Napoleon dominates narratives and discussions of the early nineteenth century. That was what he would have wanted. He had little doubt that he was an extraordinary man, and he knew how to impress his view of himself on his contemporaries. But just as he found the past a fascinating topic, so he also had an eye for the future. As a schoolboy, in his youth at the Ecole Militaire and in young adulthood as a part-time soldier he was a keen student of the doings of great men – like many of his generation he was immersed in Plutarch's *Lives* and he was instinctively drawn to a Plutarchian cult of able soldiers like Alexander the Great, Hannibal, Julius Caesar and Charlemagne. That was the sort of person he intended to be. It was also the sort of person he wanted to appear to be, and this meant that from early on in his career he devoted himself to influencing the opinions of others about himself. Initially, this involved the cultivation of men with power: Saliceti, a fellow Corsican who ran local politics first in Corsica then in the south of France; Augustin Robespierre, younger brother of Maximilien; Paul Barras, the most astute of the five Directors of the republic in the late 1790s. It was only as a figurehead that Napoleon carried out a coup d'état in the foggy month of 1799 called Brumaire, but he soon demonstrated in the aftermath that he was the figure at the head. Once made First Consul, he was in a position to use the propaganda resources of the French state to his own advantage, so that he convinced the majority of his fellow countrymen that he should be Consul for Life and later Emperor of the French. If his actions spoke louder than his words, that was because the words gave a favourable account of the actions, through government newspapers he controlled and army bulletins he drafted; and if history needed revising, he would modify the facts. A cast of mind developed as a young man became his habit of mind, and his versions of events became ever more flattering to his *amour-propre*.

Fifty years ago an American historian, Robert Holtman, wrote a book on Napoleonic propaganda. Since then, more information has confirmed the view that Napoleon was a spin doctor of genius *avant la lettre*, long before in exile on St Helena he could devote himself wholly to the task of spinning; and yet there is this difference between Napoleon and his modern successors: unlike them, he had found in himself a magnificent theme, for he either was a great man or could be a great man. During his own lifetime he appeared to be by far the most remarkable Frenchman or European of the time, so that his many achievements were bound to be measured by the highest standards of military, political, diplomatic, administrative and cultural capacity. Napoleon let many of his more intelligent contemporaries down, as Coleridge was disillusioned after the invasion of Switzerland, Chateaubriand after the execution of the Bourbon Duc d'Enghien, Beethoven after the proclamation of the Empire. For every such hostile witness, however, there was a witness converted from a sceptic into a hero-worshipper, like Jacques-Louis David, or won over to Napoleon's view of his role, like the ex-royalist Comte de Las Cases. He was an obsession both while he lived and when he died, the original Napoleon complex.

To prove this with reference to original literary sources would be a labour so life-consuming that I chose to abandon it before I started; and I quote at some length from just two sources that affected his reputation, Chateaubriand's derogatory pamphlet *De Buonaparte, Des Bourbons* and the laudatory *Le Mémorial de Ste-Hélène*. There is, I think, a simpler way to illustrate an argument, and that is by illustration. The received history of French art in the nineteenth century proceeds via David, Gros and Ingres, sometime Napoleonic artists, to Géricault (born in 1791), Delacroix (born in 1798), Courbet (born in 1819), Impressionists and Post-Impressionists including Gauguin (born in 1848), but then Horace Vernet (born in 1789), Delaroche (born in 1797), Meissonnier (born in 1815) and Detaille (born in 1848) were more widely admired and all were at some stage in their lives preoccupied by Napoleonic subjects – they were prime movers in forming the Napoleonic legend in the eyes of their spectators. Some of their paintings are familiar because being works on historical subjects they are treated as if they were contemporary comments on Napoleon's reign, rather than exemplars of a cult prevalent long after the events they depict. Other pictures mentioned take a less adulatory view, Boilly's by reason of his cheery temperament, the prints of Gillray, one anti-Bonapartist artist, by reason of their biting satire, the portraits of Lawrence, another one, by glorifying Napoleon's enemies.

Paris itself contains the most celebrated of Napoleonic images, from the Arc du Carrousel that once stood before his Tuileries palace or the column in Place Vendôme to the Arc de Triomphe at the top of the Champs-Elysées or, not far from the Ecole Militaire where he studied, under the dome of the church of Louis XIV's Les Invalides, to the tomb where his body rests. Certain buildings, like Le Vau's Collège des Quatre Nations and some eighteenth-century hôtels, were adapted to Napoleonic uses that they still retain. The Arc de Triomphe fulfils a Napoleonic function but not its Napoleonic design; and his tomb, lying beneath the gilded dome of Louis XIV's Invalides church, is a ponderous reminder that his work continued the labours of the Sun King; Paris, though not largely his creation, is the sort of imperial capital he planned. When I first saw it in 1950, it was a war-weary city, beautiful under its drabness, grand and impoverished. The re-emergence of Paris has been a sign of the re-emergence of France and of a new European order grounded in a French style of government that is recognizably a Napoleonic derivative. The memory of Napoleon still matters today.

The focus of interest, as a glance at the catalogues of most libraries or most publishers will confirm, remains Napoleon's military campaigns; and without his amazing series of victories and his even more spectacular defeats, he would never have achieved so much fame then or now. The trajectory of his career resembles that of Hannibal, with whom he liked to compare himself – he was thinking of the crossing of the Alps – and with whom he was implicitly compared by the painter William Turner. Had he died early in 1812, on the eve of the invasion of Russia, he might have seemed more like Alexander the Great, pining that there were still lands to conquer. As the literate commentator on his own achievements, he has more in common with Julius Caesar; and there are historians now who maintain that like Caesar he was assassinated, in his case slowly and with poison. A final precursor would seem to be Charlemagne, who also took an army into Italy, who came to terms with the Pope and whose empire covered much the same area of Europe as Napoleon's by the end of 1806.

Reference to Julius Caesar and Charlemagne is a reminder that Napoleon, too, was not just a general. If his art of war directly inspired Confederate leaders like Lee and Jackson in the American Civil War and has analogies with the style of von Moltke (in the Prussian wars of 1866 and 1870–71), of the German blitzkrieg and of the Israeli assaults in 1967, then that will explain why he is still studied at military academies today. With equally astonishing speed and effectiveness, he altered the way in which France and several parts of Europe were governed; and anyone familiar with the workings of the modern French state or the European Union will be aware of the abiding impact of Napoleon. But for the needs of war he might not have bothered to decide how countries, above all his own, could live in time of peace, yet when the drums were finally muffled, the troops paid off and the task of rebuilding shattered cities and replanting devastated fields could begin, he had provided a method of running a country that was of lasting utility. Democracy has made his administrative system a little less dictatorial, pluralism of belief has rendered his concordat with the Papacy not imaginative enough, the rights of workers and women have forced his code to be more flexible, it has taken two centuries to open all careers to every talent and to give France the technocratic leadership that he hoped for. Neither France nor Europe can any longer be defined in terms that he set, but, just as in the Near East, so in France and in Europe the modern world begins with him.

PART I

MAN OF WAR

1

ON TOP OF THE MOUNTAINS

No picture of Napoleon is so familiar as that by David in which the young general sits securely on a rearing horse while crossing the Alps on his way to the Battle of Marengo (1800). As a work of art it does not rank high in David's *oeuvre*. Napoleon did not sit for it, it lacks the dash of his *Count Potocki on Horseback* (an earlier equestrian portrait), it took its pose from a statue of Peter the Great and it was commissioned by King Charles IV of Spain to please a dangerous ally. It also does not tell the truth, for Napoleon crossed the Alps on an ambling mule – he was never a fine horseman – and the weather was dull, not tempestuous.

There is, however, an overt sense of the importance of the subject. The young general of David's picture was wending his way over the Alps by the St Bernard Pass en route for the Battle of Marengo. In this guise Napoleon figures on countless book covers and in documentary films – the representation is easily the most familiar way in which he is remembered. A precisian might note that this is regrettable. As First Consul, Napoleon did not bother to pose for David – he had more pressing, political concerns to attend to – and all the artist had to go on, other than his memory for a personality, were his subject's hat and cloak, in which David clothed his eldest son. David then seated his pupil François Gérard on a ladder, which helped with the angle at which the horseman would be seen, and Napoleon was gracious enough to lend his favourite grey, for he did not wish to admit that he had ridden across the Alps on that dingy mule.

The painting was not originally, it seems, Napoleon's idea, but was requested by King Charles IV of Spain, whose recent portraits by Goya had revealed him as the ugliest monarch in the whole of Europe. What Charles lacked in looks, he compensated for in the quality of the art he owned. He had equestrian paintings of his Habsburg ancestors, of Philip IV by Velázquez and Charles V by Titian; and David knew from his student days in Rome the antique sculpture that had inspired both works, the bronze of Marcus Aurelius on horseback which Michelangelo had placed on the Capitoline Hill. It was also in Italy, in Naples, that David liked to give the impression that he had met the impulsive Polish aristocrat, Count Potocki, a brilliant rider. In a late baroque masterpiece largely created in Paris, where David could refer to many paintings by Rubens, the Count indicates his skilful control by holding the reins with just one gloved hand. Twenty years before he set out to glorify the head of the French state, David revelled in the panache with which a handsome nobleman bestrides a gilded mount. The First Consul was never so well at ease on a horse, yet David, then unaffected in his simple admiration of Napoleon, remained convinced that his subject cut a heroic figure. When the painter first set eyes on the general, at that moment fresh from his first campaign in northern Italy, he had sketched his head, as if glancing at Augustus reborn. 'Oh, my friends,' he told his pupils after scrutinizing Napoleon during a sitting, 'what a beautiful head he has! Like the antique, it's pure, it's great, it's beautiful! . . . He's a man to whom people in ancient times would have raised altars. Yes, my friends, yes, my dear friends, Bonaparte is my hero!'[1]

The painting is Napoleonic in its claims of the importance of its theme. Even if the pose derives from Falconet's statue of Peter the Great (a sculpture in St Petersburg), there is no suggestion of kinship between Tsar and adventurer, if only because while the Russian was muscular and huge, the Corsican was small and sickly. Instead, words at the front left on the rocks make Napoleon the successor to two leaders who had made a similar journey before him: Hannibal and Charlemagne. From schoolday reading, Napoleon remembered Livy's account of how Hannibal had taken elephants over the mountain passes and then annihilated the Roman troops at Cannae. He also must have known how Charlemagne invaded Italy to save the Pope from the Lombards. Now he in his turn had emulated the effrontery of the Carthaginian and the civilizing mission of the Frank. In his lifetime he showed a special concern for those who had been with him at Marengo and a special concern that his own version of Marengo should be the story that they, too, recalled.

It was by the mountain ranges and in the hills of northern Italy that he had begun his march to greatness.

The Revolution had come just at the right moment to give him a chance to come to high command at a young age. Just born French in 1769 – Corsica had been annexed from Genoa the year before – he was also lucky to be a member of his nation's minor nobility, apt therefore for the patronage of the French governor, the Comte de Marbeuf, who followed up an affair or a flirtation with Napoleon's mother, the lovely Letizia Buonaparte, by offering to fund Joseph, her eldest son, to train as a priest and Napoleon, the second, as a soldier. At Autun, where Marbeuf's nephew was bishop, the boys learned French; and from there in 1779 Napoleon was sent for five years to a military school at Brienne in Champagne. At Brienne he learned to live like a Spartan; unyielding, he was a loner who could win the respect but not the affection of his contemporaries; he was always to be better with his inferiors, like the peasant children with whom he had played at home near Ajaccio; he found it easier to be commended by his teachers, for, although socially awkward, he was also industrious, a good mathematician and he read continuously. He went on to the Ecole Militaire in Paris, just by the Champ-de-Mars, where the surroundings were luxurious after Brienne and his fellow students came from much grander backgrounds. They had connections for an agreeable career in the army that he lacked. Had the *ancien régime* survived into the 1790s, Napoleon might have remained an obscure member of a provincial regiment. In 1785 this must have seemed likely when he was dispatched for grounding as an officer to the little town of Valence, where he found he had too little to do. He took to writing, he carried on with his rapid, encyclopaedic reading and he dreamed of becoming a political force in Corsica.

In Corsica, factions, then as now, were divided into two main groups: one pro-French, the other for independence. The Buonaparte family had been on the run from victorious French troops when Letizia was expecting Napoleon, but, by the time the parents had to decide how best to educate the older boys, the family saw the advantages of being pro-French. It was as a result of the efforts of Napoleon's father Carlo, which were successful, to prove the family's aristocratic status to the court of Versailles that Napoleon could go to Brienne. If in Corsica the Buonaparti were people of consequence, in France they were of not much more interest than local bandits (the behaviour of some of Napoleon's siblings later proved to be only too similar to that of members of a clan of Mafiosi). In childhood the French connection had helped Napoleon: as a young adult he thought of repudiating it. When his father died of cancer, he was the only member of the family who had a salary, however small, for Joseph had to abandon his studies, by now in the law, to take charge of family affairs at home; and the hardships the family endured encouraged Napoleon to deepen his knowledge of his native island. He made repeated visits home, originally permitted him on something like compassionate grounds – before 1789 few superiors queried an officer's need for leave – and it was only gradually that his loyalties shifted from friendship with Paoli, who was a Corsican nationalist, conservative and devout, to an alliance with Saliceti, who believed in the one, indivisible, lay republic. It was not until 1793 that Napoleon abandoned Corsica, originally as a refugee from the Paolistas, ultimately because he tied his family's fortune to that of France – the alternative, as Paoli quickly found out, was that to be free of the French was to accept the domination of the English. The Corsican years were years of apprenticeship for Napoleon: on a small stage he had political and military experience that trained him in the art of self-promotion. In 1790, while stranded by storms, he lobbied for Joseph to be elected to the town council of Ajaccio and made himself a leading member of the Ajaccio Jacobin Club. He abducted an election commissioner who would favour an opponent and he used a family legacy to bribe his way to being elected a lieutenant-colonel of the Corsican volunteers in March 1791. In 1792 he showed himself ruthless in his attempts to starve out the royalist commander from the citadel of Ajaccio, and in 1793 he led an expeditionary force that was supposed to take Sardinia – it foundered against the rocks of an outlying island when some sailors, Paolistas Napoleon thought, mutinied. Napoleon's interventions in Corsica were frustrating and frustrated, but they had taught him a lot about what not to do. All the while he had made frequent trips to his regiment in France, to the War Ministry in

Paris if need be, and had become an expert in the art of manipulation. He always seemed to be excused his independent style of action. He also became a student of current events. He watched, incredulous, as on 10 August 1792 a Paris crowd stormed the gates of the Tuileries palace and massacred the Swiss Guard. Napoleon was contemptuous of Louis XVI, for he would have known how to cope with a mob; and he was to prove it.

Between 1785 and 1793 Napoleon had dealt with riots and street fights, but he had not yet been on a campaign, other than the abortive trip to Sardinia. He had, however, continued with his reading. He was an artillery man who kept up to date with recent military thinking. It was his modernity that would give him the chance to shine.

In the last war before he had been born, France had been humiliated by its enemies, Britain and Prussia. In Europe, the so-called Seven Years War had been complemented by the Nine Years 'French and Indian' War in America and a struggle between the French and English commercial companies that vied for supremacy in India. In the colonial wars, the French and their native allies were decisively routed by the British, so that Canada became one of the dominions of George III and Bengal fell to the East India Company. On the continent the situation was even worse. Three powerful women – Maria Theresa, Queen of Hungary and by marriage the Holy Roman Empress, Tsarina Elizabeth of Russia and Madame de Pompadour, *maîtresse en titre* of Louis XV – all had their reasons for loathing Frederick II, King of Prussia; and they knew that the forces of Austria, Russia and France, if combined, far outnumbered his. But these armies proved incapable of crushing him, and even the British army, intervening on Prussia's side, beat the French at Minden – so much had changed since the previous European war, in the 1740s, had ended with a series of victories in the Netherlands for the Maréchal de Saxe, the French commander.

France, the most populous country on the Continent and naturally the most powerful, had been weak and disorganized. The protégé of La Pompadour, the Duc de Choiseul, was determined that France should have its revenge. Though she died and he was dismissed before the hour of vengeance had come, the new sense of urgency in the reform of France's armed forces and new kinds of military thinking changed the course of France's fortunes in the final quarter of the century. By aiding American rebels in their fight for independence, France hastened the end of British control of its Continental Colonies. It was Napoleon who used the new military machine to tip the Continental balance of power by defeats of Austria, Prussia and Russia. Only the lack of an adequate navy was to prevent the defeat of Britain.

Choiseul, who affected Napoleon's life directly by arranging the purchase of Corsica, affected it indirectly by his army reforms. He set up military schools like Brienne to feed into the Ecole Militaire (a pet project of the Marquise de Pompadour), and his protégé Gribeauval organized the artillery into a Corps Royal of six regiments. Though he was a nobleman, Choiseul had no doubts about the ineptitude of some of his class, so the War Ministry offered to buy many out of the service; and he gave the ministry more power over recruitment and equipment and arms and munitions factories. It was on Gribeauval's artillery pieces that Napoleon was trained. These guns, developed between 1765 and 1774, were 12-, 8-, 6- and 4-pounders, plus 6- and 8-inch howitzers – lighter by one-third than the cannon of any rival country and therefore more manoeuvrable. The French did not always have the most modern equipment. From 1777 their infantrymen had Charleville muskets, while the Prussians and later the British had begun to experiment with rifles. The decoration on horsemen's sabres changed; the weapon stayed the same.

What changed the nature of the French army was the Revolution. A professional army before, afterwards it became a national army. Before, at least half its numbers consisted of mercenaries, and its officer corps was largely aristocratic. Before, it had been the largest army in Europe, as befitted the most populous country. Now, after the revolutionaries had called for a *levée en masse*, it grew to roughly 800,000 troops, four times the size of the royal army; and initially it was all French. Much of the old officer class disappeared, and in the new army careers were open to anyone competent from any class. Augereau was a stonemason's son, Masséna a former cabin boy and supposedly a retired smuggler, Murat and Ney had begun as troopers, yet of gentle birth were Berthier, a geographical engineer long before he was Napoleon's chief of staff, and Poniatowski, a Polish prince who had served as an officer in the Austrian army. What was required of men who rose through the ranks to be Napoleon's marshals was energy and loyalty. Compared with Austrian, Prussian, Russian and British generals, they were often young, so it is worth noting that Wellington and Napoleon were of an age.

There was also a change in the military style of the new French armies. Decorous eighteenth-century soldiers looked as though they were on a parade ground while they manoeuvred for position, but what made them slow was the care their leaders took to prepare for war. This meant that long hours were spent provisioning troops for a march and a host of camp followers was laid on to transport food and look after the comforts of the soldiers. To avoid unnecessary loss of life was paramount; generals preferred to force opponents to retreat by getting them out of position rather than destroying them; as gentlemen they had a code of honour. It was poor form to devastate the countryside, as Louis xiv's forces had done in the Rhenish Palatinate in 1688, if only because it was possible that in peace negotiations, as rulers swapped a piece of territory they had inherited for one they would like, the land that was ruined might pass to the king or prince or duke whose armies had ruined it. At the end of the American Civil War, General Sherman, who had brutally marched through Georgia, said that war was hell. In the eighteenth century it was meant to be no worse than purgatorial.

Napoleon did not understand such warfare. In the long, boring hours while he was posted to the artillery school at Auxonne in 1788–9, through his commander, General du Teil, he studied the ideas of the general's brother, the Chevalier de Beaumont du Teil, expounded in *The Use of the New Artillery in Campaigns* (1778). Gribeauval's light guns could be massed at critical points in a battle; artillery also should be used at the start of battles and moved quickly along the line. A similar emphasis on speed was found in the teaching of Count de Guibert in *General Essay on Tactics* (1772) and *Defence of the System of Modern War* (1778), where Napoleon found a maxim that has been credited to him: 'the war must feed the war', by which Guibert meant and Napoleon grasped that if much of the baggage train were to be jettisoned, soldiers should live off the land. In a treatise by Pierre Bourcet – *Principles of Mountain Warfare* (1780) – he learned how a rapid way of marching through hilly terrain was possible if troops divided on the march and were concentrated for the fight.

In 1759 Guibert and Bourcet had served under Marshal de Broglie, the first man to settle on the division as the unit of manoeuvre, which was standard practice in the whole army by 1780. In defence, Guibert was in favour of lines three ranks deep or a square, with gunners in front to protect the foot; and in attack he recommended a mixed order, partly column, partly line (whereas the British, for example, stuck rigidly to their thin red lines). The column provided weight and was the easiest formation for untrained troops to master, but it could be unwieldy and was more effective racing downhill than toiling uphill. The conscripts of the Revolution charged in column, but, well before Napoleon's Grande Armée was formed, generals had reverted to using both line and column or the mixed order.[2]

Napoleon's early ventures in and near Corsica had not shown him to be anything more than a tough gunner of no particular distinction. What gave him a chance to be noticed was his very failure on home territory. A ferocious attack on Paoli's good name in the Jacobin Club in Toulon by his troublesome brother Lucien had precipitated the rapid retreat of the Bonapartes to the mainland. They lost their ancestral houses, their fields and their vineyards. Meanwhile, Paoli appealed in the Corsican National Assembly for the help of the British fleet; on arrival in the area, one of its first actions was to sail into Toulon with detachments of British, Spanish and Neapolitan soldiers in support of a royalist coup against the Parisian Jacobins; and the impoverished Bonapartes had to flee again. At this point Napoleon was able to achieve the fame he longed for in *Le Souper de Beaucaire*, a dialogue between travellers in an inn that persuasively put the Jacobin case in the south. This most ambitious of his juvenile literary efforts so far was published with the help of Saliceti, Napoleon's second Corsican patron (after Paoli), when Napoleon had realized that his political career lay in France. Saliceti showed the pamphlet to Augustin Robespierre, the younger brother of the all-powerful Maximilien of the Committee of Public Safety, and young Augustin was impressed. Saliceti also found a job in the commissariat for Joseph Bonaparte and introduced Napoleon to General Carteaux, who was besieging Toulon and who was short of an artillery man. Reluctantly, Carteaux bowed to Saliceti, who had the authority of a political commissar over him, and soon regretted his decision, for Napoleon, who had noticed that the harbour in Toulon, shaped like a conch (in this like the harbour of Ajaccio), was vulnerable if only he could take Fort Eguilette on a high cliff above both the inner and the outer harbour. Carteaux saw the point, but worried over the risk of failure, so Napoleon appealed above him to Carnot, the member of the Committee of Public Safety who was a military expert, and urged that Carteaux should be fired. His wishes were granted, but even before Carnot's reply had come, Napoleon had convinced the new commander, Dugommier, that he was right. On 13 December Napoleon opened his bombardment, on 17 December the fort fell, on 18 December Hood, the British admiral, withdrew and on 22 December Napoleon was elevated to the rank of brigadier-general. The following spring, Augustin Robespierre asked him to take charge of planning an attack on northern Italy.

He was so much in favour with Robespierre's Jacobins that when the Robespierres fell he almost fell too. He was flung into gaol but released within a fortnight for maintaining that he was only a simple soldier; besides, Saliceti had changed sides in time to bring the Robespierres down and he had uses for his youthful general. Napoleon was again sent to join the army of Italy, again asked to attack Corsica – the British fleet frustrated him – and then brought back to Paris. He was offered a posting in the Vendée, now the centre of royalist resistance, and dared to turn it down. He could see no advantage to himself in butchering French peasants, so he refused and was demoted. Riled at the way he had been treated – many soldiers kept their ranks without doing a thing – he was lucky that he had acquired a new political ally in Barras, the most unscrupulous of those who had brought Robespierre down, for he had his rank restored and was given instead a job on the Topographical Bureau general staff. It was better than nothing, but, much as he loved maps, he was not satisfied.

What made his fortune were the needs of Barras. The first need arose in October 1795. The Convention had just drawn up the plan of a new constitution that would create a bourgeois republic run by five Directors and two assemblies. Royalists, beaten Jacobins and the Jacobins' downtrodden former allies, the Parisian working class called, from their lack of breeches, the *sansculottes*, combined to challenge the government in the way that had been normal since 1789, by a riot. Barras was asked to defend the Tuileries, so he summoned his pet general, who in turn asked a Gascon cavalry major, Joachim Murat, to bring him guns belonging to the National Guard. By dawn on 5 October Napoleon had his emplacements ready, chiefly in Rue de la Convention, the road that led from Rue St-Honoré to the palace gardens. In the afternoon, as the mob advanced, it was fired on at point-blank range. The carnage was horrific, the effect decisive and Barras became one of the five Directors.

Barras's second need was to slough off a royalist mistress of whom he was weary. Rose de Beauharnais, a Creole who had been a vicomtesse and whose husband had been guillotined, was just out of prison and the mother of two children, Eugène and Hortense. With extravagant and impeccable tastes and no income, she was searching for a protector and for a time found one in Barras. In the meantime, thanks to Barras, Napoleon was made General of the Army of the Interior, in effect the man responsible for order in Paris, and thereby gained an income of 48,000 francs a year; and that made him attractive to Rose. She went further when she decided that Napoleon was a better proposition than one of her previous lovers, Lazare Hoche, a general who had gone to the Vendée, had come back in triumph but had not been so rewarded as Napoleon for killing urban *sansculottes* instead of shoeless peasants. The affair with her admirer became over-intense, she was put out when asked to marry him and was relieved when this husband of hers left for Italy.

It is not certain, but at least probable, that Barras and Joséphine, as Rose had been renamed by Napoleon, together got Napoleon a post that would take him far away. He was to attempt the near-hopeless task of defeating the Sardinians and the Austrians in Italy.

His instructions were simple. He was to detach the Piedmontese-Sardinian army from those of Austria, eliminate the Piedmontese and then turn on the Austrians (Austrian Habsburgs were by tradition the most formidable enemies of Bourbon France and were to be persistent enemies of the new France). When he met his subordinates, Masséna, Augereau and Sérurier, soldiers with experience, he boasted of his acquaintance with Carnot and Barras and made clear he would harry them. But at first he allowed them some freedom, which they used with a skill he was careful not to report to the Directory. On St Helena he would invent a speech to his troops he had never spoken – 'Soldiers, you are naked, ill fed' – but he probably promised them loot, and his official communiqués and letters gave a clear message that they would be right to trust him. While Beaulieu, the Austrian commander, divided his forces, Augereau and Masséna drove the Piedmontese west to Ceva and north to Turin. At Cherasco, the King of Piedmont, through his plenipotentiaries, sued for an armistice. Napoleon demanded gold and silver for his troops and for his masters in Paris. He also agreed to leave for the Duchy of Milan as soon as possible, to prevent too much looting. He had come, after all, to liberate Italians.

He did not go to Milan directly, but turned south into the neutral state of Parma, crossed the Po at Piacenza before the Austrians could prevent him, so breaking international law but, more to the point, putting his forces to the Austrians' rear. One of the more curious features of the first Italian campaign is that, when he used this manoeuvre, his foes did not see that, just as he had put himself between them and theirs, they were between him and his base. He thought of winning; they, old, slow and correct, thought of failing to lose. Napoleon seemed to be in charge everywhere. At Lodi he took control of the artillery barrage across a wooden bridge over the Adda river – he got covered in black powder and earned himself the nickname of *le petit caporal*. He made for Milan and, once installed there, set about wooing Italian republicans, sending more valuables to the Directors and establishing two newspapers, *Courrier de l'Armée d'Italie* and *La France vue de l'Armée d'Italie*, that were intended to boost his fame (which they did). When told to make way for General Kellerman, the victor of the revolutionary Battle of Valmy (1792), he felt strong enough to refuse and softened the blow by sending the Directors more Renaissance pictures. Confronted with the formidable defences of Mantua, he invested the city in the hope that its defenders could be starved out while he turned on easier targets, so that the Pope graciously surrendered Bologna and Ferrara, paid a large indemnity and bequeathed several masterpieces from his incomparable art collection. The Austrians, meanwhile, had replaced Beaulieu with yet another ageing soldier, Field Marshal Count Dagobert von Wurmser, and the fight for Mantua was on. While Sérurier bottled up the defenders, Augereau and Masséna were sent north to Lake Garda to intercept the relieving troops. At Castiglione, Napoleon gained one more major victory, largely because Masséna and Augereau were clever enough to take their men forward, then back, then forward again. He also gambled that Sérurier and the infantry would turn up, and they did. Thereafter he ordered that Mantua should be speedily reinvested and moved Masséna to Rivoli, Augereau to Verona, both cities on the Adige and thus to the east of Lake Garda, also posting other troops to block approaches to the rivers from the east and sending yet others to the northern shore of the lake.

Napoleon thus suggested to the Austrians that he was making for southern Germany, and Wurmser responded by deciding to attack him, unexpectedly, in the south-east, relieve Mantua and with the addition of its garrison forces turn on Napoleon from the south. This would show how risky it had been for the French to position themselves between the Austrians and their base, a risk that became even more apparent when the French corps took Trento and then found that their enemy's main counterattacking thrusts had been made to the south. By this time Masséna and Augereau had moved to opposite sides of the Brenta river, where the river was unfordable, and they were lucky that by capturing the town bridge at Bassano they could link up again. While one Austrian commander, Quasdanovich, fled towards Trieste, a second, Sebottendorf, joined Wurmser at Vicenza, and with a third, Mészáros, they concentrated at Villanuova and moved west to Legnano, a town on the Adige just east of Mantua. For a time Wurmser seemed to be in charge of the campaign. On 12 September he managed to enter Mantua, and emerged to maul Masséna on 14 September outside the city but was driven back when Napoleon himself joined the besiegers; and there Wurmser was forced to stay until he surrendered in February.

The Austrians sent a new general, Baron József Alvinczy von Børberek, a Magyar bureaucrat with experience that went back to fighting in the Seven Years War. While he could count on 50,000 men in the field, Napoleon, even when reinforced, had only 30,000 effective troops, who included those stuck round Mantua. Had Alvinczy made clever use of his numerical superiority, Napoleon could have been crushed; besides, he had scattered his corps and divisions not far apart, but separated by the hilly, inhospitable terrain just south of the Dolomites, made harder to traverse by the onset of chilly, wet, wintry conditions. Fortunately for him, Alvinczy divided and subdivided his army, so that, though he responded to Napoleon's offensive drive from Verona by pushing back the French at Caldiero, he paused long enough for Napoleon to execute one of his most daring ventures: attacking the Austrian rear through the swamps north of the Adige close to Arcola. This manoeuvre was sufficient to make Alvinczy call off his own projected attack on Verona and to retreat northwards. In a fresh attack, on 17 November, Masséna took the bridge at Arcola – Napoleon, meantime, had stumbled into a canal – and Alvinczy retreated to the east of Trento.

He made one last effort in January 1797. Having had his numbers again brought up to 50,000, he descended the Mincio towards Rivoli with 28,000, leaving 6,500 to guard his rear and sending one force to move on Verona via Bassano and another to march on Legnano. Once he had understood on 13 January that Alvinczy's elaborate moves were intended to encircle him, Napoleon attacked the main, depleted Austrian army at Rivoli, and this time the ability of his commanders to act in concert brought decisive victory, so that on 2 February Wurmser felt obliged to surrender Mantua. These defeats led the Austrians to appoint their best general, Archduke Charles, the Emperor's younger brother, but he inherited a dispirited and scattered army to fight a victorious general who no longer had to worry about the threat of Mantua behind him. In Carinthia the Archduke tried to block the way with only 10,000 men. He asked for an armistice and had to sign preliminaries of peace at Leoben on 18 April. The Italian campaign was over.

Napoleon used the Italian campaign to transform his reputation. In 1796 he had behind him some ill-starred fights in Corsica, one venture (in Toulon) that proved him as a daring master gunner, one (in Paris) that showed he could be tough, but he had never had experience of sustained leadership. When he arrived at the head-quarters of the army of Italy, he behaved like the political general his subordinates thought that he was. Throughout the campaign he made sure that whoever it was, whether a Director at home, a private soldier on the front, an Italian of republican sympathies, that man should hear what he wanted to hear or what he expected to hear. He would bully Italian princelings, his senior officers, his defeated opponents. Unlike many of the new men whose careers in a traditionally aristocratic profession had been made possible only by the social upheavals caused by the Revolution, he was just enough of a nobleman to assume that he would be obeyed and just vulgar enough to seem a man of the people. Getting grimy with gunpowder or falling headlong into a ditch suited *le petit caporal*, being embarrassingly open about his love for Joséphine gave him the air of a Rousseauite man of sensibility, paying his men wages in gold or silver at the expense of the cities he captured made the soldiers happy while the citizens were relieved that he had not asked for more.

No single set of actions shows how clever he could be as his treatment of the elderly Pope, Pius VI. He had long since ceased to think like a Christian; he also knew that the Directors had been pursuing a vigorous campaign against the devout population of the Vendée, while seeking to maintain a religious policy that would favour the constitutional Church set up by the Revolution or dechristianization or the novel sect of the Theophilanthropists. Besides, the circle to which he had attached himself in Paris, centred around Barras, had little sense of morality, let alone of religion. And yet in his dealings with the Pope he revealed a political astuteness that is surprising in a young man of twenty-eight who was elated at his own success. The most radical of the Directors, La Révellière-Lépeaux, told him to 'make the tiara of the false head of the universal church wobble', and in letters home to them Napoleon, who had seized Bologna, Ferrara and Longo from the Papal States, wrote dismissively of the 'priestly bunch', but to Cardinal Mattei he was deferential:

> I beg you, Cardinal, to assure His Holiness that whatever may happen, he can remain at Rome without fear. As the first minister of religion he will find protection for himself and the Church . . . assure all the inhabitants of Rome that in the French army they will find friends who will welcome victory only in so far as it improves the lot of the people and frees Italy from the domination of foreigners. It will be my personal care to prevent any change being made in the religion of our fathers.[3]

That France stood for freedom from foreigners was an attitude Napoleon was careful to strike. He had spoken Italian before he could speak French, and even while he dropped the Italianate 'u' from his name he liked to trace the Buonaparti back to Florentine ancestors. He may have given the Piedmontese plenipotentiary one hour to accept his terms, but he annoyed his old mentor Saliceti by not being severe enough. One of his proclamations announced:

> Peoples of Italy, the French army is come to break your chains . . . We shall respect your property, your religion and your customs. We wage war with generous hearts, and turn ourselves only against the tyrants who seek to enslave us.[4]

If some Italian patriot were to deduce from this, however, that he would have the right of self-determination, he would soon learn that nothing could have been further from Napoleon's intentions. It would be the French, or rather Napoleon, who would decide the fate of the country, not Kaiser Franz II. When the Directors sent a young soldier of Irish descent, Henri Clarke, to report on Napoleon's trustworthiness, Clarke told the Directors that Napoleon's one concern was 'the constitution', by which they would have understood the setup that kept them in power, by which Clarke himself must have meant that Napoleon was a sound republican. He was indeed a republican, for he made a point of establishing republics wherever he went. In autumn 1796, having taken from the Pope the cities of Bologna, Ferrara and the Romagna, he formed the Cispadane Republic, which, with the addition of some of the mainland territory of Venice, became in due course the Cisalpine Republic. In May 1797 a riot in Genoa gave the excuse for founding the Ligurian Republic, but, when a massacre of Frenchmen in Verona justified intervention in Venice, the French destroyed the oldest republic in Italy on the grounds that it was not democratic, at a time when the thought of democracy appalled both Napoleon himself and his masters in Paris. Napoleon was always more keen on realpolitik than idealism. In September 1797, during the revolutionary month of Fructidor, a coup against the moderates and royalists who had done well in the French elections was engineered by Augereau, acting as Napoleon's henchman in Paris. The use of military force and the breaking off of peace negotiations at Lille convinced the Austrians that Napoleon was the arbiter of Italy. The Peace Treaty of Campo Formio, in October 1797, was laid down by him. Austria ceded Belgium to France and recognized the Cisalpine Republic, but was compensated with some of the possessions of Venice – Istria, Dalmatia and the city itself – while France took the rest. Napoleon's need to dictate terms had overridden his love of republics. He had left Austria with a foothold in the peninsula. What he had changed was that Italy belonged to a sphere of French rather than of Austrian influence. Italy remained under foreign control.

In Italy Napoleon showed his instinct for propaganda. In his own newspapers his errors of judgement became deliberate mistakes by means of which he had lured his opponents to their destruction. He was not always able to dictate the course of his campaigns, for he did not have a system of communication that could tell him where at any particular moment his own troops or his enemies' troops might be; he often had to guess, and often he was wrong. When he was not certain, he took risks. His salient quality was the ability to win the final battle, and, as his victories multiplied, his soldiers became convinced that in the end they would be triumphant. Napoleon behaved like a winner and, when he had won, he congratulated them unreservedly:

> You have won victory in 70 actions and 14 pitched battles; you have taken more than 100,000 prisoners, 500 field pieces, 2,000 heavy guns, 4 bridging trains . . . contributions levied on the lands you have conquered have fed, paid and maintained the army throughout the campaign; in addition, you have sent 30 millions to the Minister of Finance to assist the public treasury. You have enriched the Museum of Paris with more than 300 masterpieces of ancient and modern Italy which it needed 30 centuries to produce . . .[5]

On St Helena, with the aid of Las Cases, Napoleon changed himself into an even more wonderful leader of men by a vivid depiction of the state of the army when he first greeted it in Nice:

> Soldiers! You are naked, ill fed; people owe us much, they can give us nothing. Your patience, the courage you show in these mountains, are admirable, but they gain you no glory. I come to take you to the most fertile plains in the world. Rich provinces, great towns, will be in our power and there you will have riches, honour and glory. Soldiers of Italy, take heart.[6]

Invented speeches were the stuff of ancient historians, many of whom Napoleon knew. One of them, Thucydides, has been described by a modern critic as a 'myth-historicus'. Frequently, Napoleon, who was the hero of his own drama, fits the term too. He was a myth-historicus before he invented his legend.

Napoleon was received in France like a general from antiquity. There was a small private matter to be resolved, for before coming out to join him in Italy and even while she was there, Joséphine had conducted an affair that was an open secret to many except her husband. Her choice had fallen on a charming dandy, Hippolyte Charles, who, though far from the equal of Napoleon as a writer of love letters, looked good, smelled good and lingered while he made love. She was already back in Paris when she became aware that Napoleon was on his way home. In her haste to intercept him, she took the wrong road, missed him and returned to their town house, only to find him back in their bedroom with the door locked. She, her son Eugène and her daughter Hortense wept and banged until Napoleon relented and let her in. The couple had learned their lessons. Hitherto he had been the wooer, she *la belle dame sans merci*. Henceforward he would be in charge, she the lover tortured by insecurity. It was also now he who mattered in politics, not she. It was in his honour that the street where they lived was renamed Rue de la Victoire.

Of his country's enemies only England fought on. The French did not know how vulnerable England was to attack in 1797, when there were naval mutinies at the Nore and Spithead, and it was a boost to England's morale that the British navy defeated the Dutch at Camperdown. To the Directors it must have seemed natural to instruct Napoleon to prepare to mount an attack across the Strait of Dover, and to this end he was made commander of the 'Army of England' in November 1797, but, after pacing fretfully along the northern shores of France, he came to the sane conclusion that an amphibious venture in the Channel was not yet feasible. Far more sensible, in his view, would be an expedition to the Levant that could disrupt England's commerce with India, which he deemed to be a more effective way of harming Britain. The Minister of Marine shared his gloomy assessment of the state of the French navy in the north. The Minister of Foreign Affairs, Talleyrand, added his suave support to the Mediterranean project. The Toulon fleet was in better shape than the fleet in Brest. Napoleon wanted only 25,000 men, and the Directors were comforted by the thought that he would be far away from France. They could rejoice in his successes and ignore his failures. They had not thought perhaps that his departure could lead old foes, in particular Russia and Austria, to re-enter a Continental war against the revolutionary government. There was only England to cope with, and at first England was foxed. The English agent at Leghorn reported that the French were going to Alexandria. Dundas sent forces to India and Pitt ordered Nelson into the Mediterranean, but the French got to Malta and Egypt without much difficulty. On 1 July they were off Alexandria, ready to disembark. On 1 August, while he was in Cairo, Nelson destroyed the French fleet off Aboukir. Within a month of his arrival, then, Napoleon was bound to fail. It is one of his more remarkable feats that he changed this inevitable defeat into a triumph for his reputation.

In one way he had already prepared the way for a favourable reaction. One of those to whom he had entrusted the text of the Treaty of Campo Formio was the mathematician Gaspard Monge, who had been sent to Italy with his friend, the chemist Claude Louis Berthollet, to be in charge of the transport of designated works of art to Paris. The two had been impressed by Napoleon's conversations with Italian intellectuals, and to them he had mentioned his early thoughts on a voyage to the East. Back in Paris he had become their colleague in the Institute and, once he had gained authorization for his Egyptian plan, he had charged them with recruiting the scientists, historians, archaeologists, linguists and artists whom he needed for his research project that lay behind the mighty *Description de l'Egypte*. It was to be his fascination with Egypt that made Egyptian-style artefacts *à la mode* all over France and led to the decipherment of hieroglyphs and the development of Egyptology and also to 150 years of French political and economic involvement in Egypt, from his investigation of the old Suez Canal, to de Lesseps's building of a new canal, the forming of the Compagnie du canal de Suez and the débâcle of the Suez war in 1956. All this was to follow from Napoleon's visionary scheme. For Egyptomania he can claim much credit; he had a knack for imaginative ideas.

What was hard to defend was the campaign itself. Though Napoleon had been given some 35,000 men instead of the original 25,000, he did not have enough horses to fight the Mameluke cavalry, who were proud of their riding skills. With their scimitars, maces and daggers, and their coats of many colours, they looked more dashing than the gorgeously apparelled hussars and they considered it a point of honour to slash off their enemies' heads so as to be covered in blood. What they did not begin to comprehend was that European discipline and firepower could reduce their charging horsemen to a heap of corpses in minutes, at most a few hours, and even in the close confines of a city's streets, such as those of Cairo, they could never be equal to the French invaders. A damascened knife was not worth a pistol.

Napoleon still found ways to broadcast his achievements. Near Gizeh he probably reminded those troops who could hear him of the forty centuries that looked down on them, even though the pyramids, after which the subsequent battle was named, were almost out of sight. In Cairo the French summarily dispatched anyone suspected of revolting, so Napoleon liked to stress his mercy to those who submitted to him. Once he had gone to Syria, he preferred to let the world know of the way he had walked unafraid among those suffering from plague rather than of how he had all Turkish prisoners shot or how he had ordered those who could not return to Egypt to be poisoned. In Syria, he did not have the siege artillery to take Acre – on St Helena he would tell of the great revolution that would have occurred had he done so – but his withdrawal, which in view of depleted numbers was prudent, could be rapidly turned to good account because back in Egypt he was faced with a new Turkish army almost three times the size of his own. On the shore by Aboukir, a charge by Murat ensured that the waves frothed with blood. Within a month he set sail for France, with Murat, Lannes and Berthier, his key officers. A more successful campaign had been waged in Lower Egypt by General Desaix, who had chased Mamelukes to the islands of Philae and Elephantine, but Napoleon did not worry about Desaix, as he was a man without political ambition.

In the war of propaganda Napoleon almost lost out to the British, who publicized his massacre of Turks in Syria and letters to and from his stepson Eugène de Beauharnais that revealed to a smirking public how Napoleon had been cuckolded. The British also let him know how in his absence the French had suffered defeat after defeat in Italy and that Jourdan had been defeated on the Rhine. When he landed back at Fréjus, the British had given him the excuse that his return was necessary and, as he arrived at the same time as the news of the victory at Aboukir, he was welcomed as a conquering hero. By the time the French forces in Egypt had to surrender to the British, few Europeans were interested; and when one of the Turkish soldiers who had survived Aboukir, a young merchant named Mehemet Ali, defeated the

British, they were even less likely to notice. It was Napoleon who had the gift for being headline news.

In Italy in 1796 to 1797 and in Egypt and Syria in 1798 to 1799, Napoleon had had the opportunity to exercise political power. He had shown himself to be a remarkably resilient general, a man who won the battles that counted, and also a masterly politician, capable of keeping any who doubted his soundness guessing. People in France had come to believe in him, so that he was more highly regarded than the Directorate, whose policies seemed to be concerned only with its own survival, while the ambience of the governing clique was sordid – racketeers were in, moral restraint was out. On St Helena Napoleon told Las Cases that 'the departure of the general in chief [that is of himself] was the result of the most magnanimous, the greatest of plans'.[7] That may well have been how many in 1799 saw his return to France and its sequel, the coup d'état that brought him to power. At the crisis of the coup, Napoleon's cause was saved by his brother Lucien, a fact that neither he nor Napoleon ever forgot. As president of the Five Hundred, the junior council of the bicameral parliament, he had seen Napoleon falter while speaking in favour of drafting a new constitution. At once Lucien rode out to the troops stationed outside the palace of St-Cloud, where the deputies were meeting, and called on them to free the building from assassins and Jacobins. He would plunge a sword into his heart, he declared, if Napoleon betrayed the republic. It was all that was needed to persuade the soldiers to turn on the deputies, who fled by any door or window they could find. Sabre rattling reduced the need for negotiation. Once he had recovered, Napoleon showed himself as shrewd as Lucien had been provocative, and in the following month he was proclaimed virtually the monarch of France, though sporting the modest antique title of consul. In modern France there were three consuls instead of the ancient Roman two. What mattered was that he was First Consul, as the Second and Third Consuls were mere advisers. The men who had meant him to be their puppet, the constitutional expert, the Abbé Sieyès, and the ex-Director Ducos, were consoled with seats in the Senate. By the new constitution, Napoleon appointed the Councillors of State, which proposed the laws. He chose the members of the Senate, which chose the members of the legislating bodies that approved the laws. He was granted the right to choose the ministers, prefects, mayors, generals, admirals and heads of the police. More emphatically than Louis XIV he could have said, 'I am the state' ('L'état, c'est moi'), but he took care not to. France was technically a republic, not a monarchy. The people in a referendum endorsed his position. He gave the impression that he did not have the right to go away to fight a war, but he knew that his assumption of such power was justified only if he could save France from its enemies. Tsar Paul I had withdrawn from the fight, furious at the British claim to stop and search any ships anywhere, so that there was only Austria to fight on the Continent. It was against Austria that Napoleon would have to prove himself once more. If Austria was out of the war, would Britain fight on? The British fleet was formidable and a good British general called Arthur Wellesley had been fighting against France's allies in India, yet Wellesley, like Napoleon, knew that the test of generalship would be taken within Europe against the leading European armies, not against Muslim fighters bedecked in exotic costumes, speaking outlandish tongues. On the Continent, as yet the British had not impressed anyone much. They were better at using their fleet to seize Malta and to isolate and starve out the French in Egypt.

In 1704, just before the Battle of Blenheim, the French had attacked the Austrians by marching down the Danube in the direction of Vienna, and this route, the Austrians were certain, would be the way along which the mass of French troops on the

Rhine was bound to go. There might be another engagement in Italy, for there was a force also in Genoa. What they did not expect was an attack across the Alps into north-west Italy, and, because they did not anticipate it, that was what Napoleon did.

As often at this period of his career, much of the success of the second Italian campaign was owed to his subordinates: early on to Masséna, an Italian veteran from 1796 to 1797; at the end to Desaix, who had fought in Egypt in 1798 to 1799. It was Masséna's job to hold Genoa against a larger Austrian force while Napoleon took men, horse and cannon across the Alps by the St Bernard Pass. For the infantry the journey was easy enough, partly because they were equipped for the journey, but it took some time for some of the cavalry and artillery to catch up. He had reached Milan by 2 June, and Masséna surrendered on 4 June. Though the gallantry of the French garrison had been exemplary, Napoleon had hoped that Masséna would survive longer, but he was confident of a quick victory against yet another old general, Field Marshal Melas, and moved at what was for him a slow pace in the direction of Alessandria, the medieval fortress town behind Genoa. Contrary to his normal practice, he divided his troops and so laid himself open to a massive frontal attack by superior forces on 14 June.

During seven long hours, from 10 a.m. to 5 p.m., he had to give way, while sending out frantic messages in the hope that some of the troops he had detached would join him. Nothing reached Desaix, but Desaix had heard the sound of firing in the distance and he marched towards it. 'This battle is lost,' he told Napoleon, 'but there is time to win another.' His judgement was soon justified. His fresh troops steadied the line while the exhausted men regrouped. It was a moment when youth triumphed over age. Melas, with a slight wound, had retired to Alessandria, thinking that victory was assured; a counterattack seemed inconceivable, so when it happened it was hard to resist. The leading Austrians were driven back on their advancing rear and, though able to escape in the darkness, with only a thousand killed, they were demoralized at their unanticipated defeat. Next day, Melas asked for and was granted an armistice. The French had had slightly more men killed out of a smaller army, among them Desaix, but they had done enough to win back control of northern Italy. The war on land was not yet won – that was not achieved for another six months till Moreau had defeated Archduke Charles at Hohenlinden – and yet once again the war at sea was lost, when the indefatigable Nelson destroyed the Danish fleet at Copenhagen. Tsar Paul I, who had supported the French by sponsoring a Baltic alliance against the English, had been murdered. Pitt, the heart of resistance against Napoleon, had resigned as British Prime Minister. It was time for all sides to make peace. Austria caved in at Lunéville in 1801, and the French and British made terms at Amiens in 1802. Now Napoleon, First Consul for Life, was securely ruler of the French.

It was while winning the Continental war against the Second Coalition that Napoleon was painted as a new Hannibal and a new Charlemagne by David. Though several versions of the picture were made, and it has become the best-known image of Napoleon, the sitter was worried. He was sure that Marengo had been his most famous victory; he named his favourite horse after the village, and he would esteem people who had been with him on the day. He had sincerely wept over Desaix, but he was obsessed by the thought that the victory had been less his than the victory of those who had arrived in the nick of time. In 1803 he ordered his staff to produce a new account of the battle, which did not please him enough, so in 1805 a third story was told. This time the Austrian army numbered 45,000, Desaix was dispatched with strict instructions to return if needed and the main French army, instead of retreating on a north–south axis, wheeled on an east–west one. In this way Napoleon had cunningly prepared the way for a flanking attack on the enemy when he deemed it opportune to do so. The occasion came when Desaix appeared as Napoleon wanted him to. The rest was history, but by now the main part of the tale was false. In truth, the strategy of the second Italian campaign had been masterly, but the tactics had been almost disastrous. Napoleon, however, was not put off by inconvenient facts, any more than he disliked being portrayed crossing the Alps on a charging grey on a stormy day. He and David had created a legend that has been believed.

2

ON THE PLAINS OF EUROPE

Napoleon's favourite painter was Antoine Jean Gros, whom José-phine first encountered in 1796 and promptly introduced to her husband as he was winning some of the more thrilling victories of the first Italian campaign. The most convincing image of the young general is shown in *Napoleon at Arcola*. Because Napoleon could not bear to be still, Joséphine had had him sitting on her knees after meals, and it was this pose that Gros had caught.

By the time Napoleon was an emperor he expected grander portrayals. It became a regular feature of the biennial Salons that there would be a number of pictures on show that were dedicated to Imperial victories, and it was for the Salon of 1808 that Gros fashioned *Napoleon at Eylau*. Under a cold sky, Napoleon appears to survey the field after the Russian retreat, but his eyes linger on some distant prospect, while the eyes of most who have survived the slaughter are fixed on him. He is rapt in a great thought: he is above noticing any of the corpses that lie before him.

In the previous Imperial Salons, Napoleon had been represented by Gros as a Christ-like figure while visiting the plague victims of Jaffa (1804) and by many as the victorious commander at Austerlitz (1806). For none of the events in his glorious campaigns did Napoleon feel so much pride as he did for his part in the Battle of Eylau. This was curious, as this was not the battle that brought the last of the big three Continental enemies of France – the Russians – to the conference table. Indeed, some commentators do not regard it as a French victory at all, just a battle Napoleon did not lose because he was left in possession of the field while the Russians withdrew. But Napoleon was so keen for it to be commemorated by a memorable work of art that Denon, director of the Musée Napoléon, arranged a competition for him to choose the best representation of the moment on the day after the battle when 'the Emperor, visiting the battlefield, comes to offer indiscriminately help and consolation to the honourable victims of the fight'. Denon was careful not to deny that the battle had been bloody. At the same time he wished to stress that Napoleon had been as compassionate as Alexander to Porus in the series on the Macedonian by Le Brun painted in homage to Louis XIV. In keeping with Napoleon's emphasis on actuality, the theme this time was from modern, not ancient, history, but the message was similar: our great ruler is even more himself when he is kind. Twenty-six artists produced sketches, most of them forgettable and lost, and there seems to be little doubt that the jury was right to choose the version by Gros. When he visited the Salon in 1808, Napoleon paused by the painter in front of his painting. Other artists had been given rewards, but Gros had received nothing, so with the kind of theatrical gesture of which he was a master Napoleon took from the lapel of his jacket the ribbon with his own cross of the Légion d'Honneur and fixed it on to Gros's coat. He had recognized a *chef d'oeuvre* in an Imperial way.

*   *   *

The Treaty of Amiens gave France and Britain a breathing space but did not bring about a permanent peace. Though both sides blamed each other, in principle neither was ready to compromise. The British had no wish to evacuate the island of Malta, which they had seized from the French. Pitt, who became Prime Minister again in 1804, objected to Napoleon's territorial gains since Amiens – he had delayed giving up the former United Provinces (the Netherlands), annexed Piedmont and the island of Elba, made himself President of the former Cisalpine Republic (now the Italian Republic), imposed a defensive alliance on Switzerland, arranged how several small German principalities and free cities should be distributed among the larger states and occupied Hanover, whose Elector was none other than King George III.

Surreptitiously, the British had brought together a royalist and Jacobin opposition, an unlikely group including the Chouan leader Cadoudal, the exiled general Pichegru, who had left France after the Directory coup in 1797, and Moreau, the victor of Hohenlinden; and it was said that a Bourbon prince was involved. A double agent revealed the plot to Fouché, until recently the head of the police, who was keen to show how useful he could be. Moreau was arrested, sentenced and exiled, Pichegru died in prison, probably by his own hand, and Cadoudal and other non-aristocratic royalists were guillotined. Fouché suggested that the Bourbon prince could be the Duc d'Enghien, heir to the Prince de Condé, the immensely rich descendant of Louis XIV's troublesome and great general. Enghien was with fellow émigrés at Ettenheim in Baden, just over the border from Alsace, poised, Napoleon believed, to invade eastern France. It took just a quick raid to capture Enghien, a brief military trial to condemn him and a firing squad to dispatch him. Napoleon wished to make clear that he would have no truck with the Bourbons; he would not be, on his brother Lucien's analogy, the Monk to some Charles II. What he achieved was a reputation for insisting on a judicial murder. Chateaubriand, the most eloquent of royalists, came to consider the incident the moment when Napoleon's moral decline set in, and Beethoven, coupling it with the proclamation of the Empire in May, struck out the dedication of the *Eroica* symphony. 'Now he will trample on the rights of mankind and indulge only his own ambition; from now on he will make himself superior to all others and become a tyrant.'[1]

For a time Napoleon gave the impression that he intended to invade the old enemy. He walked up and down on the northern coast of France, while he trained the 'Army of England' in a huge camp in Boulogne, and he evolved the elaborate strategy by which the Toulon naval squadron of Admiral Latouche-Tréville should elude Nelson's blockading fleet, join up with Admiral Villeneuve's Rochefort squadron, enter the Channel and use the six hours they might have to transport a flotilla of troops across the sea to England. After Latouche-Tréville died in August, Villeneuve was transferred to Toulon, and a modified version of the plan became possible once Spain, another major naval power, joined in the war on France's side. Villeneuve escaped in March 1805, slipped past Gibraltar, reached Martinique by mid-May and doubled back, but the Rochefort squadron failed to join him and Villeneuve could neither enter the Channel nor re-enter the Mediterranean. He took refuge in La Coruña and, on misjudging that five ships of the line he sighted were English – in fact, they were French – retreated down to Cadiz to join the Spaniards. On 21 October the allies, with slightly more ships but inferior in seamanship and armaments, sallied out in line to confront the English. Nelson broke the line in two columns, using at sea the sort of tactics that Napoleon had devised for land warfare. He lost his life, but not one ship, while eighteen French and Spanish ships were sunk or surrendered and Villeneuve committed suicide.

By then Napoleon was far from the Channel ports. On 24 August he had ordered his military force, the Grande Armée, to strike camp at Boulogne and head for the river Danube. The recently crowned Emperor of the French was going to strike at the old empires ruled by the Habsburg Kaiser Francis II and the Romanov Tsar Alexander I.

Pitt's diplomacy and gold created a Third Coalition against Napoleon, but the task had been eased by Napoleon's own behaviour. By crowning himself with Charlemagne's crown before the Pope, Napoleon annoyed Charlemagne's heir, the Holy Roman Emperor, who in 1804 reinvented himself as German Emperor; and he affronted the Habsburgs still more by crowning himself King of Italy with the iron crown of Lombardy and, in contravention of the Treaty of Lunéville, by annexing Genoa to France and making a viceroy of his stepson, Eugène de Beauharnais. The Russians were worried by the issue of a French report that claimed Egypt could be reconquered, for Egypt was legally Turkish and Turkey's affairs were Russia's concern. The French reoccupation of Naples and French meddling in Germany, above all the seizure of Hanover, threatened Russia in central Europe. Napoleon offered Prussia Hanover and an alliance; Prussia took Hanover but decided to be neutral and allied with Württemberg, Bavaria and Baden. He was poised to upset the European balance of power.

To achieve his aim, Napoleon had engineered a new French military machine, the Grande Armée.

France was at war, almost without a break, from 1792 to 1802 and from 1804 to 1814. In the early period its armies had numbered between 320,000 and 800,000 men; in the later period numbers never fell below a million. Not all the men were soldiers, not all of them were French, but at the core was a national army, the largest any nation had yet produced. The army that marched to the Danube in 1805 was the best the world had seen, excelling others not so much in arms as in its style of warfare. The weapons were those used at the end of the *ancien régime*, tactics – attacking in column or in mixed order of column and line – were revolutionary, but the organization was novel, and it was in this that Napoleon had instituted a revolution all his own. The basic unit was the corps, which had two or more infantry divisions, a brigade of light cavalry and six to eight companies of artillery and support services (engineers, doctors, supplies and headquarters). In an infantry division there should be one company of skirmishers (the *voltigeurs* or *tirailleurs*), one of *grenadiers* and four of ordinary *fusiliers*. To be a skirmisher a man had to be agile, to be a *grenadier* he had to be strong. Among the cavalry, all of whom fought with sabres, carbines or pistols there was a like distinction between light and heavy. The light, more dashing horsemen, or *chasseurs*, were the hussars (with their distinctive shakos on their heads), helmeted dragoons and (from 1809) lancers; the heavy, more powerfully built, wore the heavy body armour of the *cuirassiers* and the *carabiniers*. At the headquarters of the army there were 150 extra guns, which brought the average ratio of guns to men up to 3:1,000. There was also a cavalry reserve that was normally the concern of Murat. The chief of staff, save in 1815, was Berthier. This arrangement gave the Grande Armée cohesion but also made it adaptable. What mattered was literally esprit de corps, the way that each corps could fight its own battles as a miniature army. If there was a crisis, there was always the Imperial Guard, which never failed Napoleon before Waterloo.

Until the catastrophic campaign of 1812, the army was professional in its essence; only in 1813 and 1814 did Napoleon have to rely on a policy of massive conscription. Until 1813 he could also count on many allied troops. In 1812 only one-third of the army that crossed the Niemen was French; thereafter the French were outnumbered.

In 1805 the Grande Armée was new in its character and startling in its effect. There was no reason, however, to expect the hammer blow that hit the Third Coalition. The Austrians and Russians had time to think. The Austrians knew that Napoleon would strike in Italy, so they sent Archduke Charles there with 90,000 men; his much-less-talented brother, Archduke John, would have the lesser task of fighting in the Tyrol. Napoleon, alas, marched into Germany with almost 200,000 men, including 50,000 from his German allies – Württemberg, Baden and Bavaria – states that had profited from his recent redistribution of territory in the former Holy Roman Empire. Even when they realized their mistake, the Austrians did not panic, for the Russians under Kutuzov would soon have 90,000 men to add to the forces of General Mack, who was a competent leader of the 70,000 he had but who on Russian insistence had to defer to Archduke John, since no Russian would obey an Austrian unless he were a Habsburg prince.

Military maps of the campaign make it appear that Napoleon executed one of the most brilliant manoeuvres of his career, as the Grande Armée fanned out from Mainz to Strasbourg along the Rhine, swooped down separately on the Danube and converged a little to the east of Mack. Mack thought they would emerge from the Black Forest, but they had kept to the north. Napoleon had no plan to encircle Mack; he expected Mack to retreat to the east, to link up with Archduke John. He had not realized that Mack could cut his lines of communication. Yet another archduke, Ferdinand, forbade Mack to attack on the north side of the Danube from the west, for he wished to withdraw in safety to the Tyrol, where it would be hard for the French to reach him. So it was that Mack, trapped by a prince's indecision, fell back on Ulm, which even then could be a base from which he could cause havoc to the French, whose forces were still in disarray. Napoleon blamed his leading commanders, Murat, Lannes and Ney, for his mistakes, and in this way made them so furious that they were desperate to vindicate their reputations. Archduke Ferdinand withdrew hurriedly to deprive Napoleon, so he said, of the satisfaction of taking a Habsburg, other Austrians ran away to the south and, in this way, on 16 October Napoleon's guns opened fire on a trapped, weakened army in Ulm. On 20 October, the day before Trafalgar, Mack surrendered. Napoleon wrote to Talleyrand, his Foreign Minister: 'My plan has been executed just as I conceived it.' As so often, what he said he had conceived before the event was what in fact had happened. The masterstroke was genuine, but it was almost a fluke.

In mid-October Kutuzov reached the borders of Austria on the river Inn but, on hearing the news from Ulm, he halted. The German Emperor would not let any Austrians who had escaped from the French serve a Russian. Kutuzov heard that his own reinforcements were in Moravia; if he retreated there, he might be joined by Archduke Charles, still in Italy, so he slowly made his way to the east. Napoleon told Murat to chase the Russians and was livid when Murat, who had not stayed for the message, galloped off towards Vienna. He was not opposed, so he and Lannes paraded through the Austrian capital with their troops in gorgeous uniforms, while Kutuzov wended his way to Olmütz, where the surviving Austrians and the Tsar joined him. The Tsar took over command. Kutuzov reminded him that Archduke Charles, who had safely extricated himself from Italy, and Archduke Ferdinand, with a small force, would soon be with him. If they won victories, the King of Prussia had agreed to support the Coalition.

The Tsar, young, athletic and proud, saw no point in waiting. The French, he was convinced, had only 70,000 against his 87,000, and as late as 1 December Napoleon gladly gave the impression that his force mounted to only 57,000. In fact, Bernadotte was on his way from Prague with 10,000, and by dawn on 2 December Davout could bring another 6,000 from Vienna. If all went well, Napoleon would have more than 70,000, and in sections of the field skilful use of the terrain could outweigh any arithmetical advantage. He had also encouraged the Tsar to attack by withdrawing cavalry from the Pratzen heights, a commanding piece of land in the midst of the impending battle. With almost half his army, Alexander decided he must attack to the south, though this meant sending men into frozen marshes where the French stood safely on the far side of the Goldbach brook. As more and more of his men were bogged down in the mud and cut down in icy waters, Alexander ordered yet more and more men to replace them. At 9.30 a.m., Napoleon ordered the cavalry commanded by Soult to retake the Pratzen heights and after a tussle with the Russian Imperial Guards the commanding position in the centre was his. Other corps joined Soult, so that by 11 a.m. the French had massed artillery and cavalry ready for a decisive blow. They drove Russians down to the marshes, where their fellows were already being decimated by Davout. Meanwhile, in the north Bernadotte and Lannes drove the Austrians along the road to the little village of Austerlitz. With snow falling night drew on. The French could not see their few remaining foes to kill or capture them. Of the French, 2,000 were killed and 7,000 wounded, while the Russians had 10,000 killed, a further 15,000 wounded or captured and so many dispersed that they were no longer effective. The Tsar, however, was a stubborn man, and he marched away with only his guard. The more timid Kaiser sued for peace.

Napoleon never fought a better battle. He loved to recall the sun of Austerlitz and to regard 2 December as a special day in the year, but he was not above improving the news. An order kept in the archives, dated 1 December, states that when the enemy tries to 'turn my right flank, they will expose their left flank to me', so that 'I' can attack and destroy them. Research has shown that this order was amended after the battle had started. Originally, Napoleon had predicted that his opponents would attack his batteries and he would attack on their flanks. As a commander, he had a genius for improvization; as a military politician he also must show that he had predicted what did happen.[2]

Reactions to Austerlitz were characteristic. The German Emperor was laconic; he told his wife that 'a battle was fought today which did not turn out very well'. Pitt was prophetic – the map of Europe 'will not be needed these ten years' – and Napoleon was grandiloquent to his soldiers: 'my people will greet you with joy, and it will be enough for you to say, I was at the battle of Austerlitz, for them to say, there goes a brave type.'

Visitors to modern Paris will associate the name with a bridge and a railway station. At the time, Napoleon made a gracious gesture to the children of soldiers who had died at Austerlitz; their widows had his permission to give their children the extra name of 'Napoleon'.

At Austerlitz, for the first time, Napoleon wore the shabby grey-green redingote that came to signify his presence among his troops. He was trying to indicate that he was just one of them at the same time as he was asserting his dominance over the most powerful men in Europe. He was gratified that the German Emperor wished to treat – in the capital the *Journal de Paris* mentioned three-gun salvos announcing to popular joy the start of discussions with the Kaiser. Talleyrand, Napoleon's Foreign Minister, more attuned than his master to the diplomatic spirit of the eighteenth century, advised caution and generosity. Napoleon did not listen. The terms of the Peace of Pressburg were harsh. The Austrians had to cede Venice, Istria and Dalmatia to the kingdom of Italy; the Tyrol, the

Trentino and the Vorarlberg to Bavaria; and smaller enclaves to Württemberg and Baden. Pushed out of Italy and Germany, but given Salzburg, Francis II now chose to be Emperor of Austria. Napoleon, meanwhile, gave Hanover to Prussia in return for Cleves and Neuchâtel in Switzerland, to punish the English for financing his enemies and to reward Frederick William III for doing nothing. Of his allies, the electoral Duke of Bavaria and the Grand Duke of Württemberg became kings and the Margrave of Baden found himself a grand duke. In 1806 and 1807 Joséphine's son Eugène married a princess of Bavaria, her cousin married the electoral Prince of Baden and Napoleon's brother Jérôme married the daughter of the new King of Württemberg.

Napoleon's work in Germany was completed in July 1806 when he set up the Confederation of the Rhine, from which both Austria and Prussia were excluded.

He still had other areas to settle. Before the end of the month the *Bulletin de l'Armée* declared that 'the Queen of Naples no longer reigns', and he wrote to his brother Joseph to tell him that he was first choice for that throne. He also induced the Dutch to accept his favourite brother Louis as their king and Louis to marry Joséphine's daughter Hortense.

In establishing a new order, Napoleon had not negotiated: he had dictated. He had made clear that what mattered was what he wanted. Most peoples, most rulers or ruling classes had no choice but to accept what he determined, yet, if he thought he had finished with Austria and Prussia, they thought they had not finished with him. Kaiser Franz gave Archduke Charles the task of revitalizing the Austrian army. As commander-in-chief and head of the war council, he set about replacing the horses that had been killed and the armaments that had been lost at Ulm. To recruit more men, he increased pay. To improve organization, he started to ease out the elderly and useless officers who rendered the Habsburg armies anachronistic. To provide backup, he planned to raise a national guard that could be called up in time of war. As revenge would take time, in 1806 Austria was at pains to avoid confrontation with the French.

The Prussians were becoming more belligerent. They had not joined the Third Coalition because of the bait of Hanover, but in the end they had got their reward at the expense of territorial concessions that had not been part of the original bargain. The King, third of the Frederick Williams, was cautious, conventional and quick to do anything for a quiet life, with a beautiful and formidable wife, whom Napoleon was to call the only real man in Prussia. By repute, the King had the best-drilled army in Europe, for everyone knew the exploits of Frederick the Great, one of the few generals of the previous century whom Napoleon respected. Most of the current generals were ancient – the youngest of any importance, Blücher, was in his sixties – and the commander-in-chief, the Duke of Brunswick, was seventy-one, a veteran of the Seven Years War. In their diplomatic relations since 1804 the Prussians had appeared pusillanimous, unsure of themselves and greedy. By 1806 they had no friends, they had lost influence on German affairs in return for Hanover, they were only too aware that much of the Grande Armée was still on German soil. When they learned that Napoleon, who was short of cash and toying with the idea of a general peace, was thinking of returning Hanover to England, it was a final blow to Hohenzollern pride that even the King of Prussia could not resist. The Prussian high command agreed on just one point: they must attack.

This was unwise not just because theirs was a much smaller army than the French, but also because they could wait for the Russians, who were once again preparing to fight, to come to their aid. In the way that old men are in a hurry, the elderly generals wished to act.

In the way that old men react slowly, they were unprepared for the speed that was Napoleon's hallmark, even with the inflated forces now at his disposal. He had already left Paris to join his troops when the Prussians sent him an ultimatum. If he was rapid, he would beat them before the Russians were at hand. With a battalion square of up to 200,000 men, he moved through the Franconian forest towards Saxony, which was Prussia's ally, able to react to the enemy from whatever direction he was attacked. As often happened in his campaigns, he did not know exactly where the Prussians were, but he was sure he was ready to cope with them.

In the event he miscalculated. He was surprised that the Prussians had not waited on the river Elbe for the Russians, and he was upon them before either side expected the other. On the river Saale the corps under Lannes and Augereau, some 25,000, met Prince Louis Ferdinand with 9,000, but the Prince charged at the head of his hussars and was killed. When he had learned how small this Prussian force had been, Napoleon guessed that the main Prussian army must be further east, so he sent Murat, Bernadotte and Soult there and they found no one. He then heard that there were indeed Prussians on the Saale, further north at Jena and to the west towards Weimar, and there, he was convinced, he would meet their main army. To be certain of cutting off their retreat, he ordered Davout to place himself to its rear. He had no idea that 64,000 Prussians were bearing down on Davout's 26,000.

What followed was not one engagement but two. Napoleon, with his genius for arranging that his own reinforcements should arrive before the enemy's, sent in the first corps at Jena on a foggy October morning and it got lost. At 11 a.m. Hohenlohe tried to counterattack but did not have enough ammunition, so he determined to wait for Rüchel to bring 13,000 reinforcements from the direction of Weimar. Rüchel was too slow – he took four hours to cover six miles – and the French did not wait for him. They delivered their blow at 12.30 p.m. and the Prussians fled. Rüchel arrived too late and was quickly brushed away.

The French had lost 5,000, the Prussians 26,000. A former subject of Louis xv had got even with the successor of Frederick the Great for the humiliations French soldiers had suffered almost forty years before.

A general much less celebrated than Napoleon had done better than his master. Davout, whose solidity had been critical in deciding the outcome of Austerlitz, was yet more decisive in the double battle of 1806. It was he who fought the main bulk of the Prussian army, led first by Frederick the Great's general. the Duke of Brunswick, and, after the Duke was fatally wounded at the start, in theory by Frederick the Great's heir. For some time the French fought defensively in squares, but, at 11 a.m., when sheer numbers were about to win, Davout's last division turned up and turned the day. By one o'clock the finest army in Europe was broken. Proportionately, Davout had lost more men, but only darkness saved the lives of most of his foes.

It took Napoleon time to believe what had occurred, but then he wrote a generous letter of congratulation to Davout. To his public he was less frank. Officially there had been one battle and he its one victor. In 1808 he made Davout Duke of Auerstädt, but he talked only of Jena and on St Helena he considered that all Davout had done was to block the Prussians. In Paris there is no Auerstädt Bridge.

Not everything had worked with the precision Napoleon liked. One corps, that of Bernadotte, had moved too slowly to take part in either battle, but this was a useful omission in the aftermath, since that corps was anxious to prove itself in the headlong pursuit of fleeing troops that Napoleon set in motion at dawn on 15

October. The forces under Murat, Soult and Ney were also comparatively fresh. Bernadotte routed the last undefeated remnant of the Prussian army, the reserve stationed at Halle under the Duke of Württemberg. On 20 October the King of Prussia abandoned his men and made for the river Oder to the east, while Hohenlohe attempted to regroup at Magdeburg on the Elbe, before retreating to Stettin at the mouth of the Oder. In the race for the coast the French lost discipline and looted and ravaged at will. Napoleon himself paused at Potsdam to revere the tomb of Frederick the Great, but confiscated his sword, sash and Ribbon of the Black Eagle 'for the consolation of those of our *invalides* who escaped the catastrophe of Rossbach'. The defeat at Rossbach was an obsession of his: 'The battle of Jena,' he declared, 'has wiped out the affront of Rossbach.' He was, however, fighting a different sort of war. In the Seven Years War Frederick's aim had been survival, but Napoleon intended to annihilate his opponents. In thirty-three days that object had been achieved. The French had taken 140,000 prisoners, among them generals with famous names, Scharnhorst and Blücher, and the King and Queen had fled to the city of Königsberg in east Prussia. In the manic mood of the time, one French general was more astute than Napoleon. In the city of Lübeck, where many citizens were treated atrociously, there was a small detachment of Swedish soldiers sent by Gustavus IV to aid his Prussian ally. Bernadotte treated them with rare civility, which they never forgot, and four years later he was Crown Prince of Sweden.

Napoleon had won a campaign, but, though Frederick William talked a lot about peace, peace was not yet achieved. On 21 November 1806 Napoleon issued the Berlin Decrees that showed his main obsession: the fight against England. Just over a year after the English had defeated off Cape Trafalgar the last navies that might withstand them, he was trying to convince himself that perfidious Albion could be beaten from the land. As England depended on trade, trade should be denied it. In his Decrees, Napoleon ordered a blockade of England that he could not enforce, but possibly he could close Continental ports to English ships and he could pose as an upholder of the freedom of the seas, for the English were already blockading the Continental coast. The trade war was to have serious repercussions in England and eventually trapped the English into an unnecessary war against the United States, but it also hurt Continental traders. In the previous century Nantes and Bordeaux had been rich on transatlantic trade, and the Netherlands and north German ports like Hamburg relied on trade with the English. In France, fashionable women wished to dress in Indian muslin, to have their furniture made from Central American mahogany and to drink coffee or chocolate sweetened with cane sugar. Such luxuries were now to be denied them; and, if Napoleon's policy encouraged new patterns of transcontinental trade that were to be followed in the future, it did so at a time when the most convenient method of transport was still by boat. Until the coming of a railway network, the main beneficiary of the Berlin Decrees (and the subsequent Milan Decrees) was the country they were meant to hurt. England was forced to trade worldwide, and logically it became for many years the only worldwide power.

Before the Revolution, France had been England's main competitor for such a position. Worsted in the Seven Years War in both India and America, it had gained partial revenge by helping the North American colonists to become independent, and even after 1800 France still had a presence in the Caribbean, where the Haitians had enjoyed a temporary period when it looked as though the rights of man would end slavery, and on the North American mainland, where the huge area of Louisiana belonged to France. But the collapse of the Haitian idyll and the sale of Louisiana in 1803 to the Americans marked a turning away from what had looked like a colonial destiny. While the British gradually took over one European colony after another, in Asia and Africa as well as America, Napoleon remained obsessed by the events of the Seven Years War in Europe. His idea of France involved a purely Continental role, in which France would be not just one of the big four – Prussia, Austria and Russia were the others – but supreme over the other three. By the end of 1806 he had made first Austria, then Prussia subordinate. It was time to take on Russia.

In December 1806 Napoleon created the Duchy of Warsaw. In the eighteenth century the Kingdom of Poland, surrounded as it was by the Russians, the Austrians and the Prussians, had often been a staunch ally of France. Louis xv had married a Polish princess and, when he failed to make good her father's claim to the Polish throne, the old man was pensioned off with the Duchy of Lorraine, on condition that, when he died (which he did in 1766), the Duchy should become part of France. Louis was unable to stop the first partition of Poland in 1771, nor could the French revolutionaries prevent the elimination of the country in the two further partitions of 1793 and 1795. The arrival of the French in Warsaw on 10 December 1806 was therefore greeted by cheering crowds. A Polish aristocrat, Prince Poniatowski, was merely the most prominent of the thousands of Poles who volunteered to fight for the French – he was made a marshal in 1811 – and in January 1807 Napoleon, who had made Warsaw his base of operations, fell in love at first sight with a beautiful young Polish countess, Maria Walewska, who was persuaded to commit adultery for the good of the nation, fell in love with him and gave him an illegitimate heir. The affair had lasting results, for the handsome Alexander Walewski was to grace the court of his cousin, the Emperor Napoleon iii.

Napoleon had every intention of relaxing during the winter, and he put his troops into winter quarters. Bernadotte was to support the sieges of Danzig and Königsberg and was left stationed too far to the south to help withstand a Russo-Prussian attack, were there to be one. Sadly, Cossacks had intercepted French orders, and the new Russian general, Bennigsen, could calculate that, if he moved rapidly, he might take the French at a disadvantage. After an encounter at Ionkovo on the Alle river, Bennigsen withdrew northwards deep into east Prussia, and on 7 February Napoleon ordered Murat and Soult to let their men take refuge from the cold and dark in the little town of Eylau, not far from the main Russian army. After a costly night battle, they captured the town, but next morning they found the Russians ranged along a ridge to the east. The temperature had reached freezing point, and there were flurries of snow and more Russians than French in the area.

The eleven-hour battle that followed on 8 February was nearly a French disaster. Soult's corps, which was meant to lure the Russians to commit themselves on their right, was routed. Snow confused Augereau's relieving infantry, so that they marched straight towards Russian guns, and hundreds of them were cut down. At one moment Napoleon's command post was overrun, and he himself was saved only by the self-sacrifice of his escort. A Murat charge steadied the centre, but even the dependable Davout could not complete a move to turn the Russian left flank, as it was stabilized by the arrival of 7,000 Prussians. Napoleon was attacking as night fell, but he had not won and, had there been another day, he might well have been beaten. Many horses had been killed, the cavalry was badly weakened and the French infantry had been decimated. There is no doubt that by the evening Bennigsen commanded a considerably larger force, yet it was the Russians, not the French, who withdrew.

Next morning the survivors saw the sun rise on a scene of terrible carnage that shocked even Napoleon. 'The victory is mine,' he wrote to Joséphine, 'but I have lost many men; I am not consoled that the losses of the enemy were greater.' It is doubtful if he had won – the Russians had given up the field. It is certain he had lost more men than they had. The one consolation for him was the thought that he had felt sorry for the dead, the dying and the wounded. Eylau was a shock. Napoleon recuperated at the castle of Finkenstein, his pride nursed by the tender care of his Polish countess, planning to use the resources of the Empire to inflict a blow against Russia that would have a decisive effect. Eylau would haunt him, but he would make sure that it would be a unique occurrence.

Once he recovered his élan, Napoleon set about organizing the kind of army he would need. He would not underestimate the Russians again.

Augereau was too ill to be of use, so he was sent home and replaced by another of Napoleon's oldest comrades, Masséna, and other soldiers who had not recovered physically or psychologically were also ordered to return to France. Napoleon wanted to crush Bennigsen, and he was looking for a large, fit and enthusiastic army. From France he drafted 100,000 conscripts, and combined with allies – Italy, Westphalia and the Netherlands – he made up a total force of 200,000, besides 300,000 reserves in France and 100,00 in Germany. The Grande Armée was international in its composition, as in one new corps under the veteran Lefebvre there were two Polish divisions, contingents from Saxony and Baden and two divisions from Italy. Bennigsen, meanwhile, had rebuilt the Russo-Prussian army under himself and Lestocq to 90,000 and had in addition 30,000 near the coast at Tilsit and 20,000 close to Warsaw. On 27 May the French, having taken Danzig, were poised for attack, as his Cossack scouts told Bennigsen, and the Russians and Prussians opted to move first. Napoleon set out to deceive them by sending a fake message that could be intercepted, but his first effort to cut off the Russians from Königsberg failed after a costly struggle to take possession of the Heilsberg Heights by the Alle river. The French moved north to try once more to separate the Prussian King and Queen, in Königsberg, from their Russian protectors.

Both sides converged on the town of Friedland, a key point on the Alle, thirty-five miles from Heilsberg, a little closer to the east Prussian capital. Lannes was first to arrive and, when Bennigsen was told of the presence of a division of Frenchmen – in reality Lannes had a corps of 9,000 infantry and 8,000 cavalry – Bennigsen was sure he had his chance. Throughout the night of 13–14 June, Russians steadily moved more and more men across the river on three narrow bridges. They would have time enough for the kill.

The fight was Lannes's all morning, as he stubbornly stuck to the task of keeping the Russians engaged while Napoleon brought more and more men into play, as column after column moved up from Eylau. By next day, 15 June, the army would have reached full strength. But it was the anniversary of Marengo and 'I am going to beat the Russians as I beat the Austrians,' said Napoleon. At five o'clock in the afternoon he issued instructions, and at 5.30 a.m. the assault began, just before the Russian commander-in-chief, who now realized his precarious state, could give orders to withdraw. As the greater numbers of the French pressed the Russians into an ever decreasing area, French guns were trained on the dense mass of the opposing infantry, coming ever closer until at last they were firing at point-blank range. Counterattacks by Russian cavalry merely added horses and riders to the piles of the dead and dying; relieving attacks elsewhere on the French lines were simply blocked. A final, desperate advance by the Russian Imperial Guard was checked by French bayonets; as much of the town of Friedland had been fired, even those who could cross one of the bridges to the town were often killed before they could escape into the darkness beyond. Not until eleven o'clock was the pursuit called off.

Friedland had given the victory for which Napoleon craved. He was almost at the borders of Mother Russia, ready to treat with the man he regarded as almost his equal, the Tsar of all the Russias. On a pontoon island in the middle of the Niemen near Tilsit – it was 25 June – the two Emperors met to divide the Continent between them. The diary of Bourrienne, a somewhat suspect source, gives an exultant view of the occasion's importance: 'The interview at Tilsit is one of the culminating points of modern history and the waters of the Niemen reflected the glory of Napoleon at the height of his glory.' Not until the next day did the Tsar introduce Napoleon to the King of Prussia. In spite of the determined use of female wiles by his Queen, the King was left in no doubt that of the three monarchs present he counted the least. A treaty between the Emperors was signed and ratified two days before a treaty between Emperor and King. Napoleon would let the Russians have Finland, take as much of European Turkey as they could (except for the Ionian Islands and the Dalmatian coast) and extend their eastward expansion further into Asia. All he wanted was help to take Gibraltar and, maybe, help to remove the Kings of Spain and Portugal from their thrones and help to extend the Continental blockade against Britain in the Baltic, if necessary by putting pressure on Denmark and Sweden. To France the west, to Russia the east, but to Prussia, as previously to Austria, little in the centre. Hesse-Cassel and all Prussian territory west of the Elbe went to the Kingdom of Westphalia, which Napoleon had prepared for his brother Jérôme, and all Prussian territory in Poland was to go to a Grand Duchy of Warsaw under the King of Saxony (in the eight-eenth century three electors of Saxony had been elected Kings of Poland). From the borders of Spain to the borders of Russia, Napoleon was the dominant force. No Bourbon king, not even

Louis XIV, had ever exerted so much influence on the continent. Napoleon had changed the balance of power in Europe. Only at the periphery were others in charge: Russia in the east and, though he hated to admit it, Britain in the west.

Shortly after the Tilsit agreements were signed, Talleyrand, Napoleon's Foreign Minister, resigned. Talleyrand, to Catholic eyes still a bishop and to royalist eyes a renegade royalist, had not so devoted his energies to the support of the new régime that he was not aware of its flaws. In 1798, as Foreign Minister, he had been the chief apologist for the Egyptian venture, and his subsequent resignation had seemed to show his devotion to the new man. But he understood that there were limits to French power that Napoleon was less and less willing to accept, and he could not serve with trust a ruler who increasingly responded in only one way to a person who crossed him, by using the tactics of a bully. Napoleon was right that many on the Continent objected to the high-handed way in which the British behaved, as when they seized ships in Copenhagen, but he did not cultivate with sufficient care those who might look to France for sympathy as well as protection. If he was a protector, he made the protected pay hard for the privilege. In 1807 he demanded an enormous indemnity from the Prussians. His redrawing of the map of Germany made sense if Germany developed a sense of nationhood; more than anyone, it was he who ensured that the desire to belong to the German *Volk* would be coupled with a longing to be avenged on France.

In more southerly countries he stirred up more primitive emotions. In December 1807 he published the Milan Decrees, which tightened in law the economic blockade of England. In November he had occupied the eastern provinces of the Papal States – six months later they were added to the Kingdom of Italy – and in January 1808 he sent General Miollis to take over the Castel

Sant'Angelo in the heart of Rome. Although it was not until after he was seated in the Schönbrunn Palace in Vienna that Napoleon took the final step and deprived the Pope of his temporal power, ostensibly for religious reasons, the general drift of his policy had been clear for over a year. The attack on the Pope went hand in hand with an attack on the position of the Church in the law of Italian lands. The further south in the peninsula the French went, the fiercer opposition to them became. Though Joseph Bonaparte and after him Joachim Murat, successive Kings of Naples, made efforts to ingratiate themselves with their subjects, there was no doubt that a Frenchman in an isolated part of the kingdom was liable to have his throat cut. The bandit traditions of the *mezzogiorno*, once combined with loyalty to semi-literate clergy and British interference, proved troublesome in Calabria.

It was even harder to deal with Spain. The formerly greatest of European lands could boast the finest of court painters anywhere in Francisco Goya y Lucientes, but it had not only the ugliest royal family on the Continent, it had for a king the weak Charles IV who made with Queen Maria Luisa and his favourite (and perhaps hers) the Prince of Godoy an inept trio who had no idea how to cope with an overwhelming neighbour, other than to be overwhelmed. Many of the ablest ministers, administrators and writers were, like Goya, *afrancesados*, only too willing to work with enlightened France against Black Spain, represented by the Inquisition. Napoleon therefore expected no resistance if he moved troops into the country, ostensibly en route for Portugal, England's traditional ally. A family squabble, engineered by the loathsome Crown Prince Ferdinand, led to the abdication of the father and the succession of the son, giving Napoleon a reason for mediating. He summoned the whole royal family to Bayonne, but, while on 2 May 1808 Don Francisco, last of the royal children, was being escorted from the

capital, Madrileños took to the streets and fell upon their tormen-
tors. Murat, in charge of the French troops, knew from Napoleon
how to quell a mob, so that on 3 May firing squads disposed of the
leaders. Napoleon got rid of all the Bourbon claimants to the
throne and in their place installed his brother Joseph, on whose
Neapolitan throne he placed Murat. When he reached Madrid in
July, Joseph was greeted in silence. Many of his leading ministers
disappeared, while in the countryside priests and peasants, women
as well as men, began a new kind of harassment that led a Spanish
word for a little war – *una guerilla* – being coined afresh in many
other European tongues. The French began to suffer local defeats:
in July General Dupont's corps at Bailen in southern Castile was
routed by Spanish rebels, in August at Vimiero in Portugal Junot
was beaten by an English army under an obscure general called
Arthur Wellesley. By early August Joseph had to retreat northwards
until he was behind the line of the Ebro river.

It was time for Napoleon to teach them all a lesson. Racing
down to the outskirts of Madrid, he ordered Polish *chasseurs* to
charge Spanish guns. At the second attempt they overran them,
Napoleon had won a battle, at Somo Sierra, and the French could
re-enter Madrid. It was 4 December. A fortnight later he heard of
an English army, led by Sir John Moore, coming to the aid of the
rebels. Moore almost stumbled into the French when he suddenly
became aware that he was near an army far larger than his own. He
hurriedly began his long withdrawal to La Coruña in the north-
west province of Galicia, saved not only by his own dexterity but
by a fortunate piece of news. Napoleon had learned that he must
race back to Paris. He left his subordinates to clear the English out
of the peninsula and to put the natives in their place.

What had happened in his absence to make him race back home
was that once again a major power was preparing to take him on.

In the councils of the Austrian Empire the Emperor's third wife and the Archdukes Ferdinand and John and the Chancellor von Stadion thought they could lead a common Germanic cause against their tormentor. They knew that Archduke Charles had done a lot, if not as much as he wanted, to reform the army. He had adopted the French corps system but was not certain that his generals could make it work; he still had too many old officers with long memories and too many young ones with short memories to trust them on the same field as the veterans who ran the French army, few of them beyond their forties. Still, he could not afford not to support the war. He was given an army of more than 200,000 men, in March he proclaimed a War of Liberation and in April he invaded Bavaria. Few Germans were anxious to be free, encouraged in their moderation by the rapid arrival of the French. In April Napoleon took command of what he called with some truth the Army, later the Grand Army, of Germany, as it included Württembergers, Saxons and Bavarians as well as Poles and Frenchmen. He took the classic route along the Danube and entered Vienna, as the composer Haydn was dying, while the Austrians withdrew carefully on the north side of the river. No emissary came to meet him in Vienna, but once he had recovered from his astonishment he pressed along the river, looking for somewhere to cross, since the bridges had been destroyed. He decided to use Lobau island, in the middle of the river, close to two towns on the other side, Aspern and Essling. On 21 May, when a small French bridgehead had been formed between them, the Archduke struck. For two days there was a fierce battle. Napoleon believed that, like Kutuzov in 1805, the Archduke must have retreated, so he hurled his army unwittingly against a much larger force. Lannes led an offensive which gained a mile by 7 a.m. and a second mile an hour later, before the offensive stalled. The Austrians, meanwhile, had let loose upstream a large wooden mill which crashed through the French pontoon bridge and prevented the French troops on the south bank crossing on to Lobau island. Against superior fire, the French had to yield, as slowly as they could. Lannes had a leg shot off (and died nine days later) and at 5 p.m. Napoleon told his men to vacate the beachhead. He had lost 15,000 men and one of his best generals and he had not crossed the Danube. He had been defeated, he announced, not by the Austrians but by the river; he refused to give up Lobau island; next time he would succeed.

As it happened, he was to be proved right. He got useful help when his stepson, Eugène de Beauharnais, though defeated once by Archduke John in Italy, managed to maul his opponent while he moved back across the mountains and came first to join his stepfather in Vienna, then to pounce on and disperse Archduke John's troops from the town of Raab, where the Raab river meets the Danube. The Archdukes failed to meet up, but stepson and stepfather did. When Napoleon was ready to fight Archduke Charles again, he had about 190,000 men and 480 guns against 140,000 and 450 guns. With these advantages, the Battle of Wagram, when it came on 6 July, had an inevitable result. Though the Archduke retired in good order, he was sick with epilepsy and disheartened and he asked for an armistice, which was granted. He had not had the subordinates who had helped Napoleon win, and nor did he have so many foreign troops.

Napoleon was sure now that he was invincible. 'My victory', he wrote to Joséphine, is 'decisive and complete.' At Schönbrunn he felt that he could impose harsh terms on the Austrian Emperor. Austria ceded Salzburg and Inn-Viertel, which were given over to Bavaria; the French Empire acquired ancient Habsburg territories (Carniola and Carinthia), large parts of Friuli, the port of Trieste, parts of Croatia and Dalmatia south of the river Save; Russia got part of Austrian Galicia but most was given to the Duchy of

Warsaw. The Emperor had to pay 85 million francs for the privilege of being beaten. He could never have an army of more than 150,000 men, but, as he had lost a sixth of his subjects and dismissed Archduke Charles, there was little chance of Austria fighting another single-handed campaign against the French. Austria would have to learn more skill in diplomacy. In 1809 Count Metternich, recently ambassador in Paris, was made Austria's Foreign Minister.

It was Metternich who in 1810 negotiated what must have seemed to his master the ultimate humiliation: the marriage of Archduchess Maria Louisa to the Emperor of the French. By late 1809 Napoleon had decided that he must divorce Joséphine in the interests of France. That it was she, not he, who was sterile was proved by the pregnancy of Maria Walewska. Napoleon's first choice was the Grand Duchess Anna, the Tsar's sister, but the Tsar demurred on the grounds that his sister was only sixteen. That left as an alternative the slightly older Archduchess. The last Franco-Austrian marriage, of Louis XVI to the Archduchess Maria Antoinetta, had not left a happy memory; and there was the problem of the Pope, who had made Napoleon marry Joséphine in a private ceremony in 1804. But Napoleon was bent on joining the upper class of European monarchs. He knew that he could manipulate his uncle, Cardinal Fesch, who conveniently noticed that the religious wedding to Joséphine had not followed the proper forms, and after some unattractive family scenes, in which his sisters behaved with less dignity than his ex-wife, Joséphine was pensioned off, and at the religious marriage in the Tuileries the royal and grand ducal ladies of both the Beauharnais and the Bonaparte families were gorgeously arrayed.

In 1810 there were signs of trouble to come. In Spain and Portugal the war was not going well. Neither Masséna nor Soult could corner the English, and Napoleon was so angry with his brother Louis that he threw him off the throne of the Netherlands. But Marie-Louise was expecting a child and Napoleon an heir.

In the Salon of 1810 there was a flurry of activity in glorification of the Emperor by all the major painters. David showed *The Distribution of the Eagles*, Gérard *The Battle of Austerlitz*, Girodet *The Revolt of Cairo* and Gros *The Battle of the Pyramids*. Curiously, none of these painters tackled the subject of the hour – the Battle of Wagram – and there was no major treatment of it at a Salon until 1836, when Horace Vernet, the Bonapartist son of the Bonapartist Carle Vernet, produced his version to coincide with a period of Napoleonic nostalgia. But Napoleon had reason to be pleased with himself.

Nothing touched him so much as the key work of the previous Salon: Gros's *The Battle of Eylau*. The battle was the first occasion when Napoleon's enemies had sensed he might be vulnerable, and Napoleon had sensed it too. Not since Marengo had there been a battle over which he struggled so hard to tell the world that his version of events was the truth. In the days after Eylau he dictated to General Bertrand, who was to be one of his companions on St Helena, a pamphlet entitled *A Relation of the Battle of Eylau, by an eye witness, translated from the German*. This pamphlet was widely distributed in north German towns. Bourrienne's diary comments: 'The Emperor was exceedingly anxious that everyone should view that event as he himself viewed it.' Napoleon told his chief of police, Fouché: 'Spread the following reports in an un-official manner. They are, however, true. Spread them first in the salons and then put them in the papers – that the Russian army is greatly weakened – that the Russian army demands peace.' Curiously, at much the same time the Tsar was congratulating the 'defeated' Bennigsen for 'having beaten the man who till today has never been beaten'.[3]

Napoleon had undoubtedly been shaken. He was horrified, at

least for a while, by the pointless carnage. Gros had therefore assuaged any feelings of inadequacy or guilt by showing Napoleon as a man of compassion looking towards heaven rather than at the corpses on the earth around him. Had Napoleon been wise, he would have pondered over the snow.

3

THE ROUTE TO THE EAST
AND BACK AGAIN

—————

There is no authorized picture of Napoleon in defeat. Defeat was not a theme that appealed to him, though it would appeal to later admirers. One telling example shows how he viewed failure: his initial reaction to David's first attempt to paint a picture of the Spartan king Leonidas on the eve of the Battle of Thermopylae. David regarded art as a moral activity. He liked repeating to his pupils the dictum 'paint as men lived in Sparta'.

After Marengo, Napoleon and his brother Lucien, then Minister of the Interior, came to David's studio as Napoleon was thinking of inviting David to paint his portrait (as yet nobody had suggested the mythic scene of his crossing of the Alps). 'What are you doing now?' asked the First Consul. 'I am working on the picture of the Pass of Thermopylae.' 'That's bad. You're wrong, David, to tire yourself out painting conquered men.' 'But, Citizen Consul, these heroes were men who died for their country, and in spite of their defeat they pushed away the Persians from Greece for a hundred years.' 'No matter. Only Leonidas's name has lasted to our days. All the rest is lost to history.' 'Everything,' interrupted David, '. . . except this noble resistance to an army that could not be numbered. Everything! . . . except their devotion, which does not need the addition of their name. Everything! . . . except the habits, the austere way of life of the Spartans, whose memory is worth reminding soldiers of.' When Napoleon had gone, Lucien reassured him: 'You see, my dear fellow, he likes only nationalistic subjects, because they involve him. It's his weakness; he is not annoyed if you speak of him.' It became clear that although Napoleon was not going to pose for David, he would like to be portrayed as a man who sat calmly on a wild horse.

After 1800 David forgot about Spartan ways, became Napoleon's first painter and charged exorbitant fees. In 1814, however, after the Emperor fell, he returned to his Spartan theme and, while the Bourbon Louis XVIII held his first Salon, David put on a private exhibition of his neglected picture. *Leonidas at Thermopylae*, a slightly ludicrous work, became his final comment on the man who had been his hero.

In the Salons of 1812 and 1814 a younger, more modern painter came to attention with an exultant *Charging Chasseur* and a weary *Wounded Cuirassier*. Géricault, the painter, knew how much horses counted.

For the invasion of Russia in 1812 Napoleon produced the largest army that had ever marched. Probably some 450,000 men under his command crossed the Niemen in June 1812. Tsar Alexander could muster only 160,000 to oppose him. If the Russians were not to lose, they would have to retreat. If the French were to win, they would have to catch up with the enemy first. The kind of campaign that would be fought was determined before any shots were fired.

Napoleon would have known what had happened to the last military genius who had invaded the country: King Charles XII of Sweden had marched and marched until he was caught and pummelled at Pultava. Napoleon was sure that he had prepared with sufficient care.

Relations with Russia had taken five years to deteriorate so far that he felt obliged to attack the man he had seen as his natural ally. From the start there were three problems – Turkey, marriage and trade – that the two needed to solve. Alexander dreamed of continuing the policy of his grandmother Catherine the Great: he longed to win Constantinople, the religious capital of the Orthodox world, he had set his heart on capturing the Romanian principalities of Moldavia and Wallachia, and he wished to be a power in the Mediterranean. Late in May 1808, Napoleon told Caulaincourt, his ambassador in St Petersburg: 'If Russia had an outlet on the Dardanelles, she would be at the gates of Toulon, Naples and Corfu.'[1] The prospect worried him. In October 1808, at Erfurt, the two Emperors met again, and Napoleon found the Tsar strangely distant. When Napoleon suggested that, were he to divorce Joséphine, he might like to marry Alexander's sister, Grand Duchess Catherine, the Tsar was pointedly silent – she later married the Duke of Oldenburg, hardly a catch compared with him. Unabashed, Napoleon tried for her younger sister Anna. Again Alexander stalled, but, when Napoleon switched to the Habsburgs, the Tsar affected to be affronted. He had pressing reasons for wishing to detach himself from the French. Enforcing the Continental system hurt Russian merchants and noblemen, who exported to Britain much of the timber that was needed for the British navy.

After Austria's defeat at Wagram, there were more reasons for tension. The Russians were annoyed that Napoleon attached much of Austrian Galicia to Poland, leaving them with only a morsel of land, and, though Caulaincourt signed an agreement that France would not re-create the Kingdom of Poland, Napoleon repudiated it. In Sweden, which had a tradition of oscillating between pro-French and pro-Russian policies, the pro-French faction engineered the choice of Marshal Bernadotte as Crown Prince in 1810, which annoyed the Tsar; and he was even angrier when Napoleon annexed the old Hanseatic trading towns of northern Germany and the Duchy of Oldenburg, whose duchess was the Tsar's sister, in order to close the gaps in the Continental blockade of British goods. Simultaneously, the Tsar heard that French agents were using their new interest in Croatia and Dalmatia to make contacts with Serbs, whom the Russians regarded as their clients, while further approaches had been made in Turkey and Persia, the Muslim countries that would be most worried by Russian advances in the areas of the Black and the Caspian Seas. Napoleon knew that Alexander had approached the rich and powerful Czartoryskis in Poland and, even though he had broken his own embargo on trade with the British Isles by allowing the export there of French and Dutch wheat, he objected to the ease with which the Russians, worried by the decline of the rouble, allowed more and more so-called neutral ships to enter Russian harbours. Worse still, on New Year's Eve 1810 the Tsar placed heavy duties on foreign luxury goods, a French speciality. He did not want war, but he also did not want peace just on Napoleon's terms. He pointed out to Caulaincourt that the Spaniards had been defeated but were not beaten. He added: 'Your Frenchman is brave, but long sufferings and a hard climate wear down his resistance. Our climate, our winter, will fight on our side.'[2]

When Napoleon's son, the King of Rome, was born in March 1811, visions of Imperial Grandeur still seemed mere dreams. The Pope, deprived of the Eternal City, was a prisoner in the south of France. He had excommunicated Napoleon and would not withdraw his sentence. In the Iberian Peninsula, Spanish peasants clung to their pistols, their daggers, their pitchforks and their priests. Napoleon told his German allies that as Russia endangered the Confederation, he was requesting troops from his brother Jérôme's Westphalia, from his father-in-law's Austria and from Prussia. But the Russians demanded compensation for the loss of Oldenburg by the Tsar's brother-in-law, the evacuation of Prussia and a buffer zone between areas of Russian and French influence. They also won diplomatic skirmishes. Sweden was incensed by the economic effects of Napoleon's prohibition of any trade with the British Isles, one of Sweden's best customers, and by his seizure of Swedish Pomerania, which had given Sweden a foothold on German soil since 1648. In March 1812 Bernadotte agreed to be neutral if at some future date Sweden could have Norway (in return for Finland, which Russia had taken in 1807). Two months later, Russia signed the Treaty of Bucharest with Turkey. Only France would be the enemy.

That was not how Napoleon saw affairs. When he moved his force into Russia that June, the Grande Armée was less purely French than it ever had been. Of the 614,000 troops he raised, at most 302,000 were French, but only two-thirds of these came from within the 1792 borders of the country (others were Belgian, Dutch, Swiss or Italian). There were also some 190,000 Germans, Austrians, Prussians and Swiss (from outside Imperial France), 90,000 Poles and Lithuanians and about 32,000 from Mediterranean countries, Italians (from the east and the south), Illyrians, Spaniards and Portuguese. Of the various contingents, probably only the French and Poles were enthusiasts for the cause.[3]

Even though no more than 450,000 of these troops were in the first line of the attack, there was a difficulty that correctly caused Napoleon much concern: how could he provision such an army?

Hitherto his maxim had been to live off the land, but, even before he was faced with problems caused by scorched earth reactions to his advance, he knew that he must be able to provide his men with food and ammunition that could not be found in the vast spaces of the Russian Empire. Hundreds of carts and hundreds of thousands of animals set out with his men, along with the female camp followers, the *vivandières*, *blanchisseuses*, women soldiers, wives and lovers. Sergeant Bourgogne, a veteran of the wars in Spain, has a touching story of a gallant *voltigeur's* attempt to rescue a young Spaniard, his *cantinière*, who was struck by a bullet on her thumb while tending wounded soldiers and passed out. A gallant *cuirassier* lifted her up 'like a child' and took her off to the Emperor's surgeon, Larrey, who first amputated her thumb and then cleverly removed a bullet from the *voltigeur's* arm. Larrey and his medical team were also of key importance in the campaign, if only to mitigate the hideous sufferings of the troops, even when they seemed to be winning the campaign.[4]

At first Napoleon called his war the Polish war. The main army, under his command, 250,000 strong, was in the north, his stepson Eugène with 80,000 held the centre and his brother Jérôme, also with 80,000, the south. Macdonald and the Prussians guarded his northern flank, Schwarzenburg's Austrians the southern flank. Two days after crossing the Niemen, he was able to start building a base at Vilnius, the Lithuanian capital, while he spent three weeks pondering the future of Poland. His wing of the army pursued the main Russian army under Barclay de Tolly steadily to Vitebsk – Murat, so dashing in a charge, had not stopped to think that horses could not keep up the pace he demanded – and Jérôme veered south from Minsk in pursuit of the 50,000 commanded by Bagration – he was impeded by heavy rain. When Napoleon, wrongly believing that his brother had been incompetent, replaced him with the ever dependable Davout, Jérôme sulkily retired to Westphalia, with his wardrobe of beautiful uniforms and his crates of bottles of eau-de-cologne. The fracas enabled the two main Russian forces to link up at Smolensk. At Vitebsk Napoleon lingered again, this time to sort out principles of the government of Lithuania – Vitebsk had once been a Lithuanian city – while the indiscipline of his troops was alienating the local Lithuanian peasants. He enjoyed inspecting his men, especially the Imperial Guard, at reviews, while horses were dying and the initial stocks of food were running low. At Smolensk, he was sure, the Russians would fight.

On 17 August, when the French assaulted the *enceinte* of ancient city walls, they found it deserted. Bagration had fled without permission and Barclay had felt obliged to follow him. Junot, told to attack across the Dnieper, hesitated until he got further orders, and Napoleon, now fat, sluggish and introspective, waited at headquarters to receive further information. On 19 August Ney defeated the Russian rearguard but lost yet more horses and could not stop the enemy from escaping. After he put the army on the Moscow road, Napoleon was confronted by a heated duo, almost on the point of a duel: Murat grumbled that the infantry was too slow, Davout was furious that the cavalry set too fast a pace. In public Napoleon was soothing, but privately he sided with his brother-in-law. As a result, more and more men and horses died by the wayside, while the Russians burned houses and removed whatever crops they could take away. Though the Russian army had dwindled to 120,000 when the Tsar called the old general, Kutuzov, out of retirement, the Russian troops were in better shape than the Grande Armée, and the difference in numbers between the two sides was being rapidly eroded. The Tsar and his new commander decided that they must stand at Borodino.

*   *   *

The Battle of Borodino on 7 September 1812 was one of the bloodiest that Napoleon had experienced. By the end of the day he had lost about 30,000 men and 47 generals, fewer than the Russian 45,000, so the way to Moscow was open but the decisive victory, the elimination of the opponent's army, for which he craved, had eluded the Emperor. When he marched into the almost deserted ancient capital of Muscovy, on 14 September, Napoleon led an army of 95,000 men. While he installed himself in the Kremlin, the largely wooden city began to burn. He wrote to Alexander to tell him what had happened. The Tsar, warm in the new capital of St Petersburg, did not reply. It was too late to attack him there, too late to go after Kutuzov, wherever he was. He was told that Wellington had entered Madrid. He had planned a short campaign, he had driven the main Russian armies far from the borders of their country, but he had not won. While his men looted freely and got all the vodka, furs and jellies they wanted, they were without meat and vegetables and adequate shelter. Murat was delighted when he learned that he was the Cossacks' hero, but even his men slaughtered horses to have something to eat, while in Moscow itself maybe 20,000 horses died in a month. On 17 October Napoleon gave orders that the army should prepare to leave. Next day Murat was attacked and only just avoided capture.

On 4 November heavy snow began to fall. The retreat soon became a disaster. Men, confused by vodka or wine, fell down and lacked the energy to get up. About 15,000 horses that pulled the carts dropped dead in the five days it took to reach Smolensk by 9 November. From then on, the journey out of Russia became a series of memorable scenes that those who survived them never forgot. Ney, his 6000 rearguard blocked by 30,000 Russians, lit fires to deceive the enemy while his men crossed the icy Dnieper – only 900 of them were left. By the time he reached Borisov on the Berezina in late November, Napoleon had only a dozen guns, and his 48,000 effective soldiers were outnumbered by neighbouring Russian forces, with far more artillery. As the river had thawed, it required all the skill of French engineers to construct two temporary bridges, the larger of which broke, so that the crush on the smaller bridge caused many more men and horses to fall into the freezing waters. That the French army got away was due in no small measure to Napoleon's renewed vigour. Hounded by Cossacks and tormented by cold, a remnant of the mighty force that had crossed the Niemen in June recrossed it in December, maybe no more than 25,000 men. Napoleon lost up to 370,000 soldiers who died on battlefields, of sickness or of exposure, and about 200,000 horses, which were used by the cavalry, by the artillery and for transport.

On 5 December he left the army in the charge of Murat and was driven back to Paris, where he reached the Tuileries palace on 19 December. Three days before his arrival the twenty-ninth Bulletin of the Grande Armée, dated 3 December, had been printed in the official *Le Moniteur*. He admitted some losses at the hands of marauding Cossacks, he praised the men for their resilience, he expatiated on the heroic crossing of the Berezina, he admitted that the cavalry was mostly on foot, he blamed his difficulties on the harsh weather conditions and he finished with reassuring words: 'The health of the Emperor has never been better.'

The myth of the retreat was soon bolstered by the tales of survivors. Sergeant Bourgogne scarcely bothered with the story of how he got to Moscow, but is wonderfully eloquent about his adventures on the way home. What Napoleon did not admit was that he had lost most of his men before he reached Moscow, that his own lethargy had needlessly delayed the chase of the inferior Russian armies – he seemed more involved in parades than in pursuit – while the lack of coordination had put strains on his commanders, who were not used to thinking for themselves. He was not the general he had been, and he was going to face not only generals and troops who had beaten him but also others who knew his methods intimately – Moreau and Bernadotte – or who had learned how he could be beaten. He had claimed that God was on the side of the big battalions and yet he was unlikely ever again to be able to outnumber his enemies if they combined. His coalition of forces had failed against a national army. A coalition of national armies might produce a different class of enemy.

Napoleon set about raising another large army. He also knew he would need all his diplomatic skill to divide his enemies, so that they would not overwhelm him.

Since 1807 Napoleon had been without Talleyrand's advice. Five years later he had need of good advice, partly because his international enemies were able to call on better diplomats than he had. In the case of his most persistent enemy, Britain, this became true in 1812, for in that year Viscount Castlereagh became Foreign Secretary. Since Pitt died early in 1806, no figure in British politics had been persistently dominant. George Canning, the Pittite thought of as Pitt's preferred political heir, was too witty and indiscreet to fit comfortably into the clubbable world of the House of Commons. Besides, he had strong opinions, one of which went down badly. Like his master Pitt, he was convinced that at least some Roman Catholics, who in Ireland were in a majority, ought to have the vote. This had not prevented him from being invited to be Foreign Secretary in 1807 and as such he blamed a colleague, the War Minister Castlereagh, for military failures: Moore's withdrawal to La Coruña in Spain, and the amphibious attack on Flushing (Vlissingen) in the Netherlands. Castlereagh, who felt his honour at stake, challenged him to a duel. Both resigned, the duel took place, Canning was wounded, Prime Minister Bentinck died suddenly and another nonentity, Spencer Perceval, took over. Canning was not back in government until 1816, but in 1812

Castlereagh was recalled to the Cabinet, this time as Foreign Secretary, just before Perceval was assassinated by a madman and the office of Prime Minister passed to a peer, Lord Liverpool, who found it much easier to work with men who were abler than himself. In the crucial period of 1812 to 1815, British diplomacy was masterminded by a man who was sure that the only way to defeat Napoleon was by a coalition of all the powers and that in any alliance Britain must work closely with Continental partners. Though it was only in the Iberian Peninsula that Britain deployed an army, which in 1812 was on the verge of winning the war against the French, the navy had a vital role to play in pinning down the French; and British finance could help to support larger Continental armies, which were essential if Napoleon was to be beaten. Castlereagh was lucky that in the economic struggle against France, the worst years for Britain were over, and that, though in the same year Britain foolishly got involved in a war against the United States, its industrial problems at home, acute in 1812, were partly solved and on the Continent fresh markets were opening up to British trade, notably in the Baltic and in the Mediterranean, while the Dutch and north Germans were prepared to risk Napoleon's anger if only they could manage to smuggle goods to and from Britain in and out of their ports.

Castlereagh directed the foreign policy of a country that traditionally relied on ships to cope with international relations. Metternich, from 1809 Austrian Foreign Minister, was in charge of an Empire that was landlocked – it had lost its one important port, Trieste, to France – and, even after its losses in 1809, polyglot and polymorphous. As a noble from the Rhineland, Metternich's first tongue was French, but he had to concern himself with a group of states in which German and Magyar were dominant languages, but where there were Czechs, Slovenes and Serbs (and there had been Croats and Poles) and there were minorities of many idioms. In

73

Austria Francis I was Emperor, in Hungary and in Bohemia he was King and he had more titles than any other European monarch, including the redundant one of King of Jerusalem (a Turkish possession for three hundred years), but he knew that even a Habsburg could not pretend that he any longer dominated European affairs. It became Metternich's speciality to play a weak hand with skill. He hoped to win for his master as much influence in Europe as he could, but without Britain's economic and financial might, Russia's manpower resources, the national consciousness of France or, as it turned out, the nationalistic loyalty to which Prussia began to appeal, he needed all his charm to achieve his objectives, for he must convince others with more clout that what was good for his Austria was good for them. He was sure that revolution of any kind – social, economic or political – would upset the concert of Europe. The rulers of the ruling class, of whom emperors and kings were the natural leaders, would be wise to follow his lead, for were they to let anyone question their authority to rule, the people, whatever that expression meant, might take power for themselves. It was in this sense that he understood one of his most famous sayings: 'For a long time Europe has had for me the value of a country [*une patrie*].' His *patrie* was the antithesis of the kind of *patrie* mentioned in the first line of the 'La Marseillaise'. Napoleon wanted a Europe constituted along French lines, Metternich a Europe controlled by the upper classes who from Madrid to St Petersburg chose to speak to one another in French.

The unlikely partnership between Castlereagh and Metternich was to be a principal cause of the fall of Napoleon, but early in 1813 Metternich could provide a lifeline for Napoleon, whose new wife was Francis I's daughter.[5] There were good reasons why Habsburgs and Bonapartes should remain allies. If they did, eventually France would be ruled by the Kaiser's grandson. In January Napoleon made his father-in-law a small offer – the return of Illyria

– but he had no intention of restoring the balance of power to the days before he was Emperor. The Emperor Francis was not sure Russia could defeat France: he was also not sure that he wanted the Tsar to defeat Napoleon. He wanted peace. In April 1813 he wrote to Napoleon suggesting that their common aim should be 'stamping out the Jacobin ferment, which daily spreads, will soon threaten the existence of thrones'. In March, even though Archduke John supported it, Metternich had taken care to prevent any rebellion in the Tyrol against the French. In June he met Napoleon in Dresden, the Saxon capital, and urged him to make terms. He was pessimistic about the results of possible failure, writing to his master to say: 'If Your Majesty lose this opportunity what limit can there be to revolutions?' It was during the talks in Dresden that Napoleon told Metternich: 'Your Sovereigns born on the throne can let themselves be beaten twenty times and return to their capitals. I cannot do this because I am an upstart soldier. My domination will not survive the day when I cease to be strong and therefore feared.' He could not accept a solution for Europe that he had not proposed.

Austria had propositions of its own. Already Narbonne, his ambassador in Vienna, had told Napoleon that Austria wanted him to suppress two of his imaginative creations, the Duchy of Warsaw and the Confederation of the Rhine. Austria had no desire for either Polish or German unification. On 24 June at Reichenbach Metternich promised that if by 20 June France had not agreed to the dissolution of the Duchy of Warsaw, the enlargement of Prussia, the restoration of the North German towns and lands seized in 1810 as well as the cession of Illyria, then Austria would declare war. On 26 June Metternich and Napoleon talked for nine hours. Napoleon said that he had been mistaken to marry a Habsburg, it was like trying to wed the present to the past, 'Gothic prejudices' with modern institutions. Metternich replied that Napoleon and 'Europe' could never agree, since Napoleon wanted truces, not peace. That night he heard that his brother Joseph had been defeated by Wellington at Vittoria. Austria, he knew, would no longer stay neutral. On 14 June Castlereagh's representatives had signed treaties with Tsar Alexander and King Frederick William that stated that, provided Britain went on producing aid, neither of the Continental powers would make peace separately. A final coalition against Napoleon was almost in place, as a quadruple alliance.[6]

What was surprising, in view of his character and past events, was the vehemence with which the Prussian King undertook to fight the French. Since Tilsit his country had been transformed.

The Germany emerging from the wreck of the Holy Roman Empire was already turning into the intellectual and artistic power-house of Europe. In music, all roads in Germany still led to Vienna, where Haydn would soon end his days and where Beethoven had moved from Bonn; and no other city equalled the literary fame of Weimar, where Schiller had died in 1805 and Goethe lingered on, as the grand representative of an international culture that embraced many languages and many forms of art. In 1808 Goethe made a point of going to visit Napoleon at Erfurt, and as late as 1809 the philosopher Hegel, who had once called Napoleon 'the soul of the world', as professor at Nuremberg advised Bavarians to adopt the civil code. But there was already a new note of national-istic fervour in academic circles. From 1805 Arndt decried French cultural influence in terms that Frederick the Great, who had thought and written in French, would have found incomprehen-sible, and from 1807 Fichte's *Appeal to the German Nation* re-sounded throughout the circles of the intelligentsia. Its disparate political organization meant that Germany boasted more uni-

Boilly's portrait of Robespierre shows a strict republican, whose brother patronised Napoleon, dressing like a lawyer of the *ancien régime*.

In 1842 Bellangé placed Napoleon much closer to the Pyramids than he was in 1798.

The most virulent general opposing Napoleon was Field Marshal Blücher, who at Waterloo avenged the Prussian defeat of 1806.

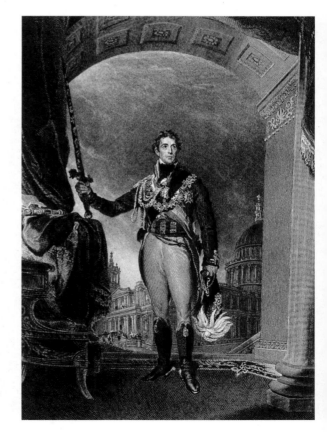

Lawrence showed the confident Wellington enjoying the defeat of Napoleon in 1814. They were yet to meet the next year at Waterloo.

Metternich, painted by Lawrence, was the skilful Austrian diplomat who prepared at the Congress of Vienna for a Europe without Napoleon.

Castlereagh, painted by Lawrence, was instrumental in keeping together the alliance against Napoleon.

Chateaubriand, as seen by Girodet, looked shifty to Napoleon. He became an outspoken critic of Napoleon and a defender of the Bourbons.

Talleyrand was Napoleon's foreign minister for many years, but later engineered the return of the Bourbons.

David painted Napoleon crossing the Alps as a hero like Hannibal and Charlemagne.

In fact the First Consul, who was not a good rider, crossed the St Bernard Pass on a mule.

After Napoleon's greatest victory at the Battle of Austerlitz (dramatised by Gérard) Emperor Francis II came to sue for peace.

At Eylau, Napoleon just withstood Russian attacks in the snow. He liked the way Gros portrayed him as a magnanimous victor.

versities than any other country in Europe – at this time England had only two – and as a corollary professors had a status that was also without parallel. Young men in small cities, in Cassel, Jena or Königsberg, became proud that they were Germans, but what is more significant is that gradually one university city was starting to outshine all the others. It was at Berlin that Fichte delivered his discourse, and it was to Berlin that Hegel would move just because he was the most original thinker in the land. Eventually, Hegel came to teach that the point to which world history was moving was the establishment of the Prussian state.

At the time of the Treaty of Tilsit such a viewpoint must have seemed ridiculous. The King was back in Königsberg, whose one claim to fame hitherto had been that Kant had taught there and the inhabitants had set their watches by his movements. There Frederick William was soon joined by a remarkable and energetic group of men: Clausewitz, the theorist of war; Scharnhorst, from Hanover, and Gneisenau, from Saxony, who were told to overhaul the army; above all Stein, who was a Rhinelander and who arrived at the end of September with a suggested plan for reform, the *Memorandum of Nassau*. They did not want an egalitarian Prussia, based on French revolutionary ideals, or a laissez-faire country that copied England. Peasants and bourgeois were allowed to own land but the King, too, gained, for he no longer conceded customary rights on his own territory, especially in forests. As for the nobility, they still retained their judicial rights – to administer local justice for example – and the effect of their pressure on the peasants they had formerly owned was that there was a steady exodus to the towns, so that the eighteenth-century country dweller was transformed in a generation or two into the nineteenth-century industrial worker.

Stein also altered the bureaucracy and political institutions. He set up five ministries and at their head created a council of ministers. The Prussian *Landtag*, the equivalent of a parliament, was to have more bourgeois and some peasants, but they voted by order, so that the rich exercised more authority – there was to be no National Assembly along the lines of the French institution of 1789 – and even this seems to have been too radical an idea for other parts of the kingdom or the King's dominions as a whole. In 1808 Napoleon forced Stein's resignation, but the idea of reform survived him. In particular, the army was the subject of changes that had permanent effect. Though Scharnhorst got rid of only some two hundred officers who had failed in the war of 1806, he had begun to prepare for a better fighting force for the future. Cadet schools were modernized, a new system of selecting officers was put in place, new training manuals were made available, discipline made less degrading and conscription by ballot was recommended. Foreign mercenaries were dispensed with, so the *Landwehr*, when it emerged in 1813, was a national army. Prussia was luckier than Austria, in that it had six years to prepare to resume war against France, not just four. Though it was constrained by the presence of French garrisons in many Prussian towns, if France had to withdraw those soldiers Prussia would be ready for a fight; and the King of Prussia could be certain that, if he fought against Napoleon, he would fight for a popular cause.

Napoleon was less sure of morale among his followers. While he was away in Russia, there was no news of him, so that a rumour of his death was easy to believe. In November 1812 a republican soldier, General Malet, tried to organize a conspiracy against him. The authorities put Malet to death, but clearly Napoleon had to make his presence felt in France. There were other urgent reasons. Since 1805 all wars had been on foreign soil and at foreign expense, and the Grande Armée had turned into a largely foreign institution.

From 1813 onwards, Napoleon had to rely on France and on the French people.

Early in 1813 Murat, who had been left in charge of the remains of the army that had gone to Russia, left orders for Eugène de Beauharnais to take command and hurried back to Naples. Never the brightest of Napoleon's marshals, his recent experiences had dented his self-esteem and he was never the same again. Though he had lost his looks, Eugène had grown in stature. He was to be faithful to his stepfather almost to the end.

Back home, Napoleon was determined to re-create an enormous army to bolster the sad remnant in Eugène's care. The previous autumn he had arranged the premature call-up of the class of 1813, so that almost 137,000 conscripts were nearing the end of their training. To these he added 80,000 National Guards. He wanted 450,000 more. The class of 1814 was ordered to report in February, but it was hard to find enough gunners, horses and horsemen. He produced the artillery by redirecting 12,000 naval gunners to serve on land and then changed 24 battalions of sailors into soldiers too. It was much more difficult to replace the cavalry. Napoleon used the gendarmerie as a nucleus, but such men would never equal those who had charged behind Murat or Ney. It was even harder to provide them with mounts. Prussia and other parts of central Germany were areas where horses were plentiful, but early in 1813 the states were indifferent to France's needs and later hostile. Caulaincourt was impressed by the single-minded way in which his fellow countrymen joined in preparations for war, but he also said that the new troops were 'an organized mob'. Most were too young or too old, some took to the hills to run away, peasants in the Vendée, whose first revolt had started off in response to con- scription, were ready to revolt again. Meanwhile, slowly Eugène retreated westwards, leaving garrisons as he moved first to the line of the Oder, then to the line of the Elbe. For a time, French troops held Dresden, but they, too, soon retired to the Saale river. So anti-French was the mood in the Prussian towns that the King felt obliged to promise to put up 80,000 to join 150,000 Russians, and the Tsar let him know he would have his pre-1806 borders back again. On 17 March, after issuing an appeal to 'my people' the King of Prussia became openly belligerent and he called up a conscript militia or *Landwehr*, a popular organization that normally he feared.

The campaigns of 1813 involved small battles and one great one, with an interval between them. Kutuzov, the victor of 1812, became the commander-in-chief but died and was not replaced. Napoleon showed some of his old dynamism and arrived before he was expected. On 2 May at Lützen he drove the allies from the field but did not have the cavalry to disperse them. He exclaimed to his Grand Marshal of the Palace, Duroc: 'I am again the master of Europe.' But he was not, and, though he scored a second triumph on 20–21 May at Bautzen, he had had to send in the Guard to win and once more he lacked the cavalry to exploit his success. He had good news when he marched into Dresden and heard that Davout had secured Hamburg, but he could not stop the Cossacks from freely roaming in his rear. When the allies appealed for an armistice at the beginning of June, he was pleased to grant their request. But when war resumed in August, Austria was committed to the allies.

Napoleon, who managed to amass three armies totalling 370,000, found himself facing Schwarzenberg with 240,000 of the Army of Bohemia, Bernadotte, now Crown Prince of Sweden, with 120,000 of the Army of the North, Blücher with 95,000 of the Army of Silesia and Bennigsen with 60,000 of the Army of Poland. Napoleon had sent Soult, who had been at Bautzen, back to Spain, where he had been before, so he summoned Murat from Naples.

He decided to tackle his main enemies separately, sending Oudinot to beat Bernadotte and retake Berlin and Ney to tackle Blücher while he would deal with Schwarzenberg. He did not know that the allies had agreed to fight subordinate armies on their own, but to avoid going after Napoleon until they could combine.

This plan was followed at Dresden in the night of 27–28 August, where Moreau, who had been giving the allies strategic advice, was killed; for, even though the Austrians outnumbered Napoleon, they disappeared in the darkness when he thought he would be in for a second day. The allies had minor victories against his supporting armies, but never let these events intoxicate them. All the time they manoeuvred to stop Napoleon picking them off one by one. While Cossacks threatened his communications in the west, the main allied armies steadily converged on him from north and east and south, driving him inexorably towards the Saxon city of Leipzig.

The great Battle of the Nations lasted over four days from 16–19 October. Every day the allies had more men and more guns, so that at the end the French had nearly 70,000 casualties while the allies had fewer than 55,000. Napoleon was able to withdraw, but he allowed Murat to return to Naples and his scheming wife Caroline, who was already half in the camp of her brother's enemies. In Germany he was finished, and, although Davout held Hamburg into 1814 and there were still garrisons in Magdeburg and Wittenberg, one by one the German allies gave way. The King of Bavaria changed sides during the course of the Battle of Leipzig, the King of Saxony kept what territory he was allowed by the King of Prussia, the Grand Duke of Württemberg also defected, Jérôme Bonaparte deserted his small Kingdom of Westphalia, the Grand Duchy of Berg disintegrated, and lesser rulers – of Hanover, Brunswick and Hesse-Cassel – regained their lands. Nobody won as much as the King of Prussia, and people in the lesser units, like free cities or margravates, had to await some general settlement.

The allies thought they had achieved enough. If Napoleon would give up Germany and Italy, he could have 'the natural borders' of France, up to the Alps and the Rhine. Were he to carry on fighting, then Russia, which had grabbed back most of Poland, would inevitably become the arbiter of Central Europe. But Napoleon was still in love with the idea of his Grand Empire and, not believing that the offer was genuine, he turned it down. On 1 December the allies pledged that they would invade France.

In 1814 Napoleon was back to where he had begun: with a small, raw army pitched against larger, confident forces. He was still sure he could win, for he would never let his enemies join up.

In the first Italian campaign, Napoleon had found himself outnumbered but had pursued the tactic of divide and rule with audacious success. Though since 1796 he had probably won more victories than any great general before him, relatively he was in a much worse state at the start of 1814. Up to 100,000 troops remained isolated and unavailable in Poland and Germany, in north-east Italy Eugène de Beauharnais was just holding his own against General Bellegarde's Austrians, only too aware that in Naples Murat and Caroline Bonaparte were likely to defect, in Spain French armies were being driven ever closer to the Pyrenees by a larger Anglo-Spanish force, while the long eastern border of France was defended by about 80,000 weakened and demoralized men who faced 300,000 allied soldiers nearing the valley of the Rhine.

His enemies had far larger resources, his country was debilitated and impoverished after over twenty years of almost continuous warfare, and he was too late to gain a peace that would leave France with its natural frontiers, the Rhine and the Alps, intact. He did not realize how little he or his country was loved in Germany or in the northern or southern Netherlands; outside France, probably only the Poles still wanted him to be their ruler. What is surprising is that the French rallied yet again, this time to support a losing cause. Defending the Emperor became the last desperate gesture of fervent patriotism.

Napoleon made diplomatic concessions to give himself time. The Pope was replaced on his throne and Ferdinand VII of Spain was offered his – Spanish envoys signed a preliminary agreement on 11 December 1813 but later withdrew their consent. He made the former ambassador to Russia, Caulaincourt, his Foreign Minister to facilitate negotiations with the Tsar; he may have guessed that an abler diplomat, Talleyrand, was negotiating on his own behalf with the Bourbons, and in any case there was less and less of a chance that he could save himself by talking. In early January the Kings of Naples and Denmark changed sides, freeing the northern and southern flanks of the allied advance. Already the allies had invaded Alsace, and within six weeks they expected to have 400,000 men in France. Many hundreds of thousands of French conscripts had fled, often into the forests, and of the 936,000 eager recruits for whom he had called Napoleon may have found that only 120,000 ever served him in the campaign that was over before the end of April.

In those four months, Napoleon marched and countermarched with the zest of a youthful commander. He was confronted by three main armies. Bernadotte was deputed to take his 100,000 men through the Netherlands – he took very little part in the decisive actions – and in the centre was Blücher, with 110,000, while to the south, marching through Switzerland, came the main army of 210,000 under Schwarzenberg. It looked a hopeless cause and in the end it proved so, but Napoleon was keen to show the overwhelming masses led by his two chief opponents that tactical brilliance could save his much smaller armies from being overwhelmed.

His intention was to disorientate them, to stop them combining and to drive them back to where they had come from. He was frequently able to achieve the first objective, surprising and beating Blücher in a first encounter at Brienne and after a setback at La Rothière mauling him in a series of actions at Chapaubert, Montmirail and Vauchamps. He then turned on Schwarzenberg at Montereau and made him retreat. He even risked putting his tiny army between their much larger forces, but in the end he could not stop them from coming together because they would not be distracted from their goal: Paris. In particular, in spite of small failures and his great age (he was seventy-two), Blücher moved forward with persistence, confident that Napoleon could not be in two places at once. In the end it was the French who were divided. Marmont and Mortier were driven back to the capital, while Napoleon had to retreat to Fontainebleau. When the marshals, including even the pugnacious Ney, concurred that further resistance was pointless and Talleyrand had persuaded the Senate to depose him, Napoleon hesitated, hoping that at least his infant heir, now in the safekeeping of the Austrian Emperor, his grandfather, might succeed him. The allies would not accept, so he abdicated. He knew how to end on a theatrical note. He tried to poison himself, but it did not work, and the world remembers only that in the front courtyard of the château, as he pressed a banner of the Imperial eagle to his heart while giving it the kiss of farewell, all the members of the Guard wept. Ever since, the site has been known as the Cour des Adieux.

It was a stoical but not a spartan end to a grand adventure. The contrast between the soldiers before him, bedraggled, dirty and tearful, and the naked athletes of David awaiting their fate before Thermopylae could not be greater. There was always something absurd about the way that David liked to idealize human bodies, without spot or wrinkle, their limbs aligned in ways reminiscent of antique statues and yet coy about their nudity as Greeks never were.

Much closer to the painful reality was *The Wounded Cuirassier*. The younger artist Géricault was more interested in actual men on actual horses than in the dream of some past perfection. His picture did not win him the favourable attention of his *Charging Chasseur* of the previous Salon of 1812, when, so far as the spectators could tell, Napoleon and his cavalry were charging against the Russians, Murat at their head, and driving the enemy to defeat. Instead, it was Napoleon who had lost and Murat who had let him down. The men and the equipment that had gone to Russia were replaced, if inadequately, but the horses could not be found again. Without enough cavalry, as in Second World War without enough tanks, no campaign could be victorious. Like Hitler, Napoleon was beaten on the eastern front and never recovered.

4

WATERLOO AND VIENNA

No portrait of Napoleon is present in the Waterloo Chamber at Windsor Castle, but by implication he dominates the room.

George, Prince of Wales, Prince Regent since 1811, had often dreamed of leading troops into a battle from which he emerged victorious. He had a passionate love of glamorous military uniforms and an aesthetic taste for French décor, for furniture, ceramics, clocks and portraits of the Bourbon royal family. In emulating and glorifying his ancestor Edward III, the first English king to claim the throne of France, he found a way of uniting these enthusiasms. When he altered Windsor Castle, instructions to the architects laid down that 'the period of Edward the 3rd . . . should generally predominate'. He longed to experience his own Crécy or Poitiers. Once he had been awarded the parliamentary funds to boost his Regency, he felt confident enough to announce that he and his court would 'quite eclipse Napoleon'. With the help of drink and drugs he eventually came to realize that he had defeated the Emperor at the Battle of Waterloo.

As Edward III had founded the Order of the Garter at Windsor and St George's Chapel is the Order's chapel, the Prince Regent had Wyatville, his architect, design St George's Hall at the Castle to be the backdrop to a Plantagenet pageant. He also invited Wyatville to provide him with a Waterloo Chamber that celebrated his supreme achievement: the defeat of Napoleon. Already in 1814 he was convinced that he was the man chiefly responsible for the Emperor's abdication, so he invited many of the principals to London, where sadly the people delighted most in greeting his chief guest, the Tsar. Undeterred by fact, the Principal Painter to George III, Thomas Lawrence, had already portrayed the Regent as, in Hazlitt's words, 'a well-fleshed Adonis of thirty-three' and now he was asked to paint a number of the illustrious visitors. Alexander I, dressed as a Russian field marshal and decorated with the Star of St Andrew superimposed on that of the Garter and with medals of the Order of St George of Russia, the Iron Cross of Prussia and the campaign medal of 1812, standing against the sky, was easily the most striking of the rulers, but Lawrence also painted a commanding image of old Blücher and of Wellington with his sword aloft, as at the service of Thanksgiving on 7 July 1814.

In 1815 the Regent knighted Lawrence, so that he would be acceptable in the most exclusive salons of the Continent, and sent him on a tour of Europe between 1818 and 1820. Lawrence had the manners of a born aristocrat and was at his ease at the council of Aix-la-Chapelle and in the Schönbrunn and Quirinale Palaces. He set the royal soldiers, Archduke Charles and the grand old Duke of York full length against dramatic skies, he gave a quiet dignity to the upright Frederick William of Prussia and the seated Francis I of Austria, he painted smaller head and shoulders of leading statesmen like Metternich and Castlereagh, but his masterpiece was a portrait of the Pope, the aged, gentle Pius VII, in front of famous sculptures from the Belvedere: the Apollo, the Laocöon and the torso beloved of Michelangelo. Whereas an English rival saw him as 'Perfumer to His Majesty', Romans nicknamed him 'Il Tiziano Inglese' and the Romans perhaps for once told the truth.

In March 1820 Lawrence hurried back from the Continent to be elected the President of the Royal Academy in succession to Benjamin West. It was the year in which the Regent succeeded his father as George IV. Both King and painter died in 1830, too soon for either of them to see the great swagger portraits gleaming in the gallery built for them. By then, George IV had further proof that he was the man who had beaten Napoleon. Nash's curving Regent Street was meant to outshine the linear boulevards of Napoleon's Paris. A grand triumphal arch, originally planned to go in front of Buckingham Palace (now called the Marble Arch), had the same dimensions as Napoleon's Arc du Carrousel; and the crowning sculpture was going to show George's conquest of Napoleon. When he died, George's imaginary heroics had deceived no one but himself. His long-suffering subjects preferred to honour Nelson and Wellington and to enjoy a poem about Sir John Moore at La Coruña. The role of British rulers in the defeat of Napoleon, however, was crucial, and for all its modish hyperbole the Waterloo Chamber does give many of the men responsible for beating Napoleon the glamour that they deserve.

Napoleon had to be defeated twice. On the first occasion, 11 April 1814, the allies signed the Treaty of Fontainebleau. Its key condition was that Napoleon, although retaining the title of Emperor, was to leave France and live in exile on the isle of Elba off the Italian coast. There he would be sovereign and his income, of two million francs, was to come from the French Crown. His wife would be Duchess of Parma, their son her heir. Bonaparte brothers and sisters were pensioned off.

The choice of Elba was the Tsar's. The Austrian Emperor was

afraid that, on Elba, Napoleon was too close to Italy, the British Lord Castlereagh thought that he was too near to France. For a few weeks Napoleon enjoyed his plot of land and was soon ready with innumerable schemes for improvement, but valuable trade with the mainland was a fantasy and the Bourbon agreement to provide financial support a hollow promise. For some days he was joined by Maria Walewska and their son, but he was distant with Maria, perhaps because he was hoping that Marie-Louise would be with him soon. He was indignant at the treachery of his sisters. Elisa, the bossy former Grand Duchess of Tuscany, and Caroline, who had slyly brought Naples into the ranks of his enemies, deserted him. He was pleased then at the arrival of the seductive and silly Pauline, especially as she had sold her beautiful Paris house to the Duke of Wellington, so that her older brother, who was then running out of money, would have the opportunity to try his luck again in France. War weariness had reduced Napoleon's popularity there, but the sluggish, ungracious and portly Louis XVIII won no friends, and his brother Charles, an erstwhile libertine whose spiritual reformation had transformed him into a fanatic, was good at making enemies. There were signs that the most reactionary clergy in the Catholic Church were gaining back the influence they had lost before 1789, the Imperial nobility were snubbed by returning aristocrats of more ancient titles, and new proprietors were worried that revolutionary redistribution of land might be questioned. Napoleon was bored, he had a gambler's temperament and he was encouraged by his mother to meet his fate. Colonel Sir Neil Campbell, a commissioner appointed by the British to oversee and protect him, warned Castlereagh that his charge might lose patience, but his warning was ignored; and it was while he had slipped away to Italy for medical treatment that Napoleon took his chance. On 26 February he took ship for France. Two days later he had landed near Antibes.

He had just over a thousand men, forty horses and two cannon to face the French royal army and the armies of the four other great powers. On his arrival on home territory Napoleon vowed that he would reach Paris without shedding blood, and he was as good as his word. As he and his small band of followers marched along back mountain roads through Grasse to Grenoble, where he had a brief introduction to a young scholar named Jean-François Champollion, the march turned into a triumphal procession. He was greeted in the capital of the former province of Dauphiné by peasants bearing flaming torches, and he left with an army of eight thousand men. As he moved into Burgundy, he could have been stopped by Ney, who had undertaken to bring his former master back to Paris in an iron cage, but once again Napoleon's histrionic gift – in this case the simple message 'I shall receive you as I did on the morrow of the battle of the Moskova' – carried the day. Sadly for him, gesture politics were not enough. News of his return had reached the allied plenipotentiaries still in Vienna, so that Britain, Austria, Prussia and Russia pledged to put together four armies of 150,000. The French could offer no such protection to their King, for the 60,000 men that Louis XVIII had raised deserted him and the fat monarch hurried away, breathless with fear, on the familiar road of exile, safe from the ogre's maw only when he reached Ghent.

Napoleon was advised that he must show himself a new man. In the later days of the Empire he had become more and more unreasonably dictatorial. Now he would be a conciliator, all things to all men other than the royalists, and a special hero for the liberals. He recalled an old adversary, Carnot, the organizer of victory in the time of the First Republic, and made him Minister of the Interior, he allowed Lafayette his favourite role as an opposition republican, he was reconciled to his prickly brother Lucien, he naively asked the treacherous Fouché to take charge of the police once more, a suitable job for a double agent, but his most imaginative act was to invite Benjamin Constant to draw up a proposal for a liberal empire.

The Acte Additionnel that Constant added to the imperial constitution made an attempt to endorse the revolutionary rights that Louis XVIII had conceded in his charter of 1814: equality before the law, equality in matters of taxation, equality of opportunity, freedom of religion, freedom of the press, the inviolability of property, the abolition of conscription. The returning royalists had not been as good as their word, since in December 1814 the Chamber had voted to give back some nationalized property to émigrés and to bring back censorship.

Napoleon now posed as more generous, for he established universal suffrage (in addition to an electoral college) as a sop to the liberals and gave Senators hereditary noble status to please the socially ambitious. His proposals were submitted to a plebiscite, a useful way of seeming a good democrat, but the Acte was hardly promulgated on 1 June when the deputies began to talk of revising it. Napoleon won his plebiscite by 1,532,527 votes to 4,802, but 5 million had been eligible to vote and in the west and the south, royalist areas, most electors abstained. The Emperor would have had to have shown how he could reign as a monarch who ruled by consent. For his future reputation he was lucky he never had to. In the short term he had to meet an emergency, so he reimposed conscription. He knew that his enemies would be upon him. The Vendéens in the west were preparing to revolt, so he had to put aside soldiers to contain them. His principal worries, however, lay beyond the eastern borders of France, for it was there that the four great powers were prepared to mass their armies for a new invasion. He reacted in the only way he knew how: he decided to be the first to attack.

*   *   *

names. The lustre of invincibility had gone, he himself was out of sorts and he was leading to their fate some soldiers worried at the thought that they might be treasonous and others desperate to show that yet again France could bring the rest of Europe to heel. His instinctive response to events was the same as ever: he must dictate them.

His intelligence told him correctly that the British and the Prussians, who had been quarrelling politically in Vienna, were not on good terms in the southern Netherlands. Each army had set up its own system of communication, Wellington was cautious and laid back, Blücher an old man in a hurry, who wanted nothing more than to capture Napoleon and have him shot. Napoleon was true to form in arriving in Belgium before he was expected, on 15 June. Wellington was unimpressed and took his time to collect together his disparate troops; Blücher would not wait for his reinforcements to arrive. The Duke stayed at the Duchess of Richmond's ball until midnight, heard that the French had taken Charleroi, gave orders for forces to concentrate on Quatre Bras, went back to his dancing, slept a little and arrived on the battlefield at 11 a.m. to find the Prince of Orange bravely resisting Ney, while five miles away at Ligny Blücher was facing the bulk of the French army under the Imperial commander-in-chief himself.

The result was what might have been expected. While Napoleon was too inventive in the action at Ligny and drove the impetuous Prussian back in disorder, Wellington was too skilful in defence for Ney to break through. On previous campaigns, Napoleon's defeated enemies had retreated towards their base and he had sent cavalry after them, so on this occasion he dispatched Grouchy to go behind Blücher and cut him off. But Blücher was wiser than in the past and instead of going north-east he moved due north, to stay as close to Wellington as he was able to be, whereas Grouchy, assuming that the Prussians had gone on a different route, veered off to the east and put himself out of touch with Napoleon until the battle that lay ahead was almost over. Meanwhile, Wellington, knowing that within a day he was likely to face Napoleon, extricated himself before the Emperor arrived and moved north-west along the Brussels road, searching for a suitably defensive position. He found it on 17 June on a ridge in front of the village of Mont-St-Jean, a little short of Waterloo, while the French came to another ridge, a mile south, centred on the hamlet of La Belle Alliance. Next day veterans of the Peninsular War would have to face the remnants of the Grande Armée, the master of defence the best attacking general of the age or any age. Wellington had taken one risk: he was counting on Blücher. Fortunately for him, Blücher, fortified by garlic and gin, had resolved to stay in touch.

On the tiny field of Waterloo the two armies were camped at less than 5,000 feet from each other; the battle zone was little over three times as wide; and altogether the troops numbered some 140,000 men. Wellington had placed his men astride the Brussels–Charleroi main road, the bulk of his forces stationed, as was his habit, on the reverse side of the slope behind a minor road that ran across the field of battle. On his right, Nassauers and Hanoverians occupied a wood and the well-fortified château of Hougoumont, but beyond them, some ten miles away, was a force of 17,000 that was meant to guard against a flanking attack, but in fact was not used. Napoleon made even worse mistakes. Persuaded that the ground was too wet for his guns to manoeuvre, he delayed any advance until one o'clock. He was also confident that Blücher would not be able to join in the battle, so his message to Grouchy, dispatched late, gave no sense that the new marshal should join his master quickly. Napoleon was too leisurely, but he was also too precipitate. All he thought necessary was a succession of frontal attacks. Ney was left to decide the details and no provision was made to cope with a possible Prussian appearance. For his part, though he heard the guns firing, Grouchy chose to linger over a large breakfast.

The main battle began around 11.30 when Prince Jérôme, the youngest and flightiest but also perhaps the bravest of the Emperor's brothers, launched into an all-out attack on Hougoumont, which took an hour to reach the château and then could not take it. When the French began to bombard the allied left centre, that, too, was ineffective, because the gunners could see few enemy to aim at – most of them were concealed behind the crests of slopes – and, besides, most of the roundshot fell harmlessly into the soft, soggy ground. Napoleon then noticed some movement off to the far right and sent Colonel Marbot to investigate what was happening. A captured courier blurted out that the men the Emperor had seen were 33,000 Prussians under von Bülow. This news made Napoleon beg Grouchy to come soon, but the request went too late. Shortly after, the main infantry attack was launched, and massive columns of battalion by division (instead of the more nimble columns of division by battalion) advanced on the allied left centre. Without adequate cavalry protection and unable to see all the forces ranged against them until it was too late, soldiers rose up from the ground before them. Four thousand were lost, but the British counterattacking cavalry charged with excessive zeal, so that the French picked off about 2,500 allied horsemen.

In the mid-afternoon Napoleon set himself one principal aim: to break through the centre at La Haie Sainte. Ney, to whom these intentions were entrusted, thought he saw Wellington's men in retreat – a few had wavered – and careered impetuously against British infantry drawn up in rectangles. As at this stage neither La Haie Sainte nor Hougoumont had fallen, Ney had too narrow a front. Still, all who saw the glittering helmets and cuirasses advancing towards them did not forget the sight. But without supporting horse artillery, the French cavalry could not break the steady masses before and around them, they charged, they were halted and they were driven back. While they were struggling to break into the British 'squares', von Bülow's relieving force pushed into the village of Papelotte on the French right. Ney charged again, eight times in all, without any useful effect, until Napoleon ordered him to use all three arms – infantry, cavalry and artillery – to take La Haie Sainte, and Ney achieved the task, two hours too late. It was a tricky moment for Wellington, but Napoleon chose not to allow Ney the extra troops he asked for. For a time the Old Guard stabilised the French right by stopping the Prussians, but with every moment Napoleon saw that his chances of victory were slipping away. His men discovered that soon the main Prussian army would be upon them, so he knew that he must make a decisive move: he ordered the nine battalions of the Imperial Guard that made up the reserve to advance. Wellington bade his hurriedly reinforced men to lie down behind the banks of the road that crossed the battle. They rose to stop the Guard, the French army fled and until darkness fell the Prussians pursued them relentlessly.

Politicians and diplomats completed the work that the soldiers had begun. The Congress of Vienna, convened before and after Waterloo, had to sort out the problem that Napoleon posed: how could one over-mighty country, in this case France, be contained within the concert of Europe?

The Treaty of Fontainebleau had been worked out on 11 April 1814 by Talleyrand, acting for Louis XVIII, and by the Tsar. Since it provided so generously for Napoleon and the Bonapartes, it was accepted with not a little reluctance by Metternich and Castlereagh. It was followed by an armistice that removed occupying forces from France in return for the evacuation of fortresses outside France's own borders that were still occupied by French troops. This led to the Peace of Paris (30 May), which left a France larger than in 1792, before the wars had begun, with 600,000 more inhabitants in the Palatinate and Savoy, and back with most of the overseas colonies that had been lost in the interim. Britain, which had spent several years acquiring colonies from France and her allies, kept French Tobago and St Lucia in the West Indies and the Seychelles in the Indian Ocean, bought the colony of the Cape of Good Hope from the Dutch, while restoring them their East Indian islands and while granting Spain the French part of Santo Domingo. A secret article of the treaty provided that Germany would be independent and organized as a confederation, a second that France would allow the incorporation of Belgium into the Netherlands, a third that Austria's borders in Italy would lie along the river Po and Lake Maggiore and that a Habsburg should again rule in Tuscany. France was freed of an indemnity and allowed to keep art treasures that it had looted. This Peace of Paris was remarkable in that its drafters concentrated not on punishment for the past but on security for the future. Castlereagh told a Swiss delegate concerned at being militarily vulnerable if a conflict arose: 'Real defence and security comes from the guarantee which is given by the fact that they cannot touch you without declaring war on all those interested in maintaining things as they are.'[1] International relations in his view linked self-preservation with peace. Though still worried by Napoleon's presence on Elba, his main concern was to calm Europe down as a preliminary to a general settlement. There was likely to be trouble from Russia and Prussia, as Alexander wished to have Poland and Frederick William Saxony, but, as France was invited to send delegates to attend the meeting scheduled for Vienna, there was a reasonable hope that what was decided there would be accepted by all. The fact that the Tsar, the King of Prussia and Metternich went off first to London showed that a key redrafter of the map of Europe was to be Britain, the power with least apparent interest in that map. The British would be there not just because they had never been beaten by Napoleon or because in every coalition against him Britain had financed the Continental members, but because how power was distributed on the Continent was Britain's chief concern in foreign affairs. By comparison, the Treaty of Ghent, which brought to an end the sad war of 1812 with the United States, mattered only in this respect, that Castlereagh prevented America from intervening in European disputes. He would use whatever influence he had to make and keep the peace of Europe, so that outside Europe Britain could be the dominant world power. Unlike some of his successors, he saw that the first aim was a condition and a corollary of the second.

The other diplomat who saw clearly that the achievement of peace was the priority was Metternich. In 1812 and even in early 1813 he had believed that Austria had an interest in Napoleon's survival as Emperor of the French. Metternich's master's daughter was Napoleon's wife, so that the heir to the French Empire was Francis I's grandson. Even if there was a tradition of Franco-Austrian rivalry that went back to the early sixteenth century, there had been a diplomatic revolution before the Seven Years War, when Habsburgs and Bourbons became allies, and Napoleon had caused diplomatic revolutions, too, so that, after warring against them in 1807, he had made a partner of the Tsar and in 1810 of the Kaiser. Just because the first partnership had broken down, it did not follow that the same would be true of the second. Indeed, the fall of the French in 1812 at first alarmed the Austrians, as the catastrophe left no country on the Continent capable of withstanding the Russians, unless it were a resurrected France; and it was only when it was clear to Metternich that Napoleon would never consent to give anything up that Austria changed sides and persisted thereafter in opposing Napoleon. This new situation brought with it the old anxiety, how to keep Russia at bay, especially as Russia seemed bent on making a junior ally out of Prussia. Metternich's response was to develop a close relationship with Britain and, so far as possible, with Bourbon France. Austria's problematic connections with the Bonapartes were solved by granting Napoleon's wife the Duchy of Parma and installing at her side a count, Neipperg, to be potentially, soon actually her lover and eventually her second husband, while keeping in Vienna her son Napoleon, no longer King of Rome but instead Duc de Reichstadt, under the controlling eye of his grandfather Francis. Such inconvenient members of the family were soon forgotten and Metternich could set about trying to restrict the influence of the Tsar as far as he dare. Napoleon's mistake had been that he had been unwilling to become part of a European concert of nations. Metternich's task was to convince others, above all the Tsar and the King of Prussia, that with Britain and France it was in their interest that the Viennese settlement should settle the Continent down.

The Congress of Vienna was expected to take a short time to ratify the Treaty of Paris and to finish the business that had been left outstanding there. There was a danger that Russia would decide everything to its advantage and a danger that Britain would see no disadvantage in taking no part in any decisions. By checking Russia and by involving Britain, the settlement turned into a diplomatic triumph for Europe as a whole. Talleyrand was able to insist that not only the four principal enemies of France, but also France itself and Spain as well as smaller states should be involved. This move effectively delayed the start of the Congress, but it did not stop the five great powers, France being the fifth, from demanding and dictating the important stipulations of the treaties. Napoleon's work was to be undone, but the way in which it was undone showed how profound was his impact on the Continent.

Napoleon had revived Polish self-respect by establishing the Duchy of Warsaw – the Tsar therefore proposed there should be a Polish kingdom under his direct rule. This was received in horror by his allies, but in the end the lion's (or the bear's) share was his, while Austria and Prussia were compensated with little more than Galicia in the first case and Posen and Thorn in the second. Napoleon had also destroyed the Holy Roman Emperor, vastly reduced the numbers of small states, set up the Confederation of the Rhine, confined Austria largely to ancient Habsburg lands and Prussia to its core of Brandenburg-Prussia. In the new order there would be some national unity thanks to a German Confederation, of which Austria, no longer at the heart of a Holy Roman Empire, would regain some dignity as the president, and in which Austria and Prussia were inevitably the chief members. While the Austrian Emperor had many subjects outside Germany, not only in the Habsburg Kingdoms of Bohemia and Hungary, the Prussian King was given land that straddled most of north Germany, including more than half Saxony (with Russian assistance he had hoped to have the whole kingdom). Many smaller German states had a more drastic fate than Saxony and disappeared for ever as independent units. In one part of northern Europe, however, little was only briefly large. The southern Netherlands, Belgium, had been part of France for almost twenty years. The northern Netherlands, given later to Napoleon's brother Louis as the first King of Holland and, after Louis was sacked, was also joined to France. Now, to provide a north-east buffer state against France, the two parts of the Netherlands, the southern half united in religion and divided in race, the northern half divided in religion and united in race, were combined under the Prince of Orange as King. Even for the Congress it was too ingenious, and the scheme soon collapsed.

The corresponding buffer state at the south-west borders of France, the Kingdom of Piedmont-Sardinia, had a longer life. If the creation of the new Kingdom of the Netherlands should be considered an extension to the settlement of Germany – the Netherlands so constituted would slow down a French attack from its north-eastern plains until Prussians came – a stronger house of Savoy would slow down a French attack across the Alps until Austria intervened. This concept of the role of Piedmont-Sardinia, which explained its acquisition of Genoa, made better sense after the final defeat of Napoleon, when the transalpine, Francophone, ancestral lands of Savoy were subjected once more to Turin instead of Paris. By a curious irony of later history, this least Italian of states was home to the two men who were to be largely responsible for modern Italy: the romantic soldier-adventurer Garibaldi, from the Savoyard county of Nice (or Nizza) and the sly Prime Minister Cavour, who being a member of the Piedmontese ruling class spoke French as his first language. Working more often in opposition to one another than in consort with one another, they would achieve what Napoleon liked to claim had been his policy: the unification of Italy.

Under Le Grand Empire Napoleon had reduced the various sections of Italy to three: in the north-west, from Genoa to Rome, an extension of Imperial France; in the north-east, the Kingdom of Italy; and in the south, the Kingdom of Naples. Although the third of these sections, Naples, was kept intact, first with Joachim Murat as King, then with a restored Bourbon ruler, the other two had to be broken up. The Pope, Pius VII, who had stubbornly resisted Napoleon, even in captivity, was rewarded with the restoration of Rome, the patrimony of St Peter (now Lazio), Umbria and the Marches; and Metternich, who wanted to make common cause against the forces of revolution, allowed him the Legations – the country centred around Ravenna, Bologna and Ferrara – and struggled successfully to win back for him papal enclaves in Naples, at Pontecorvo and Benevento. The price of re-establishing the states of the Church as a belt across central Italy was that it might put in jeopardy the cause for which it was said that the Pope must have land: independence from governments' interference. It seemed only too obvious that the Pope, like other Italian sovereigns, was an Austrian client. The Austrians had put back the Bourbons in Naples, Austrian princes held Parma, Modena and Tuscany, and the Austrian Emperor himself had annexed potentially the most prosperous parts of Italy, Lombardy and Venetia. Metternich may have satisfied himself, in one of his more famous comments, that 'Italy' was merely a 'geographical expression', but he could not disprove the notion that in Italy, beyond the line of the Dolomites, Austria was an alien presence. To those who thought like that, there was always the possibility that the Italians would look for help to France and a new Napoleon.

The reappearance of the old Napoleon in February failed to interrupt the work of the Congress; indeed, it stimulated the diplomats to speed up their work. Some decisions involved lands that had always been beyond Napoleon's reach, so that Sweden was allotted Norway because Russia had taken Finland. Others, like the question of Switzerland, which the French had organised as a unitary, hated, Helvetic Republic before Napoleon wisely conceded a looser constitution under himself as the Mediator in 1803, were resolved more or less in the interests of the countries themselves – though it lost some land to Lombardy and did not get all it wanted from France and Piedmont-Sardinia, the Swiss confederation was now guaranteed in international law. It seemed logical, too, that Prussia should buy Swedish Pomerania. At no point, however, were such choices based on kindly reactions to popular requests. The statesmen at Vienna represented their masters, not the subjects. If they operated from principle, it was the twin ideas of legitimacy and of peace, at almost any price. Wherever possible the old families came back, since this was thought of as bringing stability. There were to be those, many of them admirers of Napoleon, who did not rate peace so highly. A few students in Germany, a handful of radical writers in England, some liberals in Spain, some would-be conspirators in Italy, above all the defeated but still convinced Bonapartists in France loathed the Vienna settlement. For the time, it had settled the world in which they had to survive. Their agitation would give Metternich the excuse to clamp down on dissident intellectuals, stimulate the vilification of Castlereagh that was in part responsible for his suicide, make Goya see black so much that he sought permission to live and so die in France, draw Byron and Shelley to cloak-and-dagger intrigues in Italy and bring renown to the satirical anti-Bourbon verses of Béranger while keeping in safe oblivion the anti-Bourbon sketches and prints of young Delacroix.

Though his critics would not have acknowledged it, Castlereagh was the man behind the most idealistic clauses in the final agreement: the lines on the slave trade. The British abolition of the slave trade had been the one lasting achievement of the premiership of Charles James Fox in 1806–7, for, although a Whig and a long-time Francophile, he had been unable to make peace with Napoleon. At the Congress, Castlereagh, a Tory, became Fox's spiritual heir and got the agreement of his fellows to its worldwide abolition, at least in principle. This was to be a more enduring act than the much vaunted attempt of the Tsar to set up by means of a treaty a Holy Alliance embracing Russia, the principal Orthodox power, Austria, the principal Catholic power, and Prussia, the principal Lutheran power, which bound them to treat each another and their peoples in accord with the Christian Gospel, so as to make their alliance the basis of a fraternal union between rulers that would banish warfare from the earth.

By then the allies had reacted in a less exalted fashion to the renewal of fighting brought about by Napoleon. The hundred days wrecked the relationship that Talleyrand and Castlereagh had begun to build, but a British presence in France saved France from any possibility of German, especially Prussian revenge. Humiliatingly, the corseted Louis XVIII came back to a Paris that was under British and Prussian control. In the south and the west a White Terror turned on Bonapartists, Jacobins and Protestants. It was therefore easy for Castlereagh and Wellington to argue that calming the French down must be the chief allied aim; and fortunately the Tsar agreed. The original terms proved too much for Talleyrand, who was shrewd enough to resign, but his successor, the Duc de Richelieu, whose only important previous experience had been as governor of Odessa, proved a much tougher negotiator than his predecessor expected. The Second Treaty of Paris, signed on 20 November, had to be harsher than the first, reducing France's borders to those of 1790, taking away land and fortresses for the benefit of its neighbours, arranging the occupation of the northern departments for three to five years, demanding an indemnity of 700 million francs. To be certain France would be tamed, the four allies bound themselves to keep their alliance going for another twenty years; and it was made clear that any return of Napoleon or any member of his family would be a cause of war. Napoleon by then was far away on St Helena, and none of his siblings had shown any desire to replace him. Two other clauses were more apposite to the world after 1815. One called for consultation if the Bourbons were overthrown again, an eventuality of which no one took much notice when it occurred either in 1830, with the senior line, or in 1848, with the junior line. What was to matter much more was Article 6, which provided for European reunions to promote peace and prosperity; and the Vienna settlement and Second Treaty of Paris became the reason for a post-war European Concert that was expressed through a series of conferences. The lasting effect of the fall of Napoleon had been to make concord between the powers a European value. On his island Napoleon dreamed of a Continent that was at one because of him. He was right, but not for the reason he thought he was.

The Congress, unlike the 1919–20 Paris peace conference, settled the affairs of the Continent by negotiation; and this came to suit Russia, which lacked the economic strength to use its military might. It was also unlike its successor in that it ignored affairs outside the bounds of the Continent, except in the matter of the slave trade; and this came to suit Britain, whose landed and commercial rulers, despite Castlereagh's best efforts, thought of themselves as living in a world rather than a European context. The success of the Congress meant a reversal of Clausewitz's doctrine – first elaborated in a note written in 1827 – that *'war is a continuation of policy by other means'* (his italics). The Congress made 'policy' an answer to war.

While there was some equilibrium in European affairs, with Prussia the main power in north Germany, with Austria the main power in Italy and the German Confederation, with France and Britain the main powers in the Netherlands and the Iberian Peninsula, with Russia the main power on the Continent and Britain the main power outside it, major wars were avoided. The Greek War of Independence in the 1820s and the Belgian revolt in 1830 were resolved by agreements. Canning and Palmerston, British Foreign Secretaries respectively in the years 1822–7 and 1830–41, tended to view Continental powers as rivals. When he was frustrated by French intervention in Spain in 1823, Canning was careful to stop any European intervention, other than Britain's, in the Spanish American colonies, claiming he had 'brought the New World into existence to redress the balance of the Old'. Similarly, when the Napoleonic historian Thiers, as Prime Minister, revived a Napoleonic policy in Egypt and Syria, Palmerston took the side of the Ottoman Sultan and forced France to back down. Canning and

Palmerston, in different circumstances, were adverting to the lessons learned from the Napoleonic experience, that Britain had power chiefly where it could use the navy as a threat. They had in common a liberalism in foreign policy that they did not support at home; and it was this that made them suspect the three eastern powers for their tendency always to put down rebellions in favour of preserving the status quo, however unjust. In this view the one maverick power was still likely to be France, which revived its colonial aspirations by attacking Algiers in 1830, seemed to behave like a liberal power by endorsing Belgian independence in the 1830s (but then so did the British and the Prussians), meddled, or so it seemed to Britain, in the Near East and then infuriated Britain by organizing whom the young Queen of Spain should marry. What neither Britain nor France could forget easily was the mistrust created between them by the Napoleonic period. Socially and in political culture, they were far more like each other than either was like Prussia, Austria or Russia – both had their bills of rights, their parliaments, their comfort seeking bourgeoisies – but instinctive phobic reactions to one another meant that an entente between them, as in the early 1840s, fell short of being cordiale. When another Napoleon became president in 1848, then president for life and finally Emperor (1852), the initial British reaction was to prepare for war.

The Vienna settlement, with some alterations, had survived until 1848, when most of the Continent erupted in revolution. Though as so often the French altered their regime, no other important government lost its hold on its area of influence. Metternich had to go, but Austria was able to regain control of Italy and to force Prussia to withdraw liberal concessions and Russia crushed Hungarian rebellion against Austria – it might seem that the cause of legitimacy had triumphed yet again. The period from 1851 to

1871, however, proved to be decisive in changing the state of equilibrium set in 1814–15 at Vienna.

At first it seemed that the new Napoleonic France was setting the pace of change. In the Crimean War of 1854–6, France, with Britain (in terms of its army) its junior partner, ended Russian hegemony in Europe for almost a century. In 1859 France pushed Austria out of Lombardy, so that the Austrian princelings had to give up their lands in Parma, Modena and Tuscany as well as their domination over the Pope; and the power vacuum could be filled by Piedmont-Sardinia, which rapidly took over most of northern Italy except Venetia, left to Austria, and Lazio, left to the Pope – by way of compensation France at last got and kept Savoy and Nice. In the south, Britain played a separate role by allowing the red shirts of Garibaldi free access to Sicily and Naples. Italy had become an independent kingdom because first France, then Britain had taken a lead. In the 1860s, however, it was to become clear that the new Napoleonic France could not be the most powerful country on the Continent.

Three short wars – against Denmark with the help of Austria (1864), against Austria with the help of Italy (1866), against France (1870–71) – changed international relations within Europe for good. The astute policy of Bismarck steered Prussia to becoming first the most powerful state in Germany, then, as Imperial Germany, the most powerful state on the Continent. In old age Palmerston had tried to protect Denmark, whose Princess Alexandra had just married the Prince of Wales, but a British naval force could not create any problems for an army that attacked with lightning speed. The logic of the new situation was that Britain had no role, except as an arbiter, within Europe. It could stop Russia reaching the Mediterranean and frustrate the French in Egypt, tighten its hold on India and Burma and grab more of Africa than any other European country (with the possible exception of the

French), so that its Empire became a substitute for Europe. Ultimately, the Tory Prime Minister Lord Salisbury understood that it
made sense to pursue a policy of glorious isolation. The Continent
belonged to Germany, which had allied with Austria and Russia,
made Italy a client and left France as friendless in defeat as in
1813–15. If Germany was to be a problem, then the British and
German royal families had intermarried, and a network of alliances
connected the British royal house with many of the German
Protestant princelings. Sadly, Britain's last quarrel in Africa, with
the Boers whom they had first ruled in the Cape of Good Hope
colony in 1815, turned into a war that was hard to win and harder
to justify to European neighbours. The price of isolation was that
Britain was unloved just at a moment when republican France had
gained the most unlikely of allies, reactionary Russia. Both had
their differences with Britain – France in Africa, Russia in Asia –
but what made all three nations forget their reservations about each
other was that Germany had started to do what Napoleon had
failed to do: build a navy that could challenge Britain. Kaiser
Wilhelm II, who had foolishly failed to court Tsar Alexander III, was
even more foolish when he listened to the arguments of Admiral
Tirpitz that Germany must be strong at sea. Then she could achieve
what had been beyond Napoleon and dominate not just the
continent but all Europe.

Exactly a century after their representatives had met in Vienna,
the five great powers all went to war for the first time against one
another in what is now called the First World War but then was
sometimes known as the Great European War. The war led to the
disintegration of the most 'European' of the powers, for the dual
monarchy of Austria and Hungary fell apart because it was too
multiethnic and multilingual for an age when the President of the
United States, for the first time a party in European disputes,
preached the doctrine of national self-determination. Whatever that

meant, it did not seem to imply that peoples ought to value peace with others before their own particular concerns. Wilson would have repudiated this view, since he tried to organize a lasting peace by means of a league of nations, but his good intentions were frustrated by his own countrymen, who showed that they could be more self-absorbed than Britain had been, in this case not only isolated from Europe but insulated from the rest of the world. The American dream of self-sufficiency was an impossible dream for a nation that had replaced Britain as the dominant financial power in the world. Like Russia, which because of Communism and civil war was not allowed to take part in the Paris peace conference, America was by its nature liable to be one of the only countries capable of dictating affairs in Europe, unless it were a revived and aggressive Germany, for France and Britain, though apparently great colonial powers outside the Continent, now both lacked the wealth, the industry, the numbers to impose their will on the Continent; and their mutual suspicion made it hard for them to act in concert.

The last and most terrible person to try to play a Napoleonic role in Europe was Adolf Hitler. Just as Bismarck had had Wilhelm I crowned Kaiser in the Hall of Mirrors in the Palace of Versailles, so Hitler felt, as he marched down the Champs-Elysées to the Arc de Triomphe in 1940, that he was enjoying his finest hour. The defeat of Jena in 1806 and the 'stab in the back' of 1918, when he believed that the politicians had ratted on the soldiers, were avenged. His plan was clearer, his means more fearsome, his aims more grandiose than Napoleon's; and so the collapse of his own 'grand empire' was more complete after 1942 than Napoleon's after 1812. The impossibility of defeating Britain had prevented them both from winning; the intractability of Russia had driven them both to fail. But German military hegemony disappeared more absolutely in the late twentieth century than France's after 1815, checked as it was by Russia and America, the two world powers.

The moral of the Waterloo Chamber is that Napoleon's fall stimulated a longing for peace. The Vienna settlement, constructed by the members of Europe's ruling classes, made arrangements that proved viable for a century. Those drafting the Paris peace treaties of 1919–20 had to attend to popular demands for revenge, for national self-determination (and what I want for my nation may be what you want for yours) and for a new Holy Alliance against war. The key treaty, that of Versailles with Germany, had failed within twenty years; and other stipulations, including those setting up new states in Yugoslavia and Czechoslovakia, have in time been shown to be unworkable. The curious sequel to the Second World War is that no treaties were signed, and America and Russia kept up a cold war against each other for over forty years. The victors over Napoleon's France were wiser than those who conquered the Kaiser's Germany and Hitler's Germany; and the men in the Waterloo Chamber ought to be well known as much as Wilson, Lloyd George and Clemenceau or Roosevelt, Churchill and Stalin. It was because Napoleon's ambition had known no limits that they set themselves limited and possible aims. Peace was thus, by a curious paradox, the best gift of Napoleon to the Europe of his days.

The paths of glory he had trod led possibly one million Frenchmen to their graves and maybe as many as four million men from other lands. The story of disruption caused by almost twenty years of Napoleonic warfare will never be told in all its harrowing detail. Villages had been burned down, cities razed by cannon, the monasteries of Europe closed, thousands turned into refugees, a new word – guerilla (a little war) – had come from Castilian to other European languages, savage revolts in Ireland, maybe pro-French, and in southern Italy, clearly anti-French, had been savagely repressed, Napoleon had proffered the Poles a show of independence only for them to be deceived once more by Russia, Prussia and Austria. The little states that had dotted the map of Central Europe for centuries, whether as duchies, counties or free cities, were mostly gone for good. The new men in charge, the two Emperors, one King, one Regent and the Pope, had a fear of social unrest which also disturbed the creative statesmen who brought down Napoleon, chief among them Castlereagh and Metternich. In trying to change international relationships within Europe by force of arms, Napoleon gave his conquerors an excuse for unremitting conservatism: as far as they were concerned, all change must be avoided because all change must be bad. They had not grasped one of Napoleon's most remarkable achievements: to effect changes that would outlast defeat in war.

PART II

MAN OF PEACE

5

DESCRIBING EGYPT

Long before a glass pyramid stood over the entrance to the Louvre, the people of Paris were familiar with the Egyptian style that Napoleon had encouraged. An obelisk stands at the heart of Place de la Concorde, sphinx fountains spew out water in quiet city squares, and the German ambassador's residence, Hôtel Beauharnais, once home to Joséphine's children, is distinguished by its grandiose Egyptian façade.

Napoleon developed an instinct worthy of a Pharaoh for exaggerating his own importance, but what he achieved by going to Egypt exceeded what he had expected. For him, the voyage to the east had been in part a search for the exotic, since at one time, when uncertain about his career, he had thought of taking service with the Sultan. He also liked to argue that the purpose of the trip was to undermine the British position in India, currently threatened by the Muslim ruler of Mysore, but he could never have organized the troops, the ships or the back-up needed to go from the southern ports of France via the Middle East to the waters of the Ganges. Besides, from the Mediterranean there was no ready access to the Indian Ocean, and the British East India Company sent all its ships round the Cape of Good Hope. Napoleon may have hoped to emulate the exploits of two of the greatest of commanders from the past.

Alexander the Great and Julius Caesar had gone to Egypt, and so would he. Like them he dreamed of riches disgorged by the dark brown soil of the Nile, like them he would encounter the strange gods of the east (in his case this involved coming to terms not with Amun-Ra, Horus, Isis and Osiris but with the one god Allah), like them he would have a transforming experience. In 1799, after a little over fifteen months, he was anxious to hurry home: at the end of his life he liked to say that he wished he had stayed in Egypt.

After his triumphant Italian campaigns, Napoleon was out of a job. For a time he prepared to attack the English across the Channel, though he had already thought of a much more imaginative scheme for getting at France's most intractable enemy. The Egyptian adventure began as a cure for boredom. It was soon dressed up as a well-thought-out plan. On 12 April 1798 the Directory gave the 'Army of the East' four aims.

It was to take control of Egypt, chase the English from the Red Sea, cut the isthmus of Suez and 'improve by all the means in its power the lot of Egyptian natives'.[1] That mixture of French interest with Enlightened paternalism had been typical of revolutionary policy from 1792, when the Edict of Fraternity offered help to any nation that wished to have the benefits of a republican government *à la française*, but it gave Bonaparte's expedition its unique air of glamour. Only he could have thought of taking to a distant land, unknown to all but a small group of his fellow countrymen, some of the ablest *savants* of the age. Most of the mathematicians, physicists, chemists, biologists, engineers, geographers, artists and linguists who accompanied him were young men like himself, but some of the more influential were in their fifties, like Monge (inventor of descriptive geometry), Berthollet (an expert on explosives) and Denon (*littérateur* and engraver). All of these who came back would maintain that they had had the time of their lives – to have been an 'Egyptian' would mark the rest of their careers.

It was one thing to have a bright idea. Even if he had discussed the project for several hours with Talleyrand, the Foreign Secretary and by far the ablest member of the government, Napoleon knew that a lot of luck and his own remarkable energy would be essential to carry it out. He could not have known that the wildest part of the plan was already impossible to realize. In January 1798 Tipu Sahib, Sultan of Mysore, had sent emissaries to Paris to seek an alliance. He was so keen to be rid of the British that the previous year he had allowed the French in his capital, Seringapatam, to establish a Jacobin Club, and he had been present at its first session in May 1797, when the members set up a Tree of Liberty and vowed death to all tyrants other than their patron. To Tipu there was no Englishman like a dead one; and for the man who liked to be called 'The Tiger' a French designer had made a much-loved mechanical toy of a tiger eating a redcoat. The Sultan's fantasy was never fulfilled. From Cairo Bonaparte wrote to the Imam of Muscat to have a message sent to India. 'You have already been informed of my arrival on the coast of the Red Sea, with an innumerable and invincible army and filled with the desire to free you from the yoke of England. I should like you to dispatch, to Suez or to Cairo, some clever man who has your trust, so that I may confer with him.' If the letter reached its recipient, it came too late. On 4 May 1798 General Stuart's army broke into Seringapatam and Tipu's corpse was found beneath a pile of bodies. Napoleon never admitted he could not have helped. Twenty years on he dictated his memoirs:

he told how with fortune's favour he would have reached the Indus with 40,000 men by March 1800.[2]

Another side of Napoleon was intensely practical. With his usual care and rapidity he set about organizing his expeditionary force, and on 19 May 1798 he set sail from Toulon. The fleet's trouble-free journey was a tribute to his insistence on secrecy. Before the soldiers and *savants* reached the Mediterranean coast, few knew their destination. No British ships blocked the way to Malta, still a sovereign state ruled by the Knights of St John, so nobody prevented the destruction of that state. But if British intelligence had been foiled, the French were also unprepared for what they must expect. From classical accounts they were ready for the magnificent capital of Cleopatra, but the Alexandria where they disembarked was a deserted town of 8,000 inhabitants; the famous lighthouse, the Pharos, one of the seven wonders of the ancient world, lay spread-eagled at the bottom of the harbour; even the more modern Arab city lay in ruins. The French had also miscalculated the time of year: they had arrived in mid-summer. Like Hitler's panzers in the icy cold of a Soviet winter, they were not dressed for the occasion. Napoleon had passed time on board reading a translation of the Koran and he pronounced himself impressed. He was ignorant, however, of Arab customs and did not grasp that a free-flowing jellaba allowed its wearer to breathe more easily than the 156 buttons that constricted an officer in the hussars. The French would quickly learn about ophthalmia and the plague and the threat of crocodiles basking by the riverside, but they first had to encounter sunstroke and thirst. No sooner had they been burned by the khamsin or south wind blowing fine particles of dust that obscured the sun than they were ordered to march by the desert road of Damanhur in the direction of the Egyptian metropolis. The troops were parched, hungry and bedraggled as they reached the apex of the delta, and in the heat of the afternoon they confronted the first serious military threat: the army of the Mamelukes under its leader, Murad Bey. Forty centuries may have looked down on the French as they could spot the Great Pyramids behind the enemy, but nobody was aware of the fact then. Behind the Mamelukes lay the river and beyond that the comforts of Cairo.

The Mamelukes were not Egyptian in origin. They had been brought from the area of the Caucasus mountains by the family of Saladin, the Ayubites, in the thirteenth century, after that family had acquired Egypt; they speedily replaced their masters, and even the Turkish conquest in 1517 had not dislodged them. The Turks liked to use subjects to run things for them. Greeks or Copts, the native Christians, were regarded as skilful administrators and helped gather the taxes. The Mamelukes were a warrior class and they were encouraged to fight. For much of the next three centuries they fought each other. In 1798 two of them shared political power: Ibrahim Bey, who boasted the title of Sheik el-Beled, head of the country, and Murad Bey, called Emir el-Haj, the man in charge of the yearly pilgrimage to Mecca. That July it was Murad's sacred duty to drive off infidel hordes.

Before the French could see Gizeh there was an initial skirmish on the banks of the main left arm of the Nile at Shubra Kit between a smaller, fresh Egyptian army that looked superb and a larger, exhausted French army that saw in the rich harnesses of the Arab horses, the bejewelled scimitars, the colourful costumes and the gleaming sabres, daggers, maces, rifles and pistols of their opponents the lure of booty. The French had hardly a horse between them. They therefore formed up into defensive squares, at which the Mameluke cavalry charged with reckless and pointless abandon. In the river Muslim sailors boarded several French transport ships and massacred their occupants, until *Le Cerf* hit the Mameluke flagship and, wrote Nicolas the Turk, men flew up in the air like birds. The shock of the explosion led to a less poetic flight by land and water. Napoleon was left in possession of the field, but his enemies had escaped.

It was at the Battle of the Pyramids, one week later, that the French had a chance to turn defeat into a rout. Once again they outnumbered the Mamelukes, once again they fought defensively, once again they won because of superior tactical skill and discipline. Albanians supplied artillery and infantry for the enemy – they were exterminated. While Murad Bey's horsemen charged the squares, some before they could be formed, Ibrahim Bey watched the slaughter from the opposite side of the river. A sandstorm blew into the faces of the Egyptians, and it was the wind, according to the chronicler Jabarti, that won the victory for the infidel. The shrieking sound of the cannonade terrified the people of Cairo, and next day a deputation came to sue for terms. The palaces of Murad Bey and Ibrahim Bey were ransacked and burned by looters, Murad Bey fled towards Upper Egypt and Ibrahim Bey fled to Syria and, with only the sound of ululating women to indicate that there was still a civilian population there, Napoleon entered Cairo.

As he was to show in Moscow, Napoleon tended to think that marching into large cities, especially capital cities, brought campaigns to an end. Usually he was right, but in Egypt he soon discovered that he had made an error in his calculations – not pleasant news for one who prided himself on shrewd judgement. His local enemies were out of reach. Worse still, soon France itself became out of reach to most of the French, if not of their general. On 1 August his brother Louis in Alexandria could hear an explosion from the direction of Aboukir. As modern archaeology has proved, the French fleet anchored there was stationed too far from the shore of the bay, so that some of the British ships slipped closer to the landward side and could attack from both sides. Once guns started up, the fight was bound to go Nelson's way, and yet

French resistance was not shattered even by the death of their admiral, Brueys, until fire on his flagship, *L'Orient*, reached the powder magazine. The boy who stood on the burning deck was blown up or drowned, the English took over three thousand prisoners and in Vienna Haydn ended his *Nelson* Mass *pianissimo* with the sound of muffled drums. Psychologically, the effect of the misnamed Battle of the Nile was profound. While the Turks made clear their resentment at the unwarranted invasion of one of their provinces and both the neutral powers and the Continental allies of France became less cooperative, Talleyrand wrote confidentially to the chargé d'affaires in Istanbul that France must stay in Egypt, so that it could dominate Mediterranean trade. In Egypt Napoleon was determined to stay. The defeat at Aboukir was none of his fault. He had a country to subdue and to govern.

In northern Italy he had had some experience of ruling, but it was as a conqueror, a military governor. It was in Egypt that he first tried to appear to head a civilian administration. He needed money, so he must be able to tax the fellahin, or peasants. He needed to seem friendly to Muslims other than the Mamelukes, so he must be on good terms with the imams and the ulemas of the El-Azhar mosque. The people of Egypt were used to an ancient structure of government as well as a lazy way of doing things. Napoleon would use the former and reform the latter. A little good French management would civilize the country.

Some of Napoleon's efforts did not work. A sheik who was given a tricolour scarf was outraged but leading Egyptians came to accept that they would don a cockade before coming into Napoleon's presence and doff it as they left. Napoleon tried out a kaftan and a turban, but looked ridiculous. The sixth anniversary of the proclamation of the republic – 1 Vendémiaire (the month of the *vendange* or grape harvest) in the revolutionary calendar, 22 September in the old – was to be marked with the ascent of a balloon, but the balloon soon drifted to the ground. The Egyptians were unimpressed. They also found French behaviour odd. French soldiers surprised Arab chroniclers by preferring Armenian or Georgian women or black slave girls to local boys. The average soldier's requirements were easily fulfilled by wine, women and song. The puritanical Napoleon, though not against his own first attempt at adultery (with the wife of one of his junior officers), had more exalted ideas.

One of his first actions had been to establish the Institute of Egypt in a series of buildings and gardens centred on the palace of the absent Qassim Bey – he was fighting the French in Upper Egypt – and meetings were held in his harem. The library was open to local scholars, Jabarti among them, who were delighted to acquaint themselves with the new learning; and in their turn many among the French *savants* were keen to improve their knowledge of Arabic. As the first person to bring the technology of printing to Egypt, Napoleon was quick to bring out the news he wanted people to know. *Le Courrier de l'Egypte*, edited by the mathematician Joseph Fourier, perpetual secretary of the Institute of Egypt, gave a correct view of current affairs to readers in Egypt. *La Décade Egyptienne*, edited by the chief medical officer of the army, René Nicolas Desgenettes, another member of the Institute, who also chaired a commission to set up a hospital for Egyptians, told the world what to think.

Napoleon's gift for propaganda turned near-disasters into triumphs. After crushing a serious uprising in the city, he ostentatiously showed himself equal to Julius Caesar in clemency by pardoning the sheiks and the imams of the El-Azhar mosque, who had done nothing, while he was quietly ordering the rebels to be beheaded. As Alexander the Great had trekked through the desert to visit the shrine of Amon, so he made a point of favouring Islam. He was flattered to be called Sultan Kebir, literally the 'Great'

Sultan; he said that his defeat of the Mamelukes was predicted in the Koran; he talked of the conversion of the army, while informing the rulers of the mosque that circumcision and a ban on alcohol would not attract French soldiers. His reward came in spring 1799, when he had the ulemas of El-Azhar proclaim that Sultan Kebir 'loved the Muslims, cherished the Prophet, instructed himself by reading the Koran every day, and desired to build a mosque unrivalled in splendour and to embrace the Muslim faith'.[3]

Before this announcement was made, Napoleon had gone to Syria and back again. In December he made a quick excursion to Suez, where he claimed to be the first to find traces of the ancient canal, and met a deputation of Christian monks and Muslim traders from Mount Sinai. Two months later he left the borders of Egypt for Palestine, holy land to Christians and Muslims alike. To the Directors, in theory his political masters, he said he wished to protect the borders of Egypt, forestall an attack on Egypt by Anglo-Turkish forces and deprive the British navy of bases in the Levant. In 1805 he imagined how he could have been Alexander the Great in reverse, not coming down to Egypt, but going up from Egypt: 'I would have won a battle at Issus.' This proved only a fantasy because, unlike another great general, Richard Coeur de Lion, he could not take Acre. The tale of the Third Crusade was less familiar to Napoleon than ancient history. Crusaders knew that it was more difficult to capture a city than to win a battle; and the medieval walls proved to be impregnable when manned by a ferocious Bosnian, pasha Ahmed Djezzar, and a flamboyant émigré, Louis-Edmond Le Picard de Phélipeaux, who had always been at the top in the class of 1783 at the Ecole Militaire when one Napoléon Buonaparte was a fellow student, and as defended at sea by an eccentric English sailor, Sidney Smith.

Napoleon had a gift for forgetting what he did not like to admit. The painters who made pictures of his campaign in the Levant could linger on the battles of Nazareth, where General Junot routed a detachment of cavalry far larger than his own, of Mount Tabor, where Napoleon appeared in the nick of time, or of the Jordan, which General Murat crossed to camp in captured Turkish tents. Ten years after a secular revolution in their homeland, Frenchmen were stirred by the Christian ambience of Galilee. At Nazareth they were touched at the joy with which the Christian Arabs received them. In Jaffa, the biblical Joppa, their commander behaved with a Christ-like serenity. Desgenettes was witness to a scene, made famous by the artist Antoine Jean Gros, that Napoleon reached out without fear to put his hand on the buboes of a victim of the plague. No illustration survives, however, of an instance of his ruthlessness: the massacre of the three thousand men of the garrison after they had surrendered. Napoleon had his standards: he knew when to be kind and when to be cruel.

What he never lost was the gift for transforming reality with the spell of his tongue. Having reassured the Divan of Cairo, the community leaders of the city, that he had razed the defences of Acre, he told his troops that they had 'dispersed in the plain before Mount Tabor the horde of men from every corner of Asia who had gathered in the hope of looting Egypt'.[4] They were leaving Acre only because it was the season of the year when hostile landings could be expected, and in Egypt they would have fresh opportunities for glory. Some of the sick were to be taken by sea to the delta port of Damietta, but were intercepted by the British and allowed to proceed to their destination. Those who had to be left behind were to be dealt with more summarily: they, says his secretary Bourrienne, were to be poisoned. In the event the dose they received from the doctors was inadequate, and some lived to tell their tale. A fortnight after reaching Gaza, Napoleon and his army entered Cairo with palms in their hats and caps, with captured flags on display, to the sound of bands, through crowded streets. It was a political triumph.

By then, Napoleon should have had no doubt that he had been forced on to the defensive. British ships sailed freely round the waters of the Levant, the French government sent no aid, the Turks had declared war and the expedition to Syria had ended in retreat. Napoleon did not admit that he had lost. He advised the Divan: 'Take a good look at me, and make sure that I am really Bona-parte.'[5] He proved his point by executing several Muslim prisoners brought from Syria, hesitated over which Egyptian rebels to attack next and then got the news he wanted to hear: a Turkish fleet was off Alexandria, starting to disembark an army of 12,000 to 15,000 men. Racing up to Aboukir, he got ready to attack the invaders early next morning. 'This battle,' he informed Murat, 'will decide the fate of the world.' The battle was decided by Murat. A precipitate charge against an enemy without horse caused some two thousand to be sliced up by sabre or bayonet, and some four thousand to be drowned or shot in the sea. One of the few to get safely back to his ship was a young man who was Napoleon's contemporary: a man who was rich from trading in tobacco, a soldier from Kavallë in European Turkey who out of respect for the Prophet liked to be called Mehemet, instead of Mohammed, Ali. Within days, Napoleon learned that the French had been driven out of Germany by the Austrians and out of Italy by the Russians. The French naval commander, Bruix, was asked to evacuate the Army of the East, if it were possible. Talleyrand, the Foreign Minister, more aware of what was possible, suggested that, if it were safe, Napoleon could leave someone else in charge. Sultan Kebir passed only one week in Cairo, where the Mameluke Armenian Roustam Raza joined his service, promised his soldiers and the Divan he would be back soon and hastened to Alexandria. He had arranged a rendezvous with general Kléber, his designated successor, but, before they could meet, Napoleon was on his way back to France.

Back in France, he posed as the nation's saviour. Whereas Talleyrand had been obliged to resign, Napoleon his protégé was greeted by the lower house, the Council of Five Hundred, with an ovation and a patriotic hymn. That night all Paris was lit up. Next day, dressed in a plain uniform, he offered his services, either as a general or as a simple gunner, to the Directors, resplendent in their antique mantles and tricolour plumes. Within three weeks, a coup d'état was to make him the effective head of state. His qualification for that role was that in Egypt he had become an experienced administrator and an accomplished politician.

Despite the Battle of the Pyramids and the land battle at Aboukir, his soldiering had done little to enhance his military reputation. If there was a French hero of the Egyptian campaigns in 1798–9, that man was a general born in 1768 in Auvergne, Louis Desaix de Veygoux, by origin a minor nobleman, and one who like Napoleon had profited from the revolutionary tendency to promote young men.

Desaix has been presented as a single-minded soldier, but he could be distracted. He teased his *amoureuse en titre*, Marguérite Le Normant, with a tale of his amorous conquests: of a Georgian, blonde and gentle, fourteen years old, his 'by right of succession'; of a wild fifteen-year-old Ethiopian; of a child from the Tigris and of Fatima, 'tall, beautiful, well-shaped but very unhappy . . . Such was my seraglio.'[6] He was also susceptible to the looks of Baqil, a young black boy, and of a little Mameluke, Ismail, 'as beautiful as an angel'. It is these boys who attend him in the portrait by the Italian artist Appiani; and when he was killed, they wailed over his body with unrestrained grief.

Desaix was more single-minded than Napoleon in his determination to destroy Mameluke power. Murad Bey, the sheik of the Haj, had gone south after the Battle of the Pyramids and in August 1798, at the head of just three thousand men, without horse and with only two guns, Desaix set out after him. The pursuit was to take him, after one excursus to ancient Oxyrynchus (Bahnasa) on the so-called Joseph's Canal in the Libyan desert, further and further up the Nile. On the canal, beside a Coptic monastery, the French barely survived a bloody encounter with Mameluke cavalry. While a lieutenant in the hussars, Desvernois, was sent to woo the Bedouin and allowed himself to be wooed by Bedouin girls, a battalion under General Belliard was dispatched to reinforce Desaix, bringing with him the ageing literary factotum, Vivant Denon. It is thanks to Denon's lively work, *Voyages dans la Haute et dans la Basse Egypte*, that Desaix has had his due. Describing the pyramids and the sphinx, Denon is eloquent on the beauty of their proportions, and he proves his point with an engraving of some compatriots clambering up on the sphinx to measure it. Pyramids and even sphinxes were already fixed in the minds of well-educated Europeans. What they did not yet know lay beyond Cairo. It was Denon who, thanks to Desaix, opened the route to the ancient kingdom of Upper Egypt. Once Desaix returned from Cairo with a thousand mounted troops led by General Davout, the future Marshal, the journey became a military possibility. As Desaix had coopted a Copt, Malem Jacob, to collect taxes from the fellahin, the army would have a stomach to march on. As it went ever further south, the more likely were the Copts to be in a majority in the villages and the less popular were the financial exactions of the fleeing Murad Bey.

Malem Jacob's intelligence told him to expect that Murad Bey would stand at Girga, then the largest city in Upper Egypt, but when Desaix got there his enemy had gone. While he paused to await his flotilla, Murad Bey built up an army of 13,000 horsemen and 3,000 infantry, gathering reinforcements from as far as Hejaz in the Red Sea and Nubia in the south. A French fleet, sent by Napoleon to the port of Kosseir, was too small to stop the Meccans from alighting on the Egyptian shore and it quickly withdrew to Suez. In Girga the French took consolation from the cheap price of food; and when the yearly convoy arrived from Nubia, Denon was entranced by the liveliness, dark skin and beautiful eyes of its leader's brother. Through an interpreter he told them the prices of slaves, confirmed that there was a place called Timbuktu, six months away to the south-west, and promised them that Europeans would be welcome to trade with Africans. At last, the flotilla caught up and Desaix was impatient to fight. In the battle that followed, Desvernois swore he received nineteen minor cuts and a dozen to his horse, but Desaix reported that only Desvernois's wrist was cut. Few Frenchmen were killed. The Mameluke cavalry, as usual, made little impact on the defensive squares in which the French were massed. As usual, they fled south. The French followed as quickly as possible, much to the frustration of Denon, who had scarcely time to sketch the outline of a temple, as Desaix sped past Abydos, Tentyra, Thebes, Hermonthis and Apollonopolis Magna on the way to Syene. At Tentyra (Dendera) there was a pause in the chase, and Denon spent a day marvelling at the ruins. At the first sight of Thebes the soldiers spontaneously halted, presented arms and started to clap. Denon was proud of them and grateful as they offered their knees as rests for his sketching pad or stood between him and the overpowering light. Belliard and Denon stayed at Aswan, from where they visited Elephantine island and, despite fierce local resistance, the island of Philae, now submerged by the dam at Aswan. They had to leave in a rush, for Desaix had hastened north, vainly hoping to catch up with Murad Bey, who had doubled back. By Karnak, Meccans attacked the flotilla and raped, mutilated and hacked to pieces prisoners captured off one of the boats. Eventually, Belliard caught up with a Meccan-Mameluke force in a village called Abnud, fought them for three days and killed most of them. Desaix was already far down the Nile at Asyut, where he found the fellahin primed for revolt and the Mameluke leaders quarrelling among themselves, all too willing to sacrifice each others' lives and the lives of the fellahin. At Darfur, Desvernois attacked the caravan that had been received with such warmth by Desaix at Girga and captured 897 camels. The round of endless marching, skirmishing, slaughtering, seizing and raping got the French no nearer to controlling Egypt. Most of Belliard's party had their eyes smarting from ophthalmia, but Belliard himself was still willing to staunch the flow of sanguinary Meccans through Kosseir, once Desaix sent him the supplies he needed. Once the port was taken and a small garrison installed, Belliard wrote to the sherif of Mecca that the French republic was a close ally of the Turkish Empire, then returned to the valley of the Nile. The Mamelukes had not been destroyed; they had merely retreated into oases in the desert or to the Sudan. When the main body of the French southern expedition had returned to Cairo, Murad Bey had marched as far as Gizeh, waiting to attack them.

The French expedition to Egypt failed to conquer Egypt not because of native resistance but because of the intervention of the hated English. Nelson's victory at Aboukir Bay prevented ultimate victory, but, as long as Napoleon could defeat any land forces that the Mamelukes or the Turks could produce, ultimate defeat was postponed. After he left, that event may have become inevitable. The rough Alsatian whom he left in charge, General Kléber, was told by Napoleon that the Grand Vizier had been assured that France would evacuate Egypt, yet privately he encouraged Kléber to delay, to stop France losing out to another European power (which could only be England); and when Napoleon became First Consul, this became French government policy. Kléber was harsh, firm and unimaginative. At El Arish, on the borders of the Holy Land in

January 1800 on Kléber's authority Desaix negotiated with the Grand Vizier and Sidney Smith a treaty of withdrawal. Its terms were repudiated by the English government, but Frenchmen left Egypt with valid Turkish and unofficial English passports, among them Desaix. There ensued yet one more victory over the Turks, at Heliopolis on this occasion, and yet one more rising in Cairo; and there Kléber was killed, by Soliman, a Muslim from Aleppo. What astonished the chronicler Jabarti was that the French gave the young man a trial.

Kléber's successor was General Menou, an aged gentleman notable for his interest in the Rosetta stone, which he kept under his bed, and his conversion to Islam. Though he declared Egypt a permanent French possession, when it came to maintaining France's position by fending off a British expeditionary force, he was too slow and too hasty, so that he gave the British time to establish themselves and then attacked them with inferior numbers. Denon's friend, General Belliard, suggested an alliance with Murad Bey, who promptly and inconveniently died, and his successor preferred the English. When Menou agreed to a treaty with the English, much on the same lines as the agreement of El Arish, French scientists were allowed to keep their specimens, but he had to relinquish the Rosetta stone.

In 1801 it must have seemed that all Napoleon had achieved had been that he had given the British the excuse to take control of the country that would most ease their passage to India. Anyone who in 1801 prophesied that this would be so was misled by the turn of events.

The French broke Mameluke power without replacing them as rulers of Egypt. At this stage poised to profit from French discomfiture, the English were to suffer a similar fate, for the principal beneficiary of the European intervention proved to be a Muslim subject of the Sultan: Mehemet Ali, the tobacco merchant from

Kavallë who led three hundred men from European Turkey to defeat at the Battle of Aboukir. He survived to carry on fighting, and in 1805 he was invited by Egyptian sheiks to be pasha of Egypt, a position soon confirmed by the Sultan. Two years later, when the French had regained influence in Istanbul, Great Britain, recently created out of the union of England, Wales and Scotland with Ireland, declared war on Sultan Selim. Mehemet Ali defeated a British army at Rosetta and forced it to evacuate Alexandria. In 1811 he disposed of the Mamelukes. He invited four hundred of their leaders to the citadel of Cairo before joining in a war against the Wahabis of Arabia, who were preventing the devout from making the hajj to Mecca. From the citadel, the Mameluke beys had to pass down to the city through a narrow defile. Once they were in this passage, gates at either end were locked and they were trapped. Soldiers opened fire on them and all but one of them was killed. In 1813 Mehemet Ali was able to send the Wahabi leader in chains to Istanbul. He loyally intervened to support the Sultan during the Greek rebellion, only to be frustrated by the pro-Hellenic intervention of France and of Britain, for once cooperating, and of Russia, so instead he decided to concentrate on strengthening Egypt. He regained lands to the south, starting with Nubia, he held the island of Crete and he almost provoked war between France and Britain by routing his old master, the Sultan, in Syria.

His heirs decided to be pacific. Abbas opened Egypt to free trade, Said initiated the reconstruction of the ancient canal to Suez that Napoleon had been told to build, and under Khedive Ismail the French company of de Lesseps completed the task. Once more the British undermined a French project, for, when the Khedive found himself in debt, Disraeli, the British Prime Minister, gained the help of the Rothschilds to buy the Khedive's shares; and so the Compagnie du canal de Suez, now an Anglo-French company, provided the British route to the Indian Empire Napoleon had planned to cut. In 1882, after the British defeated a nationalist uprising led by a belligerent war minister, the dynasty of Mehemet Ali became dependent on Britain. In the First World War, as Turkey was allied to Britain's enemies, Egypt was made into a British protectorate and the base for the unsuccessful attack on Gallipoli and conquests of Arabia (by Lawrence and his Arab friends) and of Palestine and Syria (by Allenby). After that war, France was dominant in Syria, Britain in Palestine and Egypt. In the Second World War Britain used Egypt in its fight against Italy and Germany, and it was near Alexandria that British forces won the decisive battle of El Alamein in 1942.

King Farouk, the most corrupt of Mehemet Ali's family, sensual and idle, was the last to reign in Cairo. When the democratically elected Wafd party repudiated the 1936 treaty that had given Britain control of the Suez Canal, Farouk dismissed the Prime Minister and so provoked riots. Army officers found the excuse for a coup d'état and forced Farouk to lug his hulking, flabby body off to the Riviera, where he felt at home. By 1956 one officer, Colonel Nasser, had emerged as more truly heir to Mehemet Ali. He promptly nationalized the Suez Canal and unwittingly led to one last effort by Britain and France, this time in combination, to retain control of Egypt. They failed not because they lost but because the USA would not uphold their victory. The age of Napoleon had passed. The affairs of the Middle East were no longer controlled from Europe.

Egypt was something like a French colony for only three years. What endured from Napoleon's venture was the discovery of Egypt. In the middle years of the eighteenth century French scholars had produced an *Encyclopédie* that summarized information read with the sceptical eyes of writers who considered themselves 'enlightened'. What was being tried now for the first time was an attempt to understand a non-European country in all possible ways. The *Description de l'Egypte* was to be a work of collective scholarship such as the world had never seen. In its first edition it came out from 1809 onwards in ten volumes of text and thirteen of plates. It was to broadcast the wonders of Egyptian antiquity, provide a map of Egypt and investigate modern Egyptian life. The observations of the orientalists, antiquarians, surveyors, chemists, physicists, mathematicians, geologists, zoologists, botanists and biologists were illustrated by artists who recorded with sketches that in print became the 600, eventually 900 pictures produced by 400 engravers. As a monument it was unsurpassed, but it remained little known even in France, and so Louis XVIII, Napoleon's successor, decreed that a fresh edition, even more splendid, should be produced for the benefit of those who devoted years of their lives to the project. Every year, some 2,000 people worked on preparing the publication.

The *Description* was the fruit of the labours of the Institute of Egypt that Napoleon had set up in Cairo in August 1798. The Institute had four sections: mathematics, physics, political economy, and literature and the arts. Each section was limited to a maximum of 12 members, but there was a wide periphery of *savants*, many of whom made up the original 165 members of the Commission of Arts and Sciences, who never penetrated into this inner circle, so that Napoleon was as well advised as anyone in that period could have been. He himself was elected to the mathematical section, and when he was free he attended the Institute's sessions. His chosen leaders of the venture were the mathematician Monge and the chemist Berthollet, and until his death in 1822 Berthollet was director of the enterprise. But as the *littérateur* Denon was the first artist to view the grand remains of Upper Egypt and rushed into print in 1802, the reading public gained an aesthetic rather than a scientific appreciation of Egypt. Today it is still the pictures of the *Description*, not the articles, that gain attention. The scholarship of the *savants* has been superseded; the prints retain their value.

Some artists cheated. They did not understand hieroglyphs, so they invented what the symbols might have been. They were trained in the art of perspectival drawing, so, too, they could imagine what a building could look like from an angle they could not see, and they were used to inventing what a scene ought to look like. The shrine of Kom Ombo, almost engulfed by sand, was presented incorrectly as if surrounded by an open courtyard, while the temple at Edfu, the most nearly perfect to survive, was left in its unexcavated state. On the Birth House at Edfu scenes were shown that were drawn from other similar buildings. Often, however, their evidence is the best we have. Several sites were depicted that were later destroyed: the temple of Contralatopolis, a victim of the modernizing Mehemet Ali; the temple of Antaeopolis that was swept away by the Nile in 1821; the temple of Amenhotep III, on the island of Elephantine, that lasted only until 1822. Though the paws of the Gizeh sphinx were covered by sand, the face was in far better condition than it is today, when the pollution of modern Cairo has eaten into the stone. Napoleon himself refused to enter the Great Pyramids. The artists were more intrepid, and their perspective views of some of the chambers have a haunting quality that conveys the thrill of discovery. Everywhere the French went, there was some new reason for being excited. They were amazed at the huge statues of Rameses II, whom they still knew by the Greek name of Ozymandias, Shelley's 'king of kings', and at the Colossi of Memnon. Even Karnak in a state of ruin was overwhelming. At Dendera Denon had discovered and drawn a zodiac on the ceiling; another one was found at Esna; in the *Description* astronomers discussed at length what they meant. The *savants*, fascinated by antiquities, came to grasp that no ancient civilization was so well preserved as that of ancient Egypt.

Collectively, the *savants* were not lost in the past. Even if the dirt and disease of modern Egypt depressed them, it was with modern Egyptians that Europeans would have to deal. Desgenettes and his team set up a hospital to treat the native population. The soldiers were delighted to see crocodiles for the first time and quickly appreciated that their pleasure in their new learning needed to be restricted – the engravings of the reptile, understandably, do not appear to be based on very close observation. Like the artists of the *Encyclopédie*, they were more at home recording Egyptians at work, setting blindfolded oxen to draw up water from underground reservoirs in the delta or, far south near the First Cataract, using an elaborate system of dolabs (irrigation machines) to pump water from a well on to gardens. They studied Egyptian ploughs, threshing machines, their ways of making vinegar, linseed oil, a kind of brandy, the manufacturing processes of the cotton industry that was to become so important for the economy, the techniques used to make rope, felt, mats, the craft of carpenters, potters, glassmakers, knife grinders, barbers. They also recorded the appearance of their new neighbours. The artist Dutertre made a magnificent portrait of the man whom Desaix pursued all over Upper Egypt: Murad Bey. There are fine pictures of a poet, an astronomer, a young Mameluke, a sailor from Alexandria. They captured a quiet conversation between a Greek Orthodox monk from Mount Sinai and an Arab from a nearby oasis. In accordance with biological theories of the time they studied physiognomy: the head of a boy from Alexandria, refined as a result of Graeco-Egyptian intermarriage; the grave, dark features of an Abyssinian bishop; the mobile face of a dragoman, a polyglot interpreter. They had not realized how many varieties of turban there were, how dress marked out a Jew, a Copt or a janissary, how hard it was to meet any woman of social standing – yet they knew every detail of the elaborate costume worn by the *awalem* (the female dancers or singers).[7]

Those interested in the flora and fauna of Egypt arrived there at a good moment. The botanist Linnaeus had introduced a simple scheme for classifying plants, Rousseau had given the science a poetic resonance and the prestige of Buffon's *Histoire Naturelle* had boosted French self-confidence. In the South Seas recently Frenchmen had come across species alien to Europe, so Napoleon's *savants* were mentally prepared for whatever they would find in Egypt. Geoffrey Saint-Hilaire, the zoologist, thought it would have been worth his while to have come to Egypt just to see the *polyptère bichir*, a singular creature that lived at the bottom of the Nile and could be trapped only when the water was low. He was enthusiastic also about the aquatic life he had come across in Lake Manzaleh close to Damietta. There he had spent happy hours fishing and had felt himself rewarded when he caught a fish he named a heterobranch. His companion Savigny was captivated by the sight of the birds. In September 1798 he wrote in his diary: 'I have never seen so many birds on the lake: flamingos who let out repeated harsh cries, pelicans, cormorants, ducks etc.' Four days later he was entranced by the number of herons. The noise was like the crack of a rifle.[8] The artist Henri-Joseph Redouté, elder brother of the flower painter, produced beautiful watercolours of Nile fish for Saint-Hilaire, and in the finished pictures of the *Description* there are delicate tinted engravings of many of the birds. As for the *savants* as a group, when they heard that they might have to give up their specimens to the English, they said they were willing to go to England with them. What they could not bear was the thought of losing them.

Their most important discovery the French had to surrender. In

1799 a French soldier called D'Hautpol was demolishing a ruined wall at a fort near the delta port of Rosetta when he unearthed a large slab of black basalt with inscriptions on one side. Bouchard, the officer in charge, informed his superior, Lancret, who quickly realized that in addition to Greek writing, which he could recognize, there were two other scripts, one of which was identified as hieroglyphs, the ancient priestly script, the other of which must also be ancient Egyptian. Lancret sent Bouchard to take their treasure to the Institute of Egypt. The soldiers had dug up the Rosetta stone. It was to take twenty-three years before the Egyptian writing on it could be deciphered so that the three lines of inscriptions on the Rosetta stone were equally comprehensible. What is remarkable is that the decoding was achieved so soon.

The Institute had copies made that were dispatched to the learned all over Europe, but, as the stone went to England, it is not surprising that the first scholar to make some progress with the hieroglyphs, the most difficult script, was a remarkable Englishman, Thomas Young, a linguist who was also a distinguished scientist. Young instinctively applied a method. The stela, dating from the reign of Ptolemy v Epiphanes, contained Greek proper names – Ptolemy and Cleopatra – and Young noticed that at corresponding points in the hieroglyphic text oval rings or cartouches surrounded certain signs. These signs must be the Egyptian equivalent to the Greek originals, and he could offer plausible solutions implying that, instead of thinking in purely symbolic terms as earlier students had guessed, the ancient Egyptians had used something like an alphabet, at least for foreign words. After announcing his ingenious discovery, Young could get no further.

The person who was to be the first man to read hieroglyphs as a system was only eight when Napoleon had gone to Egypt and met his hero only once, in 1815, during the Hundred Days. Jean-François Champollion, the son of a bookseller in south-west France and younger brother to a professional scholar, Jacques-Joseph, was a linguistic genius. Having mastered the classical languages in childhood, he went to join Jacques-Joseph in Grenoble. By luck, the head of the local administration, or prefect, was Fourier, a *savant* who had just returned from Egypt and the man who had been given the task of writing the general introduction to the *Description de l'Egypte*. On visiting one of the local schools he was so impressed by the enthusiasm of twelve-year-old Jean-François for all things Egyptian that he invited him to see his antiquities, which included papyri and inscribed stones adorned with hieroglyphs. The boy made up his mind that one day he would read them. For years he was held up by the rigidity of Napoleonic schooling – he had to hide his Hebrew and Arabic books from the watchman who checked up on the boarders in the lycée to see that their lights were out – but gradually he mastered all oriental languages, ancient and modern, that were known, including Aramaic, the first language of Christ, and related tongues like Syriac and Chaldean.

One language he grasped was more important for his purposes than any other: Coptic. In Egypt, the French had had dealings with Christian Copts, who made up about ten per cent of the population. The Copts were the people called by the Greeks Αιγυπτοι (Aiguptoi), native to the land. Like most other inhabitants of Egypt – the Greeks, the Romans, the Nubians and people from further south – during the fourth century most became Christians. Miles from the international, Greek city of Alexandria, early monks in Upper Egypt, near Thebes, spoke Coptic. Egyptian theologians stressed the unity of Christ, and, when in 451 the Church decreed that Christ had two natures, many Egyptians repudiated the decision. The result was a division between Greeks – the council had been held at Chalcedon, near Constantinople – and Copts. Under Greek rule, Copts were often persecuted, and they welcomed conquest by Muslims. If many did not convert to Islam, they found it politic and then normal to speak Arabic. Except in a few villages in the south, Coptic fossilized as a spoken language; it remained alive only in sacred texts. In 1805 Champollion was lucky. A former Coptic monk came to Grenoble and offered to teach him Coptic. By 1809, now in Paris, Champollion could write: 'I only dream Coptic and Egyptian . . .' The two, he believed, must be later and earlier forms of the same language: Coptic was the modern route to the ancient tongue.

In 1815 an obelisk, bilingual like the Rosetta stone, was found at Philae. Once he gained a copy of it, he was able to add extra proper names to Young's tally: Berenice and Alexander. But his triumph was to grasp that hieroglyphs operated in more than one way: sometimes they could be read from right to left, sometimes from left to right, sometimes from top to bottom, sometimes like sounds (letters or syllables) and sometimes like symbols and sometimes like marks of status. Young's procedure had been too mechanical, but he also lacked Champollion's profound knowledge of Coptic, based on a study of every manuscript that was accessible, which enabled the Frenchman to guess what an earlier form of that language might be. Soon he could read the names of Rameses ii, the Pharaoh probably known to Moses, whose own name was Egyptian, and of Thutmoses iii, the Napoleon of ancient Egypt. In 1822 he rushed into his brother's room to announce that he had found out how to read hieroglyphs – and then he fainted.

It took Champollion the rest of his short life to establish Egyptology as an academic subject. He went to study the best European collection in Turin, he led an expedition to Egypt in 1828–9 and died in 1832, leaving his brother to publish his work on an Egyptian grammar. He had made possible future attempts to describe ancient Egypt in ancient Egyptian terms.

Within weeks of leaving Egypt, General Bonaparte was First Consul of France and in 1804 became Emperor Napoleon i. Now that he had the power to do so, Napoleon put one of his official artists from Egypt, Denon, in charge of the Musée du Louvre that housed Egyptian antiquities as well as more familiar European works once the property of the Bourbons or of other rulers who had endured defeat and spoliation at the hands of the French. Denon proved to be the most influential of the group of designers who favoured the spread of the 'Egyptian' style, but he was just one of the 'Egyptians' who were important in the new France.

6

ANCIENT ROME RESTORED

———⇒⊷⊶⇐———

At some moments Napoleon made out that the expedition to Egypt had been the most exciting period of his life. It changed him from being a mere soldier-adventurer into a man with experience as the ruler of a country. Though never an aesthete, Napoleon encouraged a taste for the Egyptian style that was evident in the porcelain on Joséphine's table, the cabinets in Parisian rooms, the façades of Parisian houses; and on St Helena he decorated a wall of his bungalow with a map torn from a page of the *Description de l'Egypte*. He retained a special relationship with men who had been with him in Egypt. If he might have found it hard to thank Desaix for rescuing him at the crisis of the Battle of Marengo had Desaix not been killed immediately afterwards, the boost to Desaix's fame in Denon's *Voyage dans la Haute et dans la Basse Egypte* was balanced by Denon's tactful dedication of his book to Napoleon as 'a hero'. Denon had returned to France with Napoleon, and in 1802 he was rewarded by Napoleon with the post of director of museums.

Denon was only one of the 'Egyptians' to be promoted. Duroc, aide-de-camp in Egypt, was made governor of the Tuileries palace, Berthier, chief of staff in Egypt, became Minister of War, Berthollet, the chemist who had organized the scientific commission, became vice-president of the Senate, and his mathematical companion Monge was elevated to the ranks of Senator and Comte de Péluse (after Pelusium on the borders of Egypt). Even Menou, who had surrendered to the British, was given posts in Italy.

There were limits to Egyptomania. Napoleon did not think of himself as the heir to the Pharaohs but to the ancient Greeks and Romans. His culture was classical. As a boy, he played at Romans and Carthaginians and in invading Italy he vied with Hannibal, whose campaigns he knew from Livy. In going to Egypt, he recalled how Alexander the Great and Julius Caesar had preceded him. He was authorized by a 'republic', run by five 'directors', and when he displaced them as head of state by the coup d'état of Brumaire, while eschewing for a time the role of a 'dictator' or, on the American model, a 'president', he revived the Roman titles of 'consul' (the first in a 'triumvirate') and of 'emperor'. To justify these constitutional changes, he revived the antique device of the 'plebiscite', while using modern skills to ensure that the people always chose what he intended them to want.

It took time for the artists to devise an appropriate iconography. In the 1790s there was a sophisticated fashion for wearing classical dress, favoured by the artist David and the actor Talma, but Napoleon, who had looked ridiculous in Arab costume, was not going to choose a toga in place of trousers, so that Prud'hon's vision of him riding bewreathed in a triumphal chariot was a product of artistic imagination. David's star pupils produced modern portraits that more accurately dramatize Napoleon's new roles. Gros's *Bonaparte as First Consul* has a sense of panache, as the youthful leader twists his body energetically to the left while indicating with his right hand a table strewn with treaties that he has signed (quills are dipped in an inkstand towards the back of the picture). The same subject, as treated by Ingres, is much more staid. Napoleon, with his left hand, characteristically, inside his red and gold cut-away coat, stands beside a table similar to that in the Gros painting, while the document to which his right hand points and the townscape viewed through the window behind him refer to districts of Liège, once part of the Austrian Netherlands but now since the Treaty of Lunéville (in 1801) a city that was the seat of a French prefecture. Between them, the two works suggest Napoleon's new civilian powers as the man bringing peace to and governing the larger nation that by that date France had become.

It was some time before Ingres's likeness was shown in public, for in 1804, the year when it was finished, with the help of a referendum First Consul Bonaparte transformed himself into Napoleon, Emperor of the French. In theory, France was still a republic, but Napoleon was more than just a first citizen, a latter-day *princeps* in the style of Augustus; he was the successor of the successors of Augustus. The Russian ruler was a Caesar or Tsar, the monarch of the Third Rome (after Rome itself and Byzantium). In 1806 the other European Emperor, the Holy Roman Emperor, Latin equivalent to the Basileus of Byzantium, last in a series that went back a thousand years to Charlemagne, saw his Empire collapse before Napoleon's military and diplomatic onslaught and had to make do as a simple Austrian Kaiser. Napoleon seemed like a new Caesar, a new Basileus, a new Charlemagne, and it was as such that Ingres painted him in the grandest, most disturbing of all Napoleonic images.

Well before he proclaimed himself Emperor, Napoleon had made sure that he was not to be replaced as First Consul. His title suggested an ancient republic, but the reality was that he was a modern enlightened despot, closer to Frederick the Great, King of

Prussia and Catherine the Great, Tsarina of Russia, or to Joseph II, Holy Roman Emperor, than to Presidents Washington and Jefferson. Already in 1802 he was made Consul for Life – there was to be none of the annual elections that the Romans had instituted to prevent any one man from becoming too powerful. His metamorphosis to Emperor by act of the Senate, yet another antique formula, was reminiscent of the process by which Octavius Caesar, heir to Julius, had become first citizen in the Roman Republic and then by gradual degrees the master over it. He took care not to alienate his followers who hated the Bourbons; and to demonstrate his opposition to the royal family he had seized the Duc d'Enghien, heir to the Prince de Condé, and summarily executed him. Whereas in 1789 the kings had been Kings of France, from 1804 he was the Emperor of the French, his rule less territorial than personal. As Emperor, however, he claimed a status higher than theirs, less national than universal, and the logic of his position was that he aspired to be a ruler who dominated Europe by means of what historians call Le Grand Empire.

By 1806, when he painted *Napoleon I on His Imperial Throne*, Ingres was a fluent artist, with a wonderful sense of linear design and a loving eye for detail. He had begun to enjoy the forgotten art of the past, helped by France's systematic plundering of the churches, palaces and galleries of defeated countries. He had merely to go to the Louvre to study the van Eycks' altarpiece of *The Adoration of the Lamb*, fresh from Ghent, and he made drawings of Byzantine ivories, of the emblems of Frankish kings – of Dagobert as well as of Charlemagne – besides one of a more conventional, classical image of Jupiter enthroned. From such eclectic sources he invented a Napoleon that nobody had seen, 'Gothic' in the opinion of his critics, more divine than human. Clad in purple, ermine and gold, frontally seated astride a throne, holding a sceptre of Dagobert and the hand of justice of Charlemagne, wearing laurel on his brows, with an eagle on the carpet at his feet, the person of Napoleon is swamped by his myth. This is not an imitation of appearance – Ingres did not copy Napoleon's features – but the icon of one invested by God with godlike majesty and power. Officially, Napoleon's court was embarrassed, and the painting was hung in the Palais Bourbon, home of the legislature, safe from public view.

More than his contemporaries, Ingres intuitively grasped the variety of ways in which political power was exercised in France, a country with ancient traditions before the Revolution remodelled it as antique.

The country that Julius Caesar conquered he called Gaul and its people Gauls. Among the Germanic barbarians who mastered both country and people in the course of the fifth century, one of the latest arrivals among the tribes were the Franks, who controlled areas of land on both sides of the Rhine. Gradually, Franks, while keeping control of their original territory, extended control over all Gaul and, in the reign of Charlemagne, added to it Saxony, northern Italy and the county of Barcelona. Customs of inheritance and family quarrels led to the rapid disintegration of this empire, until by the end of the tenth century the Carolingian king of the west Franks possessed nothing beyond the Ile-de-France, and it was only a miniature domain that was seized from him by Hugh Capet, nominally a duke but in fact the power behind the shaky throne.

France had been created by the steady extension of the authority of the kings of the west Franks over most of ancient Gaul, a process that took eight hundred years to complete. During the late eighteenth century France was still organized by an irrational administrative system that reflected the random way in which this had happened. In 1300 there was a supreme court, based in Paris, with jurisdiction over the northern third of France, but, as more provinces became subject to the king, each was allowed its own *parlement* or *cour souverain*. *Parlements* had the same name but a more restricted function than the English Houses of Parliament, and their advisory role was taken by the Estates General, which rarely met, and mimicked by local estates, of which only two, those of Brittany and Languedoc, survived in strength. There was no uniform taxation. The universal tax on salt, the *gabelle*, was levied at different rates in different parts of France, more heavily in central areas than at the periphery. There was a standard tax on property, the *taille*, from which nobles were exempt on the principle of noblesse oblige (in other words they should offer help), but it did not apply everywhere, for in some parts of France the *taille* was *personelle*. The incidence of indirect taxes called *aides*, often on wine, also varied from region to region. If there was a general rule, it was that there were always exceptions. Privilege or private right was endemic, and when Kings Louis XIV, Louis XV and Louis XVI tried to tax everyone equally, the privileged classes considered them tyrannical.

When it came to running everyday administration, the theoretical limits to royal power were few but in practice many. The provinces were the responsibility of military governors, but as they were nobles they could use their position and local connections to build up a power base that could threaten the king. Steadily, the first Bourbons, Henri IV and Louis XIII, cut down the numbers of the governors, and Louis XIV went further. He forced nobles to move far from their estates to the court at Versailles, where he made their way of life as expensive as possible. He even reduced the time they spent in their hôtels in Paris, so curbing aristocratic influence at the centre at the same time as in the localities. In their place, much to their disgust, he insisted that a new class of nobleman, the *noblesse de la robe* (nobility of the gown), should run the affairs of the kingdom. It was from their ranks and the related class of the *haute bourgeoisie* that he drew his ministers, men like the Colberts and the Le Telliers, who could aspire to the upper reaches of society. At a lower level they became the *intendants*, the professional administrators who were given charge of the *généralités*, large districts that overlapped with the provinces. At the lowest level they were simply *officiers*.

France seemed a well-run kingdom, controlled by a king whose will was law. The reality was more chaotic. The King ruled with the aid of the privileged classes. By a famous edict of 1604, for a small charge *officiers* were allowed to make their offices hereditary, enabling them so to draw a regular income and to achieve noble status. In the eighteenth century *intendants* became more independent by building up dynasties of their own, and at the heart of France the *parlementaires* of Paris waged a war of attrition against royal edicts. The more Louis XV or Louis XVI tried to impose a system of government and taxation that treated all Frenchmen alike, the more the privileged resisted them, and it was they who after an interval of 175 years forced the King to recall the Estates General in 1789. The Revolution began as a protest against equality in the name of liberties, not of liberty; and it was only as the self-seeking of the ruling class was exposed and their privileges abolished that an administration fair to everyone was possible. When the Estates General, whose members were elected by rank, was turned into the National Assembly (later the Constituent Assembly), open to all but dominated by the bourgeois, it was time to restructure France.

Between 1789 and 1791 the work was done. France was rationalized. In August 1789 members of the Assembly renounced their privileges and voted for the Rights of Man and the Citizen. In October 1789 the women of Paris brought the King and the

Assembly from Versailles to Paris. Paris, the city around which France had been formed, was once more capital of the kingdom, and modern France came into existence there.

In autumn 1789 France consisted of 35 provinces, 33 fiscal *généralités*, each under its own *intendant*, 175 *grands bailliages*, 13 *parlements* and 38 *gouvernements militaires*.[1] By the following spring the country had been split into 83 departments, most subdivisions of former provinces, and these in turn were subdivided into districts and the districts into communes. Large communes like Paris or Lyon dominated their departments, a few were villages, but most were medium-sized market towns or cities that had been the focus of provincial life. Modern France was to be 'natural', so most departments took their names from local rivers or mountains, the Allier or the Puy-de-Dôme. In so far as it was possible, departments were made equal in size and population, but, what mattered more, they were self-governing. So keen was the Assembly to prevent opportunities for arbitrary power that about four and a half million Frenchmen – all men over twenty-five who paid in taxation the local equivalent of three days' wages – were given the vote. They directly chose the officers of the commune, at the head of which was the *maire*, and indirectly they chose who was to run the district or the department or who should sit in the Assembly. The larger communes, with populations of more than 25,000, were broken up into sections: Paris had 48, Lyon and Marseille 32, Bordeaux 28, Toulouse 15.[2]

The Revolution had begun with acts of mob violence, as when on 14 July 1789 a mob forced the governor of the royal arsenal, the Bastille, to surrender and rewarded him for not firing at them by lynching him, or when peasants broke into *manoirs* and châteaux, destroyed records of their feudal obligations to their lords and burned the buildings down with sometimes the owners inside. The attempt to replace absolute with constitutional monarchy, which went hand in hand with a regime in which power was taken from the King and the privileged and given to the people and their representatives, was ended by a mob invading the Tuileries palace, massacring the royal Swiss Guard and arresting the King, the Queen and the Dauphin. In August 1792 France became a republic, a fact given prominence by the decision in 1793 to backdate a revolutionary calendar to that event. Like the new departments, the new year was to be 'natural', the names of the months suggesting rain or fog or snow, the seed time, the flowering or the harvesting of crops. The King, renamed after his distant ancestor Louis Capet, and his Queen, Marie-Antoinette (a Habsburg) were executed. Terror became the ruthless method of dealing with the enemies of the republic, who could be found anywhere. A nun, a viscount, a journalist, a mayor or a national politician (member of the Legislative Assembly from 1791 or of the Convention from 1792) were no more safe than a prostitute, a murderer or a thief. All power went to the political clubs, which came to mean the Jacobin Clubs; the guardian of virtue, while the republic was in danger, was Maximilien Robespierre; the supreme scourge of vice was the guillotine. As the number of victims rose, hysteria mounted. There was civil war in the Vendée and the Lyonnais; émigrés, most of them royalists, threatened invasion with or without the help of foreign armies; the country was in chaos; the economy wrecked; state finances, as the paper currency fell in value, were no longer able to sustain the weight of government. In the hot month of year II, Thermidor 1794, members of the Convention, scared that they themselves were about to die, combined to denounce Robespierre and his associates. The Terror in Paris came to an immediate end, but there was a vindictive anti-Jacobin White Terror, especially in the south; Napoleon, a protégé of Robespierre's younger brother Augustin, was lucky to escape with a spell in prison. Cruel idealism gave way to cynical manipulation. In 1795, with a whiff of grape-shot, Napoleon dispersed the last Paris crowd that tried to decide national policy. A five-man Directory aimed to do nothing more than stay in power and carried out coups d'états whenever they were threatened by the impact of popular votes on either of the two chambers that made up the latest form of Assembly. In the end, the Directors fell to the one coup that they had not engineered, when Napoleon, back from Egypt, forced them to resign. He was determined to rule France. There would be equality, but no more liberty than he thought acceptable.

It was under Napoleon that a modern administration was founded.

The attempt in the 1790s to make administration representative was doomed to failure because local officials felt no obligation to obey any central authority, while in Paris periodic mob interventions threatened the independence of the various Assemblies that were elected to order national affairs. The obsessive fear of an overpowerful executive like the Most Christian King Louis XIV made the management of France more arbitrary than the *ancien régime* upheld by the Bourbons.

On 17 February 1800 the law of 28 pluviôse of year VIII laid down that the prefects at the head of each department were to be nominated by the First Consul. The prefect was to be assisted by a general council responsible for the budget of the department and a prefecture council of three to five members meant to cope with administrative disputes. Subprefects were in charge of the subdivisions of the departments, the *arrondissements*. All these officials were state nominees.

To make this system effective and just, there was an attempt to ensure that administrators followed rules: they must consider discussions to be confidential, they must not act on the whim of the moment, they must cultivate an esprit de corps – in Napoleon's

France there was no room for individualistic caprice. There were tangible rewards for those willing to conform: a state councillor had an income of 25,000 francs, a prefect between 8,000 and 24,000 francs, while in Paris the average worker earned 3 francs a day. Provided he was loyal, industrious and efficient, a man who worked for the State could look forward to a lifetime of security.

Disapproving strongly of the instability of the ten years from the fall of absolute monarchy in 1789 to the coup d'état in 1799 that made him supreme, Napoleon was lucky that many survived who had worked for Louis XVI before 1789, while many had been politicians, ministers or civil servants who had served the constitutional monarchy of 1789–92 or the republic of 1792–9 or both. In 1799 his fellow consuls were carefully chosen. Cambacérès, the Second Consul, had worked for the republican Convention and came from Montpellier, but Lebrun, the Third Consul, was a Norman ex-royalist. Cambacérès was instrumental in nominating eight prefects in the south, Lebrun ten around Paris, in the east and in the conservative west. Under the Empire, Lebrun's two sons-in-law and a relation of his wife's became prefects. Napoleon did not care about people's past but about their present willingness to work for him. Some prefects had supported Robespierre, some his enemies, yet others had been royalists.

Charles Delacroix, the painter's father, began his career as secretary to Turgot, reforming *intendant* of the Limousin who had been summoned to Paris to head a reforming government under Louis XVI. After Turgot fell, Delacroix stayed on as principal first secretary in the Ministries of Finance and the Navy until he retired in 1779 at the age of fifty-eight. It was the Revolution that brought him back into public life. In 1792 he was chosen as representative of his native Marne in the Convention. In 1793 he sided with Robespierre in voting for the execution of 'Louis Capet', but in 1794 he opted for Robespierre's opponents. Under the Directory, he became Foreign Minister but, after being ousted from that post by Talleyrand, he was dispatched to be Minister Plenipotentiary to the Netherlands, renamed the Batavian Republic by France. Unfairly blamed for the outbreak of rebellion there, he was recalled, only to be used, for the last time, by Napoleon, as prefect of Bouches-du-Rhône, based at Marseille, and of the Gironde, based at Bordeaux. It was at Bordeaux that he died.

Such a career was typical of a man who had survived. Fifty-three Napoleonic prefects were from the military, half of those from the old nobility, sixty had worked in the Council of State. Frochot, first Napoleonic prefect of the Seine (so the man who ran Paris), had been gaoled in the Terror and taken part in the coup of 1799. Pasquier, prefect of the Seine in 1814, came from a family distinguished in the old *parlement* of Paris. Chabrol, his prefect of police, was a modern technocrat fascinated by the economy, statistics and town planning. As France settled down, so did its new bureaucracy. Charles Delacroix's son-in-law, Raymond de Verninac de St-Maur, had been ambassador to the Sultan's court in Istanbul, the Sublime Porte, as well as prefect of the Rhône, but after losing his job he never recovered. Bresson, however, once a member of the Convention and under the Directory a member of the Council of Five Hundred, the lower house, became director of the finances of the Ministry of Foreign Affairs in year VIII and stayed at his post until 1825, ten years after the fall of Napoleon. The principle Napoleon established by his appointments was that the business of a governing class was to govern. Governments, including his own, would come and go: the bureaucracy would go on for ever.

Paris housed normal Ministries – of Justice, Finance, the Treasury, War, the Navy, Colonies and Foreign Relations – but for the control of France none equalled the Ministry of the Interior, to which all prefects had to answer. By 1810, when the Grand Empire reached its largest extent, this minister was in charge of 130 departments, from the Netherlands, France and Switzerland to parts of Italy, from the Rhine to Rome. Wherever possible, Napoleon chose stability. He had only one Minister of Finance and of the Navy and Colonies, two Ministers of Police, of Justice, of War and of the Treasury, but there were six Ministers of the Interior between 1799 and 1814. Apart from Lucien Bonaparte, who was rewarded for his decisive action in favour of his brother during the 1799 coup and then sacked for sponsoring a pamphlet that compared Napoleon with General Monk, who had restored the Stuarts in 1660, the Interior Ministers had some standard credentials: as intellectuals (Laplace, who lasted for only six weeks, and Chaptal); as a diplomat (de Champagny); as a director of engineering projects (Cretet); as a lawyer, a prefect and a Councillor of State (de Montalivet). While he was away campaigning, it was above all on these men that Napoleon relied to keep France quiet, and most made sure they succeeded. Provided that they were not troublemakers, like the temperamental Lucien, the appointments worked well. The way to get on in Napoleon's France, outside the ranks of the army, was to be a docile meritocrat.

Characteristically, Lucien was a member of a body that Napoleon got rid of: the Tribunate. In the ancient Roman republic, the Tribunes had been the representatives of the plebs. The most famous Tribunes, Tiberius and Gaius Gracchus, had stirred up such strong popular feeling that their aristocratic enemies had eliminated them. Whether as First Consul or Emperor, Napoleon had no intention of allowing a French citizen to copy either of them. According to the constitution of year VIII, which was designed to follow the Bonapartist principle that constitutions should be short and obscure, legislative authority was vested in four bodies: the Council of State (with 30 to 40 members); the Tribunate (with 100, of whom a fifth was changed annually); the *Corps Législatif* (with 300, of whom a fifth was also changed annually); and the Senate, made up of 60 men, all over 40. The first drew up laws, the second discussed them and voted in favour of or against them, the third voted without debating and the fourth, which chose the Tribunes and the members of the *Corps Législatif*, could annul acts it deemed unconstitutional. This scheme admirably suited the First Consul, since it stopped everyone from interfering in the passing of his laws, while giving to professional talkers opportunities for vocal exercise and too, it made the silent majority feel important without doing anything. The Tribunate, more courageous and intelligent, did not like its quasi-passive role, revolted and was abolished. The *Corps Législatif*, larger and more malleable, survived as a nonentity. Under the Empire, social prestige gave some value to the Senate, but the Council of State mattered because it gave advice. Not, however, until the Bourbons came back in 1814 and 1815 did France enjoy a modern parliamentary form of government. Napoleon wished that government would not be impeded by discussion: Louis XVIII ruled in an age golden in political eloquence.

What Napoleon restored was the practice of giving faithful Frenchmen the pleasures of title and rank. As his rule was always personal, so all perks were signs of his special condescension. In 1802, as First Consul, he took the tricky first step when he invented the Legion of Honour. Most of the recruits were soldiers. The name of the new institution implied its military bias. As late as 1814, at the end of the Empire, just 1,500 of its 32,000 members were civilians, and most of the 16 cohorts were commanded by a marshal. But many prefects and Senators belonged – and so did bishops.

During the time of the *ancien régime* soldiers who were conspicuously brave were granted the *Croix de St Louis*, set up by Louis XIV, or, if they were Protestant foreigners, such as Swiss Guardsmen, from 1760 they could be commended by means of a medal for military merit. The revolutionaries had been keen to do away with anything that distinguished one soldier from another, but in Italy Napoleon gave out inscribed, damascened swords to those he thought deserved them. In 1802, now First Consul, he decided to create a system of rewards that would apply to soldiers serving in any part of Europe. He deliberately chose the Roman term 'legion' rather than the traditional term 'order' since the latter word had overtones of Bourbon rule – he liked to hint at antiquity. Sadly, article 87 of the recent consular constitution seemed to provide that only soldiers could be marked out, whereas what Napoleon presented to the Council of State for its consideration was a scheme for any kind of citizen.

The passage of the necessary law was not an easy process. To fellow Tribunes the ready tongue of Lucien Bonaparte, still highly regarded by his brother, argued that the new decoration had no political meaning; the legionaries would take an oath to combat any attempt to return to the feudal past, with titles and consequent personal control over land; and the property to fund the Legion belonged to it collectively, not to a single member in particular. Speaking to the *Corps Législatif*, General Mathieu-Dumas appealed from medieval remains to the more distant and acceptable past. In the eighteenth-century *Encyclopédie* he had found under the word 'honour' the story of how Marcellus, 'the sword of Rome', had erected a Temple to Honour that could be reached only by passing the Temple of Virtue. The general compared with him 'the sword of France', Napoleon Bonaparte, who had the same idea. He had sounded the right note, for the assembly clapped him for ten minutes. Another Tribune, Girardin, was more incisive: the Legion would not be a state within a state. All the same, the vote in favour of the motion was only 166 to 110, and the new decoration was soon derided by the agents of Louis XVIII, the king in exile. 'Bonaparte wishes to rebuild a monarchy for himself and his successors. In accord with this view, he takes as a model the *ancien régime* that has been so vilified these last ten years. The *ancien régime* had a nobility; the Legion of Honour will replace it.'[3] The point was a shrewd one, but luckily for the First Consul most Frenchmen had concerns other than debating points. One was the plebiscite on the lifelong Consulate, the other the high price of bread. Napoleon won his vote easily and the food crisis passed. Within a few years the Bourbon journalists were proved to be right, but not in the way that they had thought.

The Legion of Honour quickly proved popular with those invited to join it, initially not so much for the recognition that came as for the income that was promised. Land allocated to the Legion worth 76,390,000 francs was to yield 3,574,497 francs, but, by the time legal charges and disputes over property rights had eaten into this sum, there was not enough left to create the new nobility the royalists had predicted. In 1806 the council of the Legion cautioned that a sixth of the revenue disappeared in expenses. Money grew scarcer, as more and more campaigns led to the creation of more and more members. In 1809 the chancellors and treasurers who had run the Legion's finances were dispensed with, and its property was reallocated so that individual legionaries would receive a small personal addition to their incomes. To be a legionary had to be an honour beyond price.

In year XII Napoleon's first list of nominations suggested that he wished to create a national elite, for the names put forward included Senators, Ambassadors, Councillors of State, archbishops, *savants* from Egyptian days, even members of the old nobility like d'Aguesseau and Choiseul-Praslin; and to these were soon added names of Tribunes and prefects. To appease republicans the date chosen for the first investiture was to be 14 July, but the place chosen – the royal military hospital of the Invalides – and a shift of the date to 15 July suggested a break with the revolutionary past. As ceremonies became grander, so numbers were inflated; and as most of the new recipients of the blue ribbon were soldiers, the

Legion reverted more and more to the model established by the consular constitution, though that had been superseded in 1804 by the proclamation of the Empire. The Legion became popular with all ranks in the army. In his memoirs, Baron Marbot tells of the reaction of a grenadier to a promise from the Emperor: 'I shall make you a knight of the Empire with the gift of 1,200 francs.' . . . 'But, Sire, I prefer the cross.'

In modern France the Legion of Honour has been given to people of all kinds, in recognition of many different kinds of service to the state. It is true that Napoleon, once Emperor, wished to inaugurate a new class of nobility, but he had to find another way of doing so than by means of the Legion of Honour. His purported aim of ruling Frenchmen by appealing to their vanity led him to reconstruct a system of titles that involved wealth as well as rank.

In 1808, a year when he was not distracted by any campaign other than a certain little conflict in Spain, Napoleon issued decrees to establish an Imperial nobility. This time he recognized, as a lawyer or politician in kingdoms not controlled by him would have said, that an aristocrat must be rich. Once he got into the way of ennobling, he developed a habit: 744 titles in 1808, 502 in 1809, 1,485 in 1810, 448 in 1811, 131 in 1812 (a bad year, not just for nobles), 318 in 1813, 55 in 1814 (the worst year of all). Even so, he did not have enough time to equal his royal predecessors. In 1789, for every 10,000 commoners there had been seven nobles: in 1814 for the same number of citizens there was only one noble.

As with the Legionaries of Honour, the Napoleonic nobility was above all a *noblesse de l'épée*, a nobility of the sword like the original French medieval aristocracy. Most generals expected to be counts or barons, and most lieutenants or captains never got beyond the rank of knight. Twenty-two per cent came from the old nobility that had rallied to the new regime, fifty-eight per cent were of bourgeois stock, the group with social aspirations that from the time of Molière had always longed to be *bourgeois gentilshommes*, and just twenty per cent came from the lower classes. When the Bourbons were restored, temporarily in 1814, finally in 1815, Napoleonic nobles were despised as *parvenus*, but at the time it was exhilarating to be enriched from the proceeds of Napoleon's foreign conquests, addressed as one of the grand and bedecked in gorgeous robes. The subject of a fine portrait by Jacques-Louis David, Count Français de Nantes, was typical of many. He had been a Jacobin with Robespierre, a member of the Legislative Assembly, an opponent of the Catholic faith, a member of the Council of Five Hundred under the Directory and an opponent of the 1799 coup, but, once reconciled to Napoleon, he was a prefect, a Councillor of State, a count of the Empire and in 1811 grand officer of the Legion of Honour.[4] One glance at the painting will convince the viewer that he enjoyed his position, for David has so posed him that he looks down on everyone and everyone must look up at him.

The language in which Napoleon's generation, in France as in the USA, had been taught to think was classical, but in France there was another way of talking that derived from its eight-hundred-year history. In founding his nobility Napoleon had recourse to medieval French titles – *prince*, *duc*, *comte*, *baron*, *chevalier* – but his initial instinct had been to revert to ancient Roman ones. In either case he was not reviving the past: he was modernizing. The systems he set up would cope with contemporary realities: they would usher in an efficient government and reward faithful service. The relics of medieval France were destroyed in 1789. In Italy, however, there had been no bonfire of remains. To a Frenchman, Rome, despite archaeological ruins, was a medieval city, ruled not by a radical consul or emperor but by a Pope, whose office bound him to cling to tradition.

7

THE CORONATION

——————

Napoleon never visited Rome. Instead he made Rome come to him.

There is no more extraordinary episode in the life of Napoleon than his coronation. The previous coronation in France, that of Louis XVI in 1774, had been in the cathedral of Reims, where Most Christian Kings were anointed with the oil of St Remigius, who had baptized and anointed Clovis, first Catholic King of the Franks; and the unction was repeated one last time in 1825, at the coronation of Louis's youngest brother, Charles X. For Napoleon, at best a deist and at worst an atheist, such a ceremony had no meaning. He had not inherited a throne by divine right: it was the people of France who had chosen him to be their Emperor. Except as residents of Avignon, Popes had seldom come to France, but there was one precedent that was relevant to the situation of 1804. By coming to Pepin, the usurping King of the Franks and father of Charlemagne, Pope Stephen III had legitimized the seizure of the throne; and his journey was complemented by Pope Leo III's coronation of Charlemagne in Rome on Christmas Day 800. For the new Emperor of the French, Charlemagne, King of the Franks, Holy Roman Emperor, was a predecessor with whom he could identify; and he had gone to Charlemagne's capital at Aachen, aware that there many of Charlemagne's successors had been elected and crowned. He adopted as his symbols the bees of Childeric I, the father of Clovis, in place of the Capetian fleur-de-lys, and the Carolingian eagle for his seal. But he was no sentimentalist. Neither Reims nor Aachen had any role in his government. His chief palace was the Tuileries, and he had made Paris the centre of his administration. He had no intention of admitting that his authority derived from anybody beside himself; by 3,572,329 votes to 2,569 the people of France collectively had merely endorsed his right to rule, and the Pope had played no part in his rise to power. If Napoleon had a weakness, however, it was that he craved to be recognized. There was no better way of demonstrating to his rivals in Imperial dignity, Kaiser Francis II and Tsar Alexander I, that he was their equal than a public endorsement of his new status by the Pope, Pius VII, and he was determined that he should have it.

The Empire was proclaimed in April 1804, the referendum results were delayed until November, the first approaches to the Pope were made in May and in June, after consultation with his cardinals, the Pope replied that he was willing to come. He set out on 2 November and arrived on 28 November. As the coronation was fixed for 2 December, there was less than a week to work out the ritual to be followed. The Reims pontifical was inappropriate, so instead a modified Paris customary was used, as the event was to occur in Notre-Dame. Multiple genuflexions and prostrations normal to a Capetian did not suit a Bonaparte and so were omitted. The Pope would anoint the heads and the hands of the Emperor and the Empress and bless the Imperial sword, mantles, rings and crowns, but Napoleon was to crown himself and his wife and would not take Communion. The Pope insisted on one preliminary. When he learned that Napoleon and Joséphine had been married civilly, he made their Christian wedding a condition of his blessing. This was quickly carried out on the eve of the coronation, in private and without a witness, by Napoleon's uncle, Cardinal Fesch, and the great occasion could proceed. The elaborate cortège, the stark redecoration of Notre-Dame in neoclassical taste, the resplendent costumes, the music that had been specially composed, the one-hour wait from the moment of the arrival of the Pope to that of the Emperor in the cathedral, the three and a half hours spent there, the slow return of the carriages to the Tuileries, the night-time of fireworks throughout the city – all confirmed that Napoleon knew how to value grandeur.

He wanted this grandeur to be captured in paint. Only one artist had the ability to do so: Jacques-Louis David. The miniaturist Isabey and the architect Fontaine had designed the coronation costumes, and the engraver Dupréel had depicted them as well as the principal scenes of the coronation in an official publication. A pupil of David's, François Gérard, the most compliant of courtier painters, had painted Napoleon in his robes, like a cynosure of fashion, but when it came to a colossal work of art, only his master had the energy to plan it and carry it out. David had wavered between the crowning of the Emperor and that of the Empress. In the end he seems to have accepter Gérard's idea of concentrating on the second event, but the title equivocates: *Le Sacre de l'Empereur Napoléon 1er et Couronnement de l'Impératrice Joséphine*. It has been shortened to the more familiar *Le Sacre de Joséphine*, a form of words that is justified by the central action that unifies the scene, for the eyes of the spectator are drawn to the poignant, graceful figure of the Empress, eyes cast down, kneeling before her standing husband, who holds the crown above her, wreathed in laurel, while to the right, before the altar, sits the impassive Pope, himself only a spectator like the fifty-four other dignitaries visible in or over-looking the sanctuary.

Napoleon liked to convey the conviction that what he wanted recorded was nothing but the truth – according to Jules David, the painter's biographer and grandson, he criticizsed *The Intervention of the Sabine Women* because it displayed an ignorance of the way in which soldiers wielded weapons. At first glance, in *Le Sacre de Joséphine* David seems to have been careful to be accurate, for he was stationed where he could see the chief actors and made sketches on the spot. In fact, his overriding concern was to narrate a story that his Emperor wished him to tell. He did not worry that Napoleon's brothers, Joseph and Louis, were furious that they were not prominent enough. He was diplomatic in concealing the furious hatred that Napoleon's sisters felt for Joséphine – in *Le Sacre* they carry her train with demure respect – and even more diplo-matic in inserting a portrait of Napoleon's mother, Madame Mère. In December 1804 she was not even in Paris, for by then Lucien Bonaparte had quarrelled with his overbearing brother and had gone to sulk in Italy, and Madame Mère had accompanied him into temporary exile. But David was told that she must be painted in, and so there she is. Compared with this embellishment of reality, there is a far lesser departure from literal truth in that David had himself inserted by Isabey opposite the place where he had been. And yet despite these slight falsifications, the painting captures the spirit of the event. The participants were shown life-size, David took trouble over the details of their costume, their decorations (for the men) and their jewellery (for the women), and the overall effect is of a sumptuous pageant. Some in the imperial entourage disliked the prominence given to Joséphine but when Napoleon saw the finished work, he remarked, with a display of gallantry:

David, you have guessed precisely what I intended. You have

made me into a French knight. I am grateful to you for preserving for the future the proof of affection that I wished to give her who shares with me the troubles of rule.[1]

The same source, however, makes clear that the experience that had moved David more than any other while he had prepared his magnum opus was his encounters with the Pope.[2] The anticlerical David was struck by the simplicity of the man, so much more like St Peter than the pontiffs Julius II and Leo X who had patronized Michelangelo and Raphael. And besides, this Pope, too, loved the arts. He was faithfully served by the sculptor Canova, and fifteen years after David drew and painted him his character would impress a master of swagger portraits, the Englishman Thomas Lawrence. If Napoleon noticed the enthusiasm with which the people of France acclaimed the Pope, he ignored it. In Paris Pius VII was set at the edge of the court circle, just one prelate by the altar – this world, like the sacred orb he had held, revolved around Napoleon.

The Pope lingered on in Paris, for he hoped to win concessions from the Emperor, but, as the man who had denied them was Napoleon himself, he had little hope of success. Pius returned to Rome with nothing to show for his journey; his conservative critics concluded that they were proved right – he should never have left Rome.

Pius VII was a kind man, but he was also no fool, and his desire to make peace if possible with the new order in France was based on a well-tried maxim, that, if an ideal cannot be realized, it is good to make the best of reality. As far as he was concerned, the clerical governance of the Church should be free of any interference from lay rulers, such as Pius VI, his predecessor, had had to endure from the Holy Roman Emperor, Joseph II. As a protest against Joseph's suppression of monasteries and regulation of clerical education, Pius VI had travelled to Vienna and achieved nothing. In the case of France, before 1789 the relations of Pope and King were usually based on a spirit of accommodation rather than of confrontation. In 1516 Pope Leo X had hurried to Bologna to make peace with Francis I and conceded to the King the right to name, though not to appoint, the bishops of France, a deal that suited both Leo and Francis. Leo could not stop the King from choosing the bishops he wanted: Francis did not want to break with the Pope. What pleased both was that the local clergy in French cathedrals would have little say in Church affairs. By 1791 this concordat had become unworkable because the National Assembly of France did not want it.

In the eighteenth century there was still a respectable group of French clergy who wished to preserve some independence from papal control. They looked back with some nostalgia to one period of the reign of Louis XIV, when in 1682 the assembly of the clergy had voted for the four Gallican Articles drawn up by Bossuet, the foremost preacher at court. The articles set limits to papal authority: the Pope has no right to depose the king; Church councils could have authority over Popes; the French Church had its special customs; and the Pope's judgements in matters of faith were not irreformable. Before the end of his life, Louis XIV found that he had need of the Pope and the articles were quietly set aside. But a century later an ambitious cleric must be a 'Gallican' at heart if he planned advancement in the French church, and he must conceal the fact if he meant to represent the French Church in Rome.

There was another group of 'Gallicans' in France: the lawyers who sat in the *parlement* of Paris. Ever since Philip IV's advisers had claimed in the fourteenth century that there is no authority on earth above the King – *rex est imperator in regno suo* – *parlementaires* were suspicious of any move to restrict the authority of the nation vested in the King. In particular they hated the fourth vow that one religious community, the Jesuits, could demand of its members. The normal three vows of poverty, chastity and obedience caused little trouble, but, if a Jesuit in France promised to go anywhere in the world that the Pope asked, that seemed to restrict the operation of the law of France within the land of France. In the sixteenth century the *parlement* of Paris unsuccessfully resisted the efforts of the King to bring Jesuits into the country, but in 1764, after Ricci, the General of the Jesuits, had refused to take an oath to accept the articles of 1682, it had its revenge: Louis xv was forced to proscribe the Society in France.

In the minds of many delegates to the National Assembly these disputes belonged to the Dark Ages of mankind. In the modern enlightened France that they were creating, there would be no need for theological debates. Voltaire had taught that there was only one true religion: the religion of mankind. The Declaration of the Rights of Man and the Citizen had enshrined universal principles. Just before 1789 Louis xvi had revoked Louis xiv's revocation of the 1598 Edict of Nantes, so that Protestants once again were grudgingly tolerated; there had even been moves to ease the situation of the Jews. In the revolutionary order, both could be citizens. By a foolish oversight, the same right was not conceded to the largest religious group in France, the Roman Catholics.

What was unacceptable to them was the theory behind the National Assembly's reorganization of France: that the nation it represented was sovereign.

In 1767 a painter called Doyen, fresh from a triumph at the Salon for painting the patroness of Paris, Ste Geneviève, was invited by a young courtier, probably the Baron de St-Julien to paint a picture of himself gazing at his mistress on a swing that was pushed by a bishop. The commission went instead to a much more accomplished painter, Fragonard, who substituted the cuckolded husband for the bishop, but the story is in keeping with the common view of the sophistication of the unbelieving clergy of eighteenth-century France. No cleric of the later part of the century is as well known as the young Bishop of Autun, whose louche behaviour was in keeping with his neglect of his diocese. Once elected to represent the first order at the meeting of the Estates General in 1789, that bishop, Charles-Maurice Talleyrand de Périgord, visited his see on only a single occasion, and then by accident, when his carriage broke down. Talleyrand, it is often forgotten, was typical in just one way: like all his fellow bishops he was an aristocrat. Others may have been a cause of scandal, like Bishop Rohan of Strasbourg who was duped by a prostitute into paying for 'the Queen's' necklace; others, like Brienne, Archbishop of Toulouse, were politicians who made it to the top. One eminent ecclesiastic from the family of de la Rochefoucauld, the Archbishop of Bourges, generous in feeding the poor and entertaining his guests, was a calming voice in theological quarrels. From time to time there were modernizers like the Bishop of Langres, who at the Assembly of Notables in 1787 argued in favour of recognizing Protestant marriages. Everyone agreed that the golden age of episcopal preaching was past – there were no more Bossuets to reduce the court of Louis XVI to tears of repentance or of boredom – but one thing was certain. As the Abbé Siéyès argued on the eve of the Revolution, there were only two divisions among Frenchmen: 'those who have privileges and those who have not.' The bishops and the abbots of the richer mon-asteries ranked with the lay aristocracy, the curés and insignificant members of religious orders with the bourgeois and the peasants. In 1789 curés, monks and friars rebelled, and it was thanks to them that in the summer of that year the liberals created one unicameral National Assembly out of the three estates of the Estates General. At the centre of his projected picture of *The Tennis Court Oath* that set up the new institution, David placed three clerics, the monk

Dom Gerle, who had not been present but who stood in for the regular clergy, the Abbé Grégoire, representing the secular clergy, and Rabaut St-Etienne, a Protestant pastor. As three Frenchmen, all were equal to one another. None was a member of the hierarchy that with the Pope had hitherto directed the religious affairs of France.

What followed none could have anticipated. Privilege was renounced one night in August – nobody dared flout the self-sacrificing gesture – and three weeks later the Rights of Man and the Citizen were defined. That religious rights were to be elucidated by the state acting in accord with the national will became clear in the autumn. The Pope lost the right to the financial support of the faithful who had paid him Peter's pence; and the liberal noble, the Comte de Mirabeau, declared that all the clergy should be salaried officials of the state. In November all the property of the Church was nationalized and in February monastic vows were forbidden. When in April 1790 Dom Gerle tried to move that the Catholic faith should be declared the national religion, Rabaut St-Etienne, the current president of the Assembly, helped defeat the attempt; no religion was to be preferred before another. Rabaut was from the town of Nîmes, which had suffered much from Louis XIV, and when Catholics tried to gain control of the surrounding department of Gard by force, they were routed. Meanwhile, many subjects of the Pope in the enclaves of Avignon and the Comtat Venaissin demanded to be made citizens of France and, once in control of the city council of Avignon, brought local law into line with the laws of the nation. Soon, with no respect for international treaty, the whole area, except a part of the Comtat, had joined France.

Pius VI did not like the prospect of losing his property by the Rhône, but what led him to mistrust the propensity of the Revolution was the Civil Constitution of the Clergy, which was passed by the Assembly in July 1790 and condemned by him in May 1791.

The assembly unilaterally abolished the concordat of 1516 and did not see the point of a new concordat. In the deputies' minds the Pope was a foreigner and what the French nation decided was no affair of his. The long pause before he made up his mind what to do over the Civil Constitution of the Clergy was put down to worries over Avignon and the Comtat Venaissin, a view that was excessively cynical. It was axiomatic in the curia that the Pope needed the Papal States to keep his independence from the pressures Catholic monarchs could put on him, as when the Kings of Portugal, Spain, Naples, France and Maria Theresa, the Queen-Empress (Queen of Hungary and Holy Roman Empress), had forced through the suppression of the Jesuits. The French properties did not count for much; the lands in central Italy were vital. What is surprising is that the deputies did not understand that condemnation of the Civil Constitution was inevitable. To be a Catholic was to be in communion with the see of St Peter, and this implied at least some papal authority over the French or Gallican church. The Church that was established by the law of the Civil Constitution of the Clergy was by definition purely national and therefore not universal or Catholic.

The Church was to reflect the new structure of the nation. Already its property had been taken away, so that clerics no longer had any role as a distinct part of the nation. Henceforward they were to be salaried by the state in a way that benefited parish priests more than bishops. As for bishops, there should be one per department, eighty-three in all, and ten archbishops, and every town of fewer than 6,000 inhabitants was to have only one parish. Chapters of canons, like monasteries and convents, were useless and therefore abolished, for the clergy had one function: to minister to the faithful. For this reason a bishop should have served fifteen years in a parish and a curate five years before he became a parish priest; and the clergy were to be elected by district or departmental assemblies whose members might be Protestants, Jews or atheists. No Frenchman was allowed to have contact with any foreign bishop or his agent, but this was without prejudice to 'the unity of the faith, and the communion to be maintained with the visible Head of the universal church'. Before 1790 the Pope had confirmed all episcopal appointments. Now he would be told that they had been made.[3]

Privately, in July 1790 the Pope wrote to the King that, if Louis signed the act, he would lead the French Church into schism. In France itself well before the Pope had reacted officially, the new religious order had become a cause of division among Frenchmen. Former religious houses were convenient for political meetings, so that the so-called Breton Club acquired a new name – by taking over the house of St-Jacques belonging to the Dominican friars it became the Jacobin Club – and its rival, the Cordeliers, replaced Franciscan friars. Government paper notes, the *assignats*, were floated on the compulsory acquisition and sale of Church lands (euphemistically renamed *biens nationaux*). There was an even vaster exchange of land consequent on the abolition of the tithe, which under the *ancien régime* had financed the incomes of the clergy. Everywhere, people, above all the bourgeois, gained an interest in the despoliation of the pre-Revolutionary Church.

What the revolutionaries failed to appreciate was that they were ending a way of life. From time immemorial the French had been baptized, married and buried by the Church, educated by it and, if poor or sick, cared for by it. Though many Catholics gave up observing certain practices that had been popular in previous centuries – in Provence the pious burned fewer candles – there was a new pattern of spending more on the welfare of others. Monasteries were not attracting new recruits, but many clergy indulged in a little gentle research into Church history or in a taste for religious music or religious building without forgetting their spiritual duties. For the mass of the population, the Church's calendar set the rhythms of the year – its holy days were their holidays – and the pattern of the day for artisans in towns and peasants in their villages was laid down by the ringing of church bells. As a new law from Paris attacked another familiar custom, many felt overwhelmed by change. The republic ended the Jewish-Christian seven-day week. Dechristianizers shattered church glass and statues, desecrated altars and burned vestments, renamed churches 'temples of reason' and for the Trinity substituted the worship of the Supreme Being. Opposition hardened the resolve of the revolutionaries, so that the ultimate test of loyalty to the state became a readiness to take the oath affirming the Civic Constitution of the Clergy. Pius VI protested, yet Louis XVI had to sign it, with great reluctance. Abroad, émigré nobles rediscovered the religion of their childhood, none more spectacularly than the King's youngest brother, the future Charles X. At home there developed a strange alliance between non-juring priests – those who would not swear to the new constitutional Church – and dispossessed aristocrats and the more conservative peasants. More than any other action of revolutionary governments, including the execution of King Louis XVI, was as potent an argument as the promulgation of the nationalized Church in lending credence to the view, so dear to the younger royalists, that the wellbeing of the Church went hand in hand with the good of the Bourbon family. Nothing else elicited such violent reactions from the French people.

In Anglo-Saxon countries, with help from Thomas Carlyle and Charles Dickens, the most horrific part of the Revolution is the Terror, which in Paris alone accounted for 2,621 executions in 15 months during 1793 and 1794. The civil war in the west, centred on the Vendée, however, dragged on for eleven years, until 1804,

In his portrayal of an officer of the Mounted Chasseurs charging, Géricault expressed French confidence in 1812 when they invaded Russia.

By 1814, Géricault knew that his wounded cuirassier quitting
the field expressed the bitter truth of French defeats.

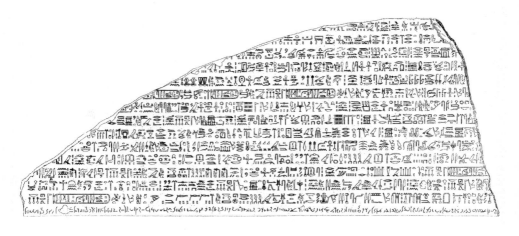

The Rosetta Stone, found by a Frenchman and taken by the British,
proved to be the key to Egyptian hieroglyphs.

Napoleon housed the Institut in a building opposite the Louvre,
that Le Vau designed in the seventeenth century.

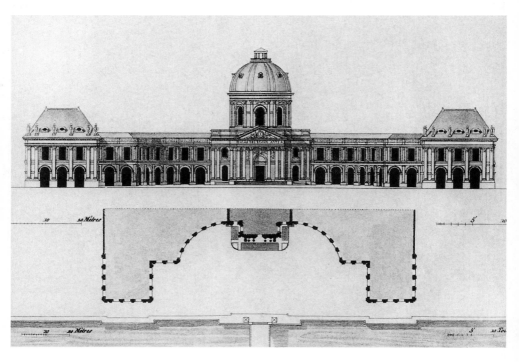

Napoleon as First Consul, was seen by Ingres as awkward in his civilian role.

David's representation of Le Sacre de Joséphine shows Napoleon's proudest moment, when before the Pope he received the homage of his Empress.

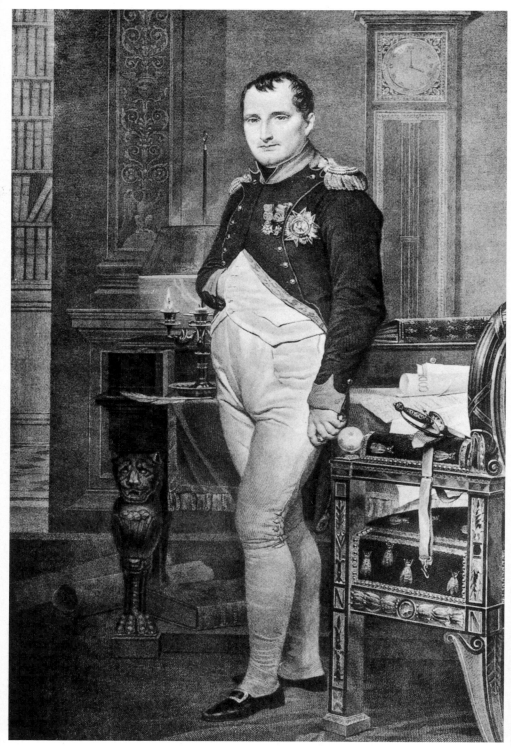

In *Napoleon in his Study*, David captured the Emperor's
ideal version of himself as a lawmaker.

Gillray's *The Plumb-Pudding in Danger* foresaw a division of the world between Pitt, who takes the sea, and Napoleon, who takes the land.

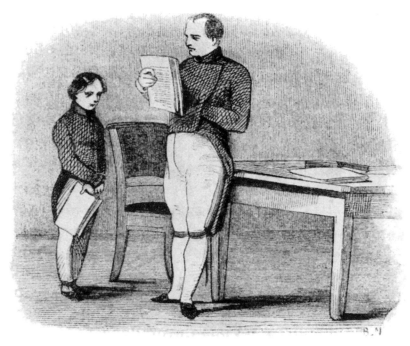

The Napoleonic legend owed more to Las Cases than to any other writer. Las Cases's son later came back to St Helena to collect the Emperor's body.

Napoleon's tomb in Les Invalides became the focus of the cult of the Emperor.

and may have led to the deaths of over half a million people. The immediate cause of the uprising was the attempt to conscript for the revolutionary armies, but the force behind the resistance came from a virulent hatred of the new. One of the first victims of rioting in the market town of Machecoul was the local constitutional priest – he was bayoneted in the face for ten minutes before being finished off – and the republican general Turreau who was to be among the most brutal soldiers in repressing revolt, said: 'It was a true crusade.' What the Vendéens achieved was repeated, to a lesser extent, by the chouans in Brittany and the White Terror in the Lyonnais. A revolution based on reason stirred up extreme emotions. 'La Marseillaise', brought to Paris by recruits from the southern port, who had got it from Montpellier, urged the purging of impure blood – *Qu'un sang impur abreuve nos sillons* – in the name of a bloody banner (*l'étendard sanglant est levé*). The Revolution was to be supported by blood-letting. It was acceptable to think that the cause of trouble came from invasions by foreign tyrants: they were less hard to cope with than guerilla action from within. A foreign army was hard to sustain and, after a decisive battle, could be easy to repel. Local peasant revolts, bolstered by occasional aid from abroad, went on and on, until someone had the wit to see how to make peace.

Peacemaking was the only sensible, but not the easiest option. The crushing of all Catholic resistance would not make a victorious general, even a Bonaparte, friends with the devout: overt favouring of Catholics could lose him the support of the dechristianized, whether they were deists or Theophilanthropists or atheists.

The best solution, Napoleon saw, was to negotiate a fresh concordat with the Pope. In 1799, after seizing power, he sought to bring about national reconciliation. Emigrants, apart from the most hardened royalists, wished to come home. While dechristianization had turned many parts of France permanently against the Christian Church, any people who wished to practise the Catholic faith were divided between those in the official constitutional Church, which was too nationalistic for some and not republican enough for others, and the non-juring Church true to the Pope, whose members disliked being considered unpatriotic. The Directory strengthened the case that throne and altar were inseparable by their actions in 1799: deporting 9,000 non-juring priests, changing the Papal States into the Roman Republic and imprisoning the old Pope, Pius VI, in Valence, where he died on 29 August. After these events concessions that Napoleon made were bound to appear gracious, and he was helped by the election of a new Pope, Pius VII, in March 1800. As Cardinal Chiaramonti, he had concluded a sermon with the words: 'Be good Christians and you will be excellent democrats.'[4] Such a man could come to terms with change.

In 1800 Napoleon was in Italy for the campaign of Marengo. It gave him the chance to make a tentative approach to the Pope. He made a point of behaving like a good Catholic. He celebrated victory over the Austrians with a Te Deum in Milan Cathedral and through the Bishop of Vercelli made an approach to the Pope that the Pope reciprocated. On his return to France the discussions became more specific, as Pius sent Monsignor Spina to Paris. Both sides were anxious about the wording of any agreement. Napoleon demanded the right to appoint bishops, Pius the pre-eminence of the Catholic faith. Papal lands were indirect causes of difficulty – when Pius had been made Pope, Austria dominated the peninsula, but a year later it was France – but neither side allowed politics to frustrate the project of an agreement. When this came, it gave something to each. The Catholic faith was deemed the religion of the majority of Frenchmen; it could be freely and publicly practised if there was no threat to public order. In exchange for an oath of loyalty to the state and prayers for the state, the bishops, chosen by the state, and curés, chosen by the bishops, were given a salary by the State, and bishops were allowed a cathedral, a chapter and a seminary. The most difficult part of the agreement, so far as the Pope was concerned, was that he asked all non-juring bishops to resign their sees. As far as the First Consul was concerned, what was hard to sell was the idea of a concordat as such. Consalvi, the chief adviser to the Pope, warned that, beside Napoleon, hardly anyone in Paris liked it.

The Pope did not care for toleration but, by accepting that the Catholic faith was not the state religion, he admitted that Protestants and Jews were Frenchmen too. It was a first step to the modern belief in liberty of conscience. What Pius may not have anticipated was that the faith could become chic. In 1802, when the State solemnly celebrated the concordat and the Treaty of Amiens with Great Britain, Chateaubriand published *Le Génie du Christianisme*. As a junior member of a noble family, he had seen his mother die in prison in Paris, siblings prisoners in Rennes and a brother and sister-in-law guillotined, and he had been a lonely, hungry émigré in England. Napoleon's amnesty to émigrés had encouraged him to return to France. There he found himself a habitué of the salon of Napoleon's sister Elisa, soon that of Madame de Récamier, and his book, while irritating ideologues of all persuasions, made fashionable the aesthetic appeal of Christianity. Young people began to become pious.

The new Emperor was not interested in piety but in power. The Pope had gone to Paris in order to discuss religious affairs: Napoleon wanted him there only to legitimize his Imperial name.

One corollary of the concordat had been that the Pope had abolished the 135 sees of the *ancien régime*, demanded of the non-juring bishops who had been faithful to Rome that they should resign and created 60 new dioceses that the Civil Constitution had envisaged. After these sacrifices, the Pope probably thought that he had conceded enough, but he was wrong. The First Consul wrote to the Pope to say that, at the moment when he had made the Treaty of Amiens with Britain, it was opportune to promulgate the concordat and so to re-establish the practice of the Catholic religion in France. Though some supporters, like General Augureau, begged Napoleon to let them miss the solemn Mass in Notre-Dame that marked these happy events, Napoleon stood firm. He would celebrate his compromises, without placating either republicans or clerics. To show that he meant to have his way, along with the papally approved document, however, he published seventy-seven 'Organic' Articles that had not been negotiated with the Pope; and the forms in which ten new bishops who were former constitutionals were to be reconciled with the Pope were not correctly observed. The Pope was irritated at the lack of courtesy, but still promoted Napoleon's five nominees for the rank of cardinal. He had gone to Paris hoping for concessions. While there, he sought restitution of papal lands that had been incorporated into the French Empire – and Napoleon rebuffed him. What concerned him more was the claims made by the Organic Articles.

He had conceded in 1801 that for the good of public order the practice of Christian worship could be regulated by the police. The articles had used this as an excuse to lay down how the clergy should behave. Bishops were to control their dioceses. They would appoint all curés, who were to live only in sizeable towns (as they were paid by the state, this would save money) and could not leave the diocese, preach or say a novel prayer without the bishop's permission. In their turn, bishops were subordinate to the state. Without ministerial permission, they could not ordain priests, set up cathedral chapters, convoke synods, go outside their dioceses, attend a metropolitan council, use a catechism other than the one laid down for all France, wear clothing other than that prescribed for French clerics, keep any feast that was not ordained by the government or say any prayers other than those drafted by the government. And finally the Pope too was kept in his place. The Gallican Articles of 1682 were official in all seminaries, and the Pope needed government permission for representatives or representations.

No more than the drafters of the revolutionary Civil Constitution of the Clergy did Napoleon wish to concede that the Catholic Church was by definition an international institution. He believed, as they did, in the one, indivisible, secular, sovereign republic. Unlike some of them, he was convinced that religion acted as a social bond, but it was not to limit the authority of the state, which was his authority. With greater assurance even than Louis XIV he maintained that he and the state were identical: 'L'état, c'est moi.' He believed in civic religion in the style of Rousseau, religion whose function was to give communal value to the common good. He wanted no truck with a faith that claimed to be universal.

It was less easy to unite the constitutional and the non-juring clergy than Napoleon expected. When the vicar-general of Montpellier was sent by his bishop to Albi, a see that had been suppressed, he was met outside the cathedral by the constitutional Bishop of Tarn, arrayed in full pontificals, only to process straight past on his way to take control of the building. It was not the time to prolong modern quarrels, for the clergy had lost most of their wealth, bishops were seldom of noble rank, few candidates applied to be ordained priests and no one could join a religious order by taking perpetual vows. Napoleon was averse to useless monks but he authorized the formation of several missionary congregations. 'These religious,' he declared, 'will be useful to me in Asia, Africa and America. I shall send them to gain information on the state of the countries. Their status protects them and serves to cover up political and commercial designs.' He was also pleased to have nuns to teach and care for the sick and the poor. He put them under the protection of Madame Mère, his mother, and, when he was First Consul, a new order was founded, the Ladies of the Sacred Heart, whose vocation was to educate the young daughters of the bourgeoisie. Devotion, however, seemed to be dying, if not already dead. In 1806, on the occasion of the translation of the so-called relics of Christ's Crown of Thorns to Notre-Dame, the cathedral canons were astonished when some teenage boys presented themselves for Communion. They found out that the youngsters were students of law, of medicine and of engineering, grouped into a pious congregation by a priest.

Napoleon's Church was meant to glorify him, rather than to encourage an interior life. Three Church feasts, Ascension Day, All Saints and Christmas, were State festivals, and two state occasions, 14 July and 2 December, anniversary of the coronation and of the victory of Austerlitz, were kept by the Church. The Imperial catechism also proscribed the veneration of the Emperor's name day. In the days of the *ancien régime*, the feast of St Louis, the patron of every king from 1610 to 1792, was attached to 15 August, the feast of the Assumption. Now the royal saint was replaced by St Napoleon.

The catechism went further. Napoleon, it asserted, had been raised up 'by God in difficult circumstances'; he was God's anointed, and good Christians must love him, pay taxes, accept conscription or go to hell.

'What are the duties of Christians to the princes who govern them and what in particular are our duties to Napoleon I, our Emperor?' 'Christians owe the princes who govern them and we owe in particular Napoleon I, our Emperor love, respect, obedience, fidelity, military service, the taxes ordained for the preservation and defence of the Empire and his throne; we also owe him fervent prayers for his salvation and for the spiritual and temporal prosperity of the State.' 'What should one think of those who neglect their duties towards the Emperor?' 'According to the Apostle St Paul, they resist the order established by God Himself and render themselves worthy of eternal damnation.'[5]

Napoleon resented any encroachment by the Pope on his authority, but he had no qualms about limiting the authority of the Pope. In 1804 the Pope came to Paris of his own free will. The next time he arrived in France he had had no say in the matter.

The deterioration of relations between Pius VII and Napoleon had begun before the coronation. From the coronation the Pope gained nothing, whereas after the coronation the new Emperor, who soon was also King of Italy, saw himself as successor of Charlemagne, who, he claimed, had given the Pope the Papal States and in whose name therefore he could revoke the grant. The Pope pointed out that Napoleon was recognized as Emperor of the French, not of Rome. 'There is no Emperor of Rome.' Even before Ulm and Austerlitz, Francis II renounced the title of Holy Roman Emperor and after the double defeat he could not stop Napoleon from making good the claim to be *rex totius Italiae* ('King of all Italy'), as he annexed Venetia and gave his brother Joseph the throne of Naples, an area over which for centuries Popes had overlordship. In 1807, after concluding the Treaty of Tilsit with the Tsar, Napoleon mastered the continent, having conquered two other Emperors, those of Austria and Russia, as well as the King of Prussia; and he demanded that the Pope should acknowledge the facts – renounce his suzerainty over Naples, make a third of his cardinals French, and enforce an economic blockade against the English, whom Napoleon, with unaccustomed zeal, described as 'infidels'. Sadly, the Pope did not understand the case for crusading against the leading Protestant power, so in February 1808 the

French General Miollis ejected the garrison from Castel Sant'-Angelo, in April 1808 Napoleon grabbed a section of the Papal States, in May 1809 he took back Charlemagne's 'donation', perpetually part of the French Empire, and in July 1809 General Radet took the Pope from his usurped palace of the Quirinale.

By stages, the seventy-seven-year-old Pope was moved from Rome to Florence, from Florence to Turin, from Turin to Grenoble, then back to Savona. In 1810 Rome became the second city of the Empire, and so a future Imperial prince would be its king. As the Pope would not promote this happy event by releasing Napoleon from his vows to his first wife Joséphine, the Emperor divorced her, but, when he married Archduchess Maria Louisa of Austria, thirteen French cardinals stayed away. They were exiled, the Pope ceased appointing bishops Napoleon named and even his uncle, Cardinal Fesch, refused to act as the new Archbishop of Paris. In 1812 the Pope was brought to Fontainebleau.

While the Pope was away from Rome, the Eternal City was run by the French. Napoleon's policy augmented the colony of administrators and artists in Rome (along with his own intractable brother Lucien), who look out from the elegant oil and pencil portraits of Ingres, himself a refugee from the critics in Paris shocked by his portrayal of Napoleon as a new Charlemagne.

Even in Fontainebleau, Pius VII still would not see reason, but after 1812 Napoleon had concerns that worried him more than the obstinacy of a frail octogenarian. In January he arrived at the château unexpectedly, warmly embraced the Pope and almost got the old man to agree to reside in Paris, but by then Europe had awoken from Napoleon's dream of reconstituting the empire of Charlemagne. One part of Napoleon liked the idea of being a sacred ruler, for he encouraged those painters who showed him in the Salons as a Christlike figure, granting mercy to rebels in Cairo, healing the plague victims of Jaffa, showing compassion to all soldiers butchered in the snow at Eylau. Towards the Pope, however, he had behaved simply as a bully.

David's picture of the coronation did not tell the whole truth about the occasion that it was meant to celebrate. It also fails to convey a sense that the occasion was sacred. What is striking is its concentration on a moment in the story of Napoleon and Joséphine. It was his own epic that drew Napoleon to art. This is obvious in the picture's pendent, *The Distribution of the Eagle Standards*, which glorifies the mutual dedication of Napoleon and his soldiers in a ceremony that took place only three days after his coronation. In front of the Ecole Militaire, where he had been trained, Napoleon, arrayed in full Imperial regalia, invited soldiers – marshals, generals, chasseurs, mamelukes, grenadiers and 'gendarmerie d'élite' – to take an oath of allegiance. 'Here are your eagles . . . do you swear to sacrifice your lives in their defence and to maintain them constantly on the path to victory?' 'We swear.'[6] What the Empire valued above all was devotion to the Emperor, not dedication to God.

Between Napoleon's Empire and the Catholic Church there could be only an uneasy compromise, for his ideal was ultimately secular fame. Nothing shows this so clearly as his attitude to his own divorce, a right allowed him by his own legal system, the *Code Napoléon*.

8

THE MAN OF LAW

The representation of himself that most appealed to Napoleon also came from the brush of David. *Napoleon in His Study*, which dates from 1812, is as understated as the *Le Sacre de Joséphine* is grandiose. The clock is set at 4.13 and the lighted candle makes clear that it is 4.13 a.m. 'You have understood me, my dear David; in the night I am occupied with the happiness of my subjects and during the day I work for their glory.' Papers tumble from the desk behind him. On the top sheet is written the word 'Code'.

Roman emperors had been proud that they ruled according to the law. Even if there was a despotic streak in all the imperialistic theories of jurisprudence, as when in the first century the jurist Ulpian laid down that 'what pleases the prince has the force of law' (*quod principi placuit legis habet vigorem*), Roman law was seen as having a universal application. In sixth-century Byzantium the eastern emperor, Justinian, had it codified. From the twelfth century its study was mandatory at the western universities, notably Bologna, which offered courses in law; it inspired the advisers of

Frederick Barbarossa, who offered protection to the professors; almost four hundred years later it appealed to those close to Charles v, who believed that the man who reigned over Spain, Naples, Milan, the Netherlands, much of south Germany and Austria, over islands in the Mediterranean, Atlantic and Pacific, over Aztecs and Incas would exert worldwide dominion. Of the Habsburgs it was said that Austria was to rule everywhere: AEIOU (*Austriae est imperium orbis universae*). In the time of Charles's son Philip II, whose cousins got the Germanic lands but who inherited all Portuguese possessions, the prophecy seemed about to be fulfilled.

It was not to be. During the late seventeenth century Louis XIV, half a Habsburg and wholly a Bourbon, dominated Europe, and the Dutch, the British and the French steadily reduced the area overseas held by the Iberian kings. In 1807, while Britain was the European power that was most influential outside Europe, on the Continent no monarch was the equal of Napoleon. Almost everywhere there his word was law, and the epitome of that law was the *Code Napoléon* referred to by David.

The inner life of nations is expressed in the history of their laws. In the *ancien régime* the Most Christian King was, under God, the ultimate source of law. In the thirteenth century his court had become the final court of appeal in feudal disputes, so that Philip II Augustus had deprived John, King of England, of his hereditary possessions, including the Duchy of Normandy and the county of Anjou. The King could modify the law by issuing edicts, so in 1536 François I had made French the nationwide language of law and in 1598 Henri IV had conceded to Protestants a privileged status in certain areas of France. But the arbitrary power of the king was restricted by the fundamental laws of the kingdom. In the 1590s, on behalf of the Bourbons as in the 1340s on behalf of the Valois, it was the lawyers who had upheld the Salic law according to which succession to the throne went only through the male line.

In the eighteenth century the French legal system remained as illogical as the systems of many other European countries. Louis XIV approved a determined effort to regularize civil and criminal procedure and to tidy up administrative law in matters of internal and external transport, trade and commerce, but the weight of the past frustrated attempts to give France a uniform code of practice. There were still four hundred local systems and, while northern France adhered to custom, southern France looked to Roman law. In 1685 the Code Noir, drawn up for French West Indian colonies, echoed Roman law in regarding slaves as chattels, while expressing the pious wish that their masters had no right to treat them badly. In the course of the next hundred years, many lawyers, however, began to talk a new language. Those opposed to the unpredictable or barbaric behaviour of the Crown or the courts would appeal to the general will of the people, to the nobility of the noble savage, to the universal rights of man. During August 1789 the sentiments of these liberal lawyers passed into law. In the Declaration of the Rights of Man and the Citizen, all Frenchmen acquired equality of taxation, equality of legal punishment, the right of access to public office, freedom of worship and freedom from feudalism (though not from the law of primogeniture). As one result, though the Catholic Church retained control over the register of births, marriages and deaths, first Protestants, then Jews were granted civic rights. Another result ought to have been the offer of liberty to all, but, like the founding fathers of the USA, those who drafted the new constitution of France limited the exercise of freedom to those rational enough to appreciate it. In France itself there would be no more serfs, but in the colonies no slave could be a citizen. The only men of colour who would be free were those born to free parents. Near Cap-Haïtien on St-Domingue the blacks rose in revolt, the mulattos turned both on them and on the whites and gradually the colony was devastated.

The blacks were to have their day. In 1793 Jean-Baptiste Belley, a freed slave and a Jacobin, was chosen as deputy for St-Domingue in the Convention. In February 1794 he made his maiden speech just before the Convention voted by acclamation a law to abolish slavery in the colonies and so to extend rights of citizenship to all inhabitants. Belley continued as a deputy in the Lower House under the Directory, and it was while in Paris in 1797 that his handsome, languid figure was painted by Girodet in front of a huge bust of Abbé Raynal, author of a monumental indictment of European treatment of indigenous peoples in both the East and the West Indies. Belley went home to a country which seemed ready for a bright future, leaving the beautiful portrait behind him.[1]

In France, those with modern ideas looked forward to a similarly brave new world. The attack on customs dating back to the Middle Ages was continued. From 1790 a family court shared authority with fathers. At eighteen, if emancipated, or else at twenty-one, 'liberated' children gained control of their property. Awkward women could no longer be imprisoned by the arbitrary method of *lettres de cachet*; a wife's consent was required for the marriage of her children; a wife, like her husband, could seek a divorce. A series of laws passed in 1793 and 1794 abolished primogeniture, the mainstay of feudal and noble status. Henceforth all property had to be divided equally among heirs, non-heirs could never be left more than one tenth and 'natural' children had the same rights as the legitimate.

Privileges of any kind were abolished. The learned professions were opened to all, the academies and the universities were dissolved, the craft guilds were abolished. By disestablishing the Discount Bank, which had acted as a national bank of issue, the Convention destroyed joint-stock companies in 1793. The pursuit of equality seemed liable to threaten the traditional aim of the bourgeoisie to become rich, if they did not have ancient wealth to preserve. What worried them more was the financial mismanagement of the successive revolutionary regimes. The tensions of the period 1789 to 1794, as idealism gave way to fanaticism, was followed by the unstable politics of the late 1790s, as by any means the Directors clung to power. Governments had never been democratic, but some had wanted to be representative. The Directors, however, chose to ignore the results of elections and carried out coups d'état to bolster their resistance to the general will. By one final coup Napoleon could appear to be the champion of the people, and every time he gained more power he justified it by appealing to the people and then making sure that they were seen to vote for him. In the days of the Consulate he acted with a sure political instinct. He knew that the mass of the bourgeoisie, like the peasants, wanted to keep intact a number of revolutionary achievements: equality before the law; family flexibility; the recent extension of property ownership. Morally, he would be a conservative with liberalizing tendencies.

Civil legislation had changed so often since 1789 that critics started to complain that there was need for a new legal code. The Constituent Assembly had adopted a rural code in 1791, but nothing more was done in the decade. In 1793, and again in 1794 after the fall of Robespierre, there was discussion of a new code. In 1796 Cambacérès suggested a new project, but the enormity of the task caused yet further delay. A by-product of Napoleon's seizure of power was that he had the energy to carry through the projected reform. Once he felt secure, after the victory of Marengo, he turned to the task of galvanizing the lawyers – if he was head of state, he must act not just as a soldier but as a civilian. There could be no better way of showing how he was to rule than to play the role of a Justinian and codify the law. In less than two years he set up five commissions to reform the civil code, the criminal code, the commercial code, the rural code and the code of civil procedure.

The process of codification was carried out largely under First Consul Bonaparte, but after the civil code was published in 1804 it was soon called the *Code Napoléon*; and the name is just, as it was because of him that the work of drawing it up was carried through.

Napoleon arrived back from Italy in July 1800, fresh from the lucky, decisive Marengo campaign. On 12 August he named a commission whose business was codification. His experts would represent the two main areas of French law: Tronchet and Bigot de Préameneu came from the north, Portalis and Maleville from the south. Tronchet, a vigorous old man of seventy-four, was president of the Court of Appeal and had helped defend Louis XVI. The other leading jurist, Portalis, had defended non-juring priests and was Napoleon's Minister of Religion. Bigot de Préameneu, a former member of the *parlement* of Brittany, stood firmly for customary tradition; Maleville, from the *parlement* of Bordeaux, was as stubbornly an advocate for the clarity of Roman law. All four were acquainted with the confusion of the *ancien régime*, with the variety of its regional practice, with the overlapping jurisdiction of its hundreds of courts, and also with the pell-mell attempts of the revolutionaries to change everything they could think of, so that since 1789 some 44,000 decrees had been promulgated, often contradicting existing laws. A process of sifting was essential if France was to be a cohesive country, rather than a territorial definition. In the 1790s Cambacérès had been an enthusiast for codification. As Second Consul he had a chance to live up to his intentions, but he relied on Napoleon to push him to act. Whereas when he took charge of meetings of the Council of State business ended soon, when Napoleon was presiding conversations might go on all day. So, too, when Napoleon wrestled with the niceties of law, he sometimes carried on into the early hours of the morning. He was anxious to be quick, but he also meant to be thorough. He told his commissioners: 'I give you six months to make me a civil code.' Once the draft was ready, then it was time to reflect, to argue and above all to decide.

'Citizens, the Revolution is attached to the principles that began it: it is over,' had proclaimed the three consuls. This meant that the jurists regarded certain changes made in and after 1789 as permanent. An aristocracy privileged to exact feudal dues from dependants was gone for ever, and instead all citizens had the same rights: equality before the law, personal freedom, freedom to work and liberty of conscience in a lay state. But some of the more radical experiments of the 1790s – above all the 'protosocialism' advocated by Robespierre that had set a maximum price for food, drink, fuel, clothing and even tobacco on the grounds that property rights could be restricted by the needs of others – were firmly shelved. Since 1789 there had been huge transfers of property, from the clergy, from nobles, from emigrés to bourgeois and above all to peasants, so that by 1799 there were many more property holders than there had been a decade earlier. These people planned to keep what they had gained; and Napoleon, a nouveau riche himself, had no intention of undermining their new prosperity. At the same time he was no liberal in economic affairs. One of his first schemes had been to insist that the Bank of France he set up in February 1800 should neither charge interest above six per cent nor lend too much. He intended to keep down inflation, to raise tax effectively, to balance the budget; and the stringent policies he began as First Consul he carried on as Emperor. Symbolically, he replaced the worthless paper money of the 1790s, the *assignats*, with gold coins, chief of which was the twenty-franc piece, the *napoléon*. His government would depend on the support of the well-to-do and in return the well-to-do would have to let him manage the economy and state finances. Property rights were never absolute since the government maintained the right to override them.

Napoleon was fortunate that his consular colleagues were trained in the law. Cambacérès had voted for the execution of the King, opposed Robespierre and experienced the problems of legislating in a decade of uncertainty. Lebrun's zeal for compelling change had been evident as long ago as the 1770s. At the end of Louis XV's reign, he was the secretary of the King's chief legal officer, Chancellor Maupéou, and he was said to have drafted the edicts that temporarily suspended the privileges of the Paris *parlement*. In the revolutionary period he had survived by passing his time translating Greek and Italian epics; now he saw his chance to carry out the kind of authoritarian reforms for which enlightened royal administrators had striven; he was also driven by a writer's instinct for exact expression. Compared with the two of them, Napoleon was just an amateur autodidact, but he had an astonishing appetite for absorbing new ideas, he asked penetrating questions and at this stage he did not mind being contradicted. He also had filled the Council of State, to whom the codifiers were to report, with people who would not have served a king. Besides distinguished magistrates – Treilhard, a survivor from the *parlement* of Paris, Muraire, president of the tribunal of appeal in Paris and a Piedmontese, Galli, president of the tribunal of appeal in Turin – there were former ministers – Forfait and Petiet – and many generals – St-Cyr, Jourdan and Marmont among them – and naval officers, diplomats, a chemist, a doctor, businessmen and a market gardener. At first, Napoleon found it hard to get his way with such a group, and in 1801 he had to postpone final decisions because of resistance from his advisers. In 1802 the situation began to change, for he became Consul for Life and he made less of an effort to conceal his dictatorial inclinations. Few dared to stand up to him any longer, so that what was decided in 1803 and 1804 was quickly ratified. In May 1804 the sessions were over. In the same month, First Consul Bonaparte was proclaimed Napoleon I, Emperor of the French.

In 1667 and 1669 jurists had drawn up civil and criminal *ordonnances* for Louis XIV. *Le roi bureaucrate* had not deigned to discuss the details or even the principles with his experts. Napoleon's style of ruling was much more personal. He preferred to convince those around him that he was right. In the drafting of the code he did not always succeed.

The codifiers met for three sets of sessions: from July 1801 to January 1802; from November 1802 to March 1803; and from December 1803 to March 1804. In the first period, after defining civil personality, they dealt with marriage and so with divorce, paternity and adoption. In the second period they carried on with questions of adoption before turning to matters of inheritance. The final sessions involved the law on sales and in particular on conveyancing. In more than half the meetings, Napoleon himself presided.

Napoleon asked innumerable questions, to make sure he had grasped what the professionals were telling him, but on some matters he could not be silenced. Preoccupied by the status of émigrés, mostly royalists who had fled abroad, whose numbers he computed at five or six thousand, and of criminals who were deported, he urged that the state should show compassion to their wives. If the wives stayed in France, they should not be ejected from their houses. As for those who were ordered abroad, like soldiers, he asserted that 'where the flag is, there is France'.

On marriage he became eloquent. Accepting the revolutionary view that marriage was a civil contract, he wanted to give the ceremony a moral dimension. He criticized one legal corollary of the insistence that the couple must speak their vows aloud. It was unjust that deaf mutes should not be allowed to marry. He also objected to the idea that marriage with a woman who had concealed the truth about herself must be invalid. 'There is no contract if there is violence, but the consummation of a marriage makes it a contract in intention.' Again and again, despite his misogynistic reputation, Napoleon intervened on the side of women: 'Morality could prevent the dissolution of the marriage contracted by error with an adventuress, if by continual good conduct she makes her husband happy.' He also wished to defend the wife against 'the feebleness of age and the tyranny of families', but he still was a firm partisan of the husband's authority. In 1800 this view was merely conventional. Merlin, a jurist who was regarded as too revolutionary for the commission, had argued in 1793: 'I think that woman is generally incapable of administering and that a man, who has a natural superiority over her, must conserve it.' Napoleon, who was only too aware of Joséphine's incompetence in handling money and her frivolity, could not have put his own opinion more succinctly, for he said 'women occupy themselves only with pleasure and making themselves up'. He disliked clever women and suspected that those who could look after themselves were not truly feminine.

From analysing the essence of marriage the discussion moved on to the dissolution of marriage by divorce, a right conceded in the 1790s. It is not evident that Napoleon wished to anticipate his eventual divorce from Joséphine, for he had established a way of life that gave him the freedom to have casual affairs and, if he worried about the impact of unsuitable marriages, he would have thought of his brothers Lucien and Jérôme rather than of himself. Three influential tribunals, among them the Paris Court of Appeal, demanded the retention of divorce; and Portalis argued passionately in its favour. What was at issue, then, was on what grounds divorce could be conceded. The First Consul wanted divorce by mutual consent or for incompatibility and maintained that the family must give its consent. Bigot de Préameneu rejected the first idea, Portalis the second, Tronchet the third. Napoleon then claimed that marriage does not derive from nature but from society and custom – and this, too, was rejected. In the end, though there were some concessions to his interventions – divorce by consent was permissible with the consent of parents – the law on divorce that was passed was settled by following the instinct of all – it favoured men. A man could divorce on grounds of simple adultery, a women only if the man's mistress was brought into the house. An adulterous wife could be put in prison for up to two years and let out only if her husband wanted her back, whereas all a man had to do was to pay a fine. After all, according to article 213 of the code, a woman must obey her husband.

On the rights of fathers Napoleon is often said to have stood for strict paternity in the light of the teaching of Roman law on the paterfamilias, yet already in the discussion on marriage he had emphasized a father's duties to his children. 'A rich, comfortable father always has to give fatherly support to his children,' he declared, and then, turning on those with harsher views, he added: 'You will force children to kill their fathers.' 'In this debate,' he asserted in a later session, 'who will take the side of the child, if it's not the law?' But if fathers had to protect their children, then the law had to be sure that they were the true fathers of the children concerned. As stayed the case until DNA testing became possible, he pointed out: 'The law must punish rape, but it must not go further . . . If paternity can be proved, the man should be forced to marry the mother, but this proof is impossible.' Like any jurist of the time he wished to distinguish between children born within marriage and those born outside marriage. On occasion he also took a surprisingly modern attitude to family life. 'When the behaviour of a father is self-indulgent, perhaps it may be necessary

. . . to give some authority to the mother, who, without having power, is the natural teacher of the children.'[2]

At the end of the first sessions, the consuls and the jurists must have thought that their recommendations would soon become law. They had not reckoned with the criticisms of the assemblies, above all the Tribunate. Some were survivors from more turbulent times and were not used to agreeing with one another, let alone with any government. Some were men of distinction who expected their voices to be heard. Benjamin Constant, the writer, objected to being given a simple choice: rejection or acceptance. After a short tussle, Napoleon decided to shelve decisions until the assemblies were more amenable. 'They are twelve or fifteen metaphysicians fit to be thrown in the water. They are like vermin under my clothes.' From Lyon, where he was settling the situation in Italy, he commented indignantly to his fellow consuls:

I beg you give a helping hand to those who will get rid of the twenty and the sixty bad members we have in the assemblies . . . The will of the nation is that nobody should stop the government from doing good and that the head of Medusa will not appear again among our tribunes or our assemblies.

The jurists went back to their deliberations. By the time the next lot of sessions began, Napoleon, now Consul for Life, had established the Legion of Honour and signed the concordat. He was not in a mood to allow opposition. But with his intimate advisers he was still flexible. He argued in favour of adoption, but wanted to make clear that he did not so much emphasize the importance of the continuation of a surname that he proposed to restore a caste system. 'The chief purpose of adoption is to give a father to orphans in the case of an individual who, being without close heirs, wishes to attach a child to himself, to whom he can leave his property and his name.'

A far more famous decision concerned the law of inheritance. There was no question of the restoration of the principle of primogeniture, a means of preserving noble estates intact; and Napoleon approved of the revolutionary change that had increased the number of property holders in France. The system of division that the consuls and jurists approved – that property should be divided equally among heirs – had existed before the Revolution in some parts of France, where there were many differing traditions of inheritance; indeed, it dated back to the times of the Franks. In making universal the practice of making all the heirs equal Napoleon has been blamed for the slow growth of the population of France from 1800 to 1950, which has been regarded as a reason why Germany, whose population grew much more rapidly to a position of eminence in Western Europe that it has never lost, has also replaced France as the major power in that area. The truth must be more complicated, however, since between 1950 and 1975 the French population grew at a far faster speed than that of Germany, in a time when the Napoleonic system was still operating. In that period those who had children profited from generous family allowances, but after 1975 the allowances remained high but the rate of population growth fell back. Morale and a changing lifestyle mattered more then than the Napoleonic law on inheritance.

The final sessions dealt with more intricate cases of property, such as the rights of women in marriage. One of the consequences of the publication of the Napoleonic Code was that, unless she was a registered trader, a woman did not have the same rights in the handling of money as her husband. Napoleon may have reflected that it was wise to set limits to the freedom of action for a woman like his own Joséphine, but one result of the official line was that until recent times many French women have not had chequebooks in their own name.

The printer's ink was scarcely dry on the publication of the civil code before First Consul Bonaparte was transformed into Napoleon I, the Emperor of the French. Whereas the important codes that were to regulate commerce, crime and punishment, respectively in 1807, 1808 and 1810, were overtly imperial, the 'consular' civil code has had the most lasting effect on French society. Like the American constitution, it has been often amended, but the principle of summarizing principles on which a great country, in this case France, is to run has remained intact. David intuitively understood why Napoleon was proud of the *Code Napoléon*.

What official propaganda ignored was the erosion of political freedom that was characteristic of the new regime. Napoleon was no democrat, and nor did he intend that liberty should set inconvenient bounds to the rights of the state. His censorship was severe – there was in France no equivalent to the disrespectful caricatures of Rowlandson or Gillray or Cruikshank and he reduced the number of Paris newspapers to four – and under Fouché his police force was active and effective. To enjoy the benefits of free debate, French men had to await the creation of English-style parliaments under the restored Bourbons. To argue without fear a case against the government, French politicians needed the charter of their rights that was conceded by Louis XVIII. It was the regime of the restored Bourbons who provided for the rest of the continent a model for free parliamentary debate. Napoleon, by instinct authoritarian, did not understand that politicians might value debate for its own sake. As far as he was concerned, others debated and he decided. In recent years, as the French legal system has become more liberal, it has moved away from his emphasis on paternal and property rights. He would be astonished that women have been a *juge d'instruction*, a bank manager, a voter, a deputy, a prefect, a *polytechnicienne*, a member of the Institut (Marguerite Yourcenar), a Minister of Health (Simone Veil), a prime minster (Edith Cresson, sadly), a head of a political party (the Gaullist Michèle Alliot-Marie), but as yet neither a general nor the head of state. He would also have had no respect for a Prime Minister, Lionel Jospin, who quickly gave way to the demands of striking truck-drivers – his way with social protesters was to use a whiff of grapeshot, as he had in 1795. The one democratic leader whose treatment of recalcitrant trade unions he might have approved of must have been Margaret Thatcher. She had much in common with the figure staring out from David's picture of a ruler in a study: sleepless hours of work, unwavering convictions and the belief that the law must be obeyed.

9

THE MAN OF LEARNING

———✦———

The Institut de France, built by Le Vau to be the Collège de Quatre Nations, leads across the Pont des Arts to the Louvre, Napoleon's museum of art (much of its contents looted from conquered countries), and can be approached from behind by Rue Mazarin or Rue Bonaparte. In cultural policy Napoleon looked back to the Grand Siècle and added some grandeur of his own, for it was through the patronage of the cardinal and premier ministre of Louis XIV that the original Collège had been built and it was through the patronage of the first Napoleon that the building was given a new function.

In the seventeenth century the government had steadily taken control of the careers of the most talented writers, artists and musicians in the land. Richelieu had established the Académie Française in 1634 with the prime purpose of regulating French by producing a dictionary of the language, a task that took over fifty years. Though the wits had fun at the slowness with which the job was done – the *savants* finished the letter 'A' only in 1639 – and though the Academy made a fool of itself by condemning the best play of the decade, Corneille's *Le Cid*, for its politically incorrect Spanish theme, the idea that the arts could be given official approval found favour at court. Colbert, the protégé of Richelieu's protégé Mazarin, had no difficulty in persuading Louis XIV that the system should be extended to the visual arts, so that there were academies of painting and sculpture and of architecture, and an academy of 'Inscriptions et Belles-Lettres', organizing propaganda; the court composer Lully was made *surintendant de la musique*; and there was finally an Académie des Sciences, whose members met to debate mathematics on Wednesdays and natural sciences on Saturdays.

The purpose of these institutions was to encourage the most talented artists and intellectuals to work for the Crown and for the country. The Académie des Sciences, said Colbert, was 'to work for the perfection of the sciences and arts, and to seek generally for all that can be of use or convenience to the human race and particularly to France'.[1]

Besides the Crown, the other institution that had a say in fostering the arts and learning was the Church, and for most people in the land the Church was the more important institution. It was the Church, through its priests, brothers and sisters, that took charge of education, from those whose proudest achievement was to read or write to those who themselves were teachers. The Sorbonne, the famous university in Paris, was dominated by its theological faculty, and the only sections of higher education to escape clerical control were the faculties of law and medicine. It was from the class of lawyers above all that the *haute bourgeoisie* of Paris recruited its numbers – or rather it was the lawyers who made themselves into a permanent elite, who became the nobility of the gown (the *noblesse de la robe*), who sat in the Paris *parlement*, acted as *échevins* or aldermen in the city government and might aspire to advise the King. What they envied was the social preference given to the nobility of the sword, the *noblesse de l'épée*, and the intellectual and spiritual prestige accorded the clergy. In the eighteenth century such people sometimes acted as a conservative force – the *parlement* of Paris time after time prevented imaginative attempts by royal officials to reform royal finances – but others were the most eloquent critics of the *ancien régime*. Relatively informal gatherings, in a metropolitan salon or a provincial academy, became occasions for witty subversion. At Louis XIV's court, the chief exponent of a sacred view of history was Bossuet, Bishop of Meaux, whose magnificent perorations astounded the fashionable congregations to whom he preached, but in the reign of Louis XV Voltaire taught sophisticated readers how to smirk before Rousseau taught sensitive ones how to weep. The most impressive monument to contemporary learning, the *Encyclopédie*, was so skilfully edited by Diderot that its jokes fooled the censors – long before 1789 the Church and the state no longer dictated the fortunes of the arts and the sciences. In particular the Church had been weakened by the suppression of the Society of Jesus in 1762, for the Jesuits owned many schools for the sons of the upper classes, ran many colleges for the clergy, supervised the welfare of many cultivated nuns, used many churches to charm the eyes and ears of the *beau monde*, and spoke against secular chic. In certain cases they could be replaced, as when the Oratorians tried to take over their role in secondary school teaching, but their disappearance meant that before the collapse of the *ancien régime* a whole generation had grown up that was accustomed to new ideas called Enlightened – that is, free from the superstitions of the past, putting its trust in unfettered reason and sensibility; and it was to this generation that Napoleon, born in 1769, belonged. Oddly, the last lawyer to have the manners and wear the costume of an *ancien régime avocat* was Maximilien Robespierre, but most of the leaders who came to the fore in the

1790s, like Danton or Marat, were cut from rougher cloth. Refinement did not appeal to the mob. The ablest chemist in France, Lavoisier, dressed elegantly for his 1788 portrait by David, was executed during the Terror, while David sat on the committee of public security. The most exquisite of *ébénistes*, Riesener, could not find anyone to buy his *secrétaires*, the most playful of rococo painters, Jean-Honoré Fragonard, was driven to penury, and the best of poets, André Chénier, had his life cut off by the guillotine. In times of civil hysteria, the work of teaching, researching or creating takes too much effort to be attractive. The revolutionaries could dismantle the old structures and could set in place plans for new ones, but without stability there was no chance that any worthwhile changes would be effective. It was Napoleon who undertook to make France stable.

Napoleon was neither artistic nor an intellectual, but he realized that the arts could be useful as propaganda and he understood the practical utility of intelligence. He was not without literary gifts.

His own education had been a thorough preparation for a military man. With the help of his mother's admirer, the Comte de Marbeuf, he was admitted to the college of Autun at the age of nine. Hitherto he had studied in Italian. He found it hard to learn French, and when he did he spoke it with a strong Corsican accent. From there the next year he was taken to Brienne in Champagne, where the military academy to which he was admitted was run by Franciscan friars. The boarding school was run strictly like a religious house, with the days punctuated by the hours of prayer, daily Mass and occasional confession and Communion, but it had been founded by a Minister of War, St-Germain, and it was meant to inculcate in its pupils the virtues of loyalty to the King, Louis XVI, and to the proudest traditions of France. Napoleon's history lessons taught him about a hundred-year war without any defeats at the hands of the English – it was the Gascons who had caused all the trouble – and appealed to local loyalty by stressing the prowess of Jean de Brienne, once Latin Emperor of Constantinople. He admired tales of heroism he read in Plutarch and Corneille, he excelled in two subjects – mathematics and geography – and in 1783 the Chevalier de Kéralio, after inspecting Brienne, reported that young Buonaparte 'will make an excellent sailor'. He may have almost applied to the English naval college at Portsmouth, but he went instead to the Ecole Militaire, the foremost military finishing school in Paris. He disapproved of the luxurious accommodation there, and he drafted a letter recommending the value of a more spartan upbringing. Again Napoleon won no prizes, but he achieved exam results sufficiently good to complete the course in a year; and, though forty-second out of fifty-eight, he was the fourth youngest to pass out. He gained a commission just after his sixteenth birthday.

His flair for mathematics made it natural for him to join the artillery, and he was an enthusiastic student of ballistics, but, apart from clumsy interventions in Corsica in 1791, 1792 and 1793, he had little occasion to use his military training before he became involved in the general European war that broke out in 1793. He was so often on half pay that he was able to read widely. Besides Bernardin de St-Pierre, a novelist of sensibility, he tackled Marigny's *History of the Arabs*, made notes on English history up to 1689, on Buffon's *Histoire Naturelle* and on the history of his native Corsica – he planned to tell the tale himself. He tried his hand at essays and his most ambitious literary endeavour, *Le Souper de Beaucaire*, was a political dialogue. By September 1793, when ordered to join the troops whose duty was to dislodge the British navy and the French royalists from the naval base of Toulon, a project that gave him at last the opportunity to make his name as a gunner, he was an unusually well-read soldier.

Five years later he was a famous general, victor over the Sardinians and the Austrians in Italy, and called to be the master of Egypt. Before he went, he was proud that he had been elected to the new institution, the Institute of France, as a mathematician. In Italy he had demonstrated his appreciation of painting and sculpture by looting works of art from Parma, Modena, Milan, Bologna, Venice and Rome. In Egypt he would show his love of learning. He did not bring home to France an obelisk but he set the fashion for doing so.

The Directors, who authorized the campaign in Egypt, thought that the role of France in that country would be to bring the native peoples the benefits of French civilization. Already the Commission of Italian Sciences and Arts had supervised the transport of works of art from the conquered cities of Italy to France, and within this group two men had been pre-eminent. One, Gaspard Monge, was a mathematician who had invented descriptive geometry, had been correspondent of the Royal Society of Sciences from 1772 and was Professor of Physics at the Ecole Militaire in Paris, Napoleon's former school. The other, Claude Louis Berthollet, was a chemist. Elected to the Royal Academy in 1780 and the new Institute in 1795, he held the Chair of Chemistry at the Ecole Normale, another new institution with a long future. To these two men in 1797 Napoleon had entrusted the text of the Treaty of Campoformio. To them now he revealed his oriental plans, and they undertook to help him form a commission to go to Egypt. In May the Minister of the Interior was charged with 'putting at the disposal of General Bonaparte the engineers, artists and other subordinate to your ministry, as well as the different objects he will ask you for to help with the expedition with which he is charged'.[2]

Even before the troops had been transported to Egypt, Napoleon had tried to show that his attitude to the relics of past cultures or the alien cultures of the present were not always those typical of a philistine soldier – he may have looted in Italy and brought to an end a thousand years of Venetian independence, but he wished to go to Egypt to learn from Egypt as well as to make clear to the Egyptians that they must learn from the French. On board ship he read a translation of the Koran and, though scarcely a religious man, gave the prophet his vote of approval. Even more astonishing, before he sailed to the east he had spent 80,000 livres on scientific and technological instruments, especially those linked to printing, and most of this money on books, and that the subjects he demanded information on were astronomy, topography, physics, chemistry, aerostatics, natural history, surgery and pharmacy. Once in Egypt he enjoyed confounding his entourage with mathematical puzzles; and one of the most striking of Denon's images illustrates this spirit as French surveyors balanced precariously on top of the head of the sphinx of Gizeh to measure it. Napoleon was proud of his mathematical skill. According to the old calendar, it was on 25 December 1797 that he had been elected to a seat in the division of the Institute that concerned mathematicians and scientists. When on his return to France he acquired political power, he admitted that often while making appointments he favoured mathematicians and chemists, for he felt himself to be one of them. As he grew more accustomed to the exercise of power, he realized that what supported the arts and sciences in France, the system of education to provide an infrastructure to sustain the achievements of the Institute, had been damaged and must be renewed.

In the *ancien régime* there was in theory a neat division of roles: the Church by means of schools and universities dominated education, and the Crown by means of the academies tried to regulate the professional scientists, writers and artists. The radical revolutionaries were intent on replacing this simple arrangement: the one undivided republic was to have undivided control of all intellectual and aesthetic activity. In place of the clergy who taught the catechism, argued Lakanal, teachers would instruct children on the values implicit in the Declaration of the Rights of Man and the Citizen.[3] While France's most gifted scientist, Lavoisier, was sent to his death, France's most gifted painter, David, who signed many of the death warrants that authorized the execution of such men and women by guillotine, also campaigned to end the monopoly of the Royal Academy of the Beaux-Arts. David, however, did not wish to grant artists freedom to follow their artistic whims. He was, if anything, more dictatorial than those whose reign he ended. He stood for a classical republicanism – that is, until he found in Napoleon's head the reincarnation of an antique hero and became by stages a classical imperialist who longed to do for the arts under Napoleon what Le Brun had done for the arts under Louis xiv: create beauty by ordering it.

The more idealistic ambitions of the Revolution for the educators as for David were stilled by the severing of Robespierre's head, but those who felled him in the hot August days of 1794 (Thermidor year ii), the Thermidorians, began to achieve what their predecessors had merely talked about. In April 1792 the philosopher Condorcet, while urging the liberal view that every citizen had the right to establish a school, had proposed a national system of education. Girls as well as boys should have primary education, then there would be a secondary level organized by 'institutes' and finally there would be nine lycées. At each stage, selected young people would be 'national scholars' paid for by the nation; the others would be encouraged by national festivals and lectures, the secular equivalent of feasts and sermons; and a National Society would exercise overall control of teaching and research. In 1792 Condorcet had been listened to with respect, but nothing was done. In 1793 Robespierre suggested the adoption of a plan by an ex-nobleman, Lepeletier de St-Fargeau, that envisaged a state monopoly of education. The state would take charge of girls from five to eleven and boys from five to twelve, but the school should be run by a council of fathers of families as a cooperative. The imparting of virtue rather than knowledge was the school's aim. Lepeletier, like Condorcet, never lived to see his ideas made real. Whereas he was assassinated, Condorcet may have committed suicide in prison. In December 1793 the Convention recommended free primary schooling for at least three years, to be given by a schoolmaster who would be either a citizen who offered to teach or a teacher selected by the town council. Whether he was to be a cleric or layman was laid vague. What mattered was that he took a patriotic oath.

The Thermidorians were practical. In October 1794 they decreed the opening of a 'normal' school where able teachers should train 1,300 would-be teachers sent from their districts; and in the following month they stated that for every thousand inhabitants the republic should open a school whose teacher it should pay. At the same time they made no effort to close down private schools – there were some ex-priests and ex-nuns who still taught – and the bourgeois, relieved to see the Thermidorians in power, were often inclined to avoid the institutions of the state.

In the case of higher education, they proved themselves enthusiastic. During the last fifteen months of its existence, the Convention, purged of Jacobin influence, brought into existence: the Conservatory of Arts and Crafts; the Central School of Public Services (later Works) that by specializing in the training of future soldiers and sailors as engineers was the prototype of the Ecole Polytechnique; a School of Mines; three Schools of Medicine (in Paris, Montpellier and Strasbourg); the School of Oriental Languages, an institution that proved its worth when the French encountered Arabs; the Museum of French Monuments; and the

Conservatoire de la Musique. Finally, the Thermidorians made plans for the Institute to oversee every form of culture.

Their ideas for secondary education cost less money than Condorcet's proposals, for, though each department was to have its central school, fees were no longer waived, and then in October 1795 the central government absolved itself from the duty of paying teachers' salaries, so that the success of the new schools depended on the support of the local communities through departmental funding and the support of the parents who could pay for their children's education. In the days of the Directory (1795–99), the government tried to discourage all officials from opting for private schools, since these were usually run on religious principles, and sometimes closed them down, but the rich on whom the government relied for survival were not easily converted to the ideal of lay schooling for all. Christian education had a long history and would survive. Logically, the Revolution led to a secular alternative, but as yet no class of a lay clerisy had developed a sense of its secular vocation. The France of *professeurs* and *instituteurs* had been envisaged but had not yet been brought into being.

What was in place was the coping stone of a new edifice: the Institute. Its three divisions – for the mathematical and physical sciences, for the moral and political sciences and for arts and letters – stood for all that mankind could aspire to without divine revelation. The theologians of the Sorbonne had once been the arbiters of French culture. Now the *immortels*, as the members of the Institute are known, would settle what was true, good and beautiful; and Citizen Bonaparte was of their number.[4]

While First Consul, Napoleon quickly realized that what the Revolution had promised had not been fulfilled. In 1801 one of the Councillors of State, Fourcroy, wrote:

The children of less fortunate citizens and those who live in the countryside still receive no or almost no form of instruction. Two generations of children are virtually doomed to be unable to read, write or know basic mathematics. That is why the government must take measures to remedy this evil.

His words were endorsed by reports coming in from fifty-eight departments, but what the precise condition of education was nationwide cannot be assessed. There must have been many private schools that consisted of a former nun or two who taught a handful of children their letters, somehow shopkeepers of modest means still learned to calculate and some famous schools had survived. The ancient monastic school of Pontlevoy, in its prospectus, boasted that it had never been closed down. In 1800 Paris claimed to have two hundred schools of all sorts, but of what quality is not clear. The Convention had instituted primary schools and central schools in each department; and even Fourcroy was sanguine about the central schools, stating how impressive were many of the science and maths teachers and how steadily the number of pupils was growing. A wide syllabus appealed to those with abilities that the educators of the past had neglected: those with a leaning to experimental science, those with a gift for design, those with a flair for French rather than Latin, those curious about law and political history. Religion was no longer relevant, and the course in philosophy that would replace the study of religion had not yet been devised. The programme, however, presupposed a philosophical position: that of the Enlightened *philosophes*.

Within weeks of the coup of Brumaire 1799 the Ecole Polytechnique acquired its modern militaristic character, and *polytechniciens* quickly learned the value of working for the state, for on graduation they were paid. A University of Jurisprudence was opened in Paris in 1800–01, and an Institute of Jurisprudence and

Political Economy (Economics) in 1801, soon renamed the Academy of Legislation. Soon, other learned societies were founded: a Philomathematical Society, a Celtic Academy that became the Society of Antiquaries, a Society of Medicine. What Napoleon's rule brought to fruition was the movement of intellectual energy from speculation towards useful knowledge. But there were limits to his tolerance, for after the concordat had been signed he did not approve of anti-Christian sentiment. In 1803 he closed the faculty of ethics and politics in the Institute because too many of its members had stood for the rationalist views of the late eighteenth century.

When he became Emperor of the French, Napoleon's dislike of any form of dissent made him suspicious of romantic *littérateurs* who set the mode for the sensibilities of sensitive souls. Although a devotee of *Ossian*, the 'forgery' of the Scots poet Macpherson, Napoleon and his Institute were sticklers for the 'rules' of poetry, like Louis XIV and his Académie Royale. Chateaubriand was invited to join the new Academy in 1811, but his speech of acceptance was so critical that permission to read it was withheld; and when Napoleon fell, Chateaubriand, by now a confirmed royalist, wrote a pamphlet attacking him, *De Buonaparte, Des Bourbons*, that was all the more devastating because, in identifying the Emperor by the Italian version of his surname he was both proclaiming him a usurper and implying that he was a foreigner. Another leading author of the time, Madame de Staël, had a more drastic fate. She was exiled in 1803 (along with her lover, Benjamin Constant), again in 1806 and finally in 1810, when most copies of her *De l'Allemagne* were destroyed. Her crime was heinous, for while comparing the qualities of modern French and German writers, she made appallingly clear that she preferred the Germans. Napoleon could not abide opposition, yet he was not a twentieth-century dictator. In 1804 the poet Desorgues published an epigram, 'Oui, le grand Napoléon – Est un grand caméléon', and when the eagles were distributed to the army after the coronation, a military student, Faure, cried out 'Liberty or death'. Both were interned as mad. In 1810 Napoleon brought back state prisons and a despotic feature of the *ancien régime*: arbitrary imprisonment. In 1814, though without any equivalent to a gulag, France probably had 2,500 prisoners whose only offence was political.[5]

Napoleon wanted technocrats of arts and letters. If the three best-known authors of the day defied him, none of the major architects or artists did; and he gave them work. Percier and Fontaine, who had renovating the château of Malmaison for young General Bonaparte's wife, gained their just deserts by becoming in the days of the Empire the chief propagators of the Empire style in interior décor. At a time when arches of triumph were springing up all over France, they erected the most elegant one, the Arc du Carrousel, at the entrance to the Tuileries palace. They extended and adapted that palace to make it Napoleon's principal residence in Paris and, when his legitimate son, Napoleon (II) was born, it was they who planned the immense palace that would be fitting for a King of Rome. In painting, David and his pupils prospered; indeed, David made sure that he earned large sums for huge masterpieces like *Le Sacre de Joséphine*. While many pictures at the biennial Salons glorified Napoleon, he had every reason to express his pleasure with them. In 1808 Denon organized for him a competition for the best representation of a scene from the Battle of Eylau (1807). Gros, who was declared the winner, seemed to be ignored by the Emperor until Napoleon stood in front of the painting. The Emperor paused before removing from his lapel his own ribbon of the Légion d'Honneur and placing it on Gros. Gros found himself made Baron de l'Empire.

Napoleon had some literary appreciation but was not a refined judge of the visual arts. Those whose gifts he prized the most were those with a scientific training. He took care that young French men should be educated in ways he approved of. They should model themselves on him.

As Emperor, Napoleon had grandiose ambitions for French education. He had a vision of a teacher as somebody who was in part a lay priest, in part a member of the professional classes, imbued therefore with a sense of esprit de corps. 'I wish for a body of public instruction,' he noted in 1806, 'that will have its feet on the benches of the college and its head in the Senate . . . I want a corporation, because a corporation does not die . . . My principal aim . . . is to have a means of forming political and moral opinions . . . The essential point is that only the University, for that is what it will be called, will have the privilege of teaching.' In 1806 two clauses were enough for the law that created the University; and by a vote of 210 to 42 the legislative body established it.

Campaigns in Germany and Poland distracted the Emperor until he issued a decree in 1808 that established the University as an institution that would be 'Catholic, Gallican, loyal, conservative, liberal and uniform'.[6] On the same day he appointed Fontanes, the president of the legislative body, as grand master, Villaret, Bishop of Casale, as chancellor and Delambre, perpetual secretary of the first class of the Institute, as treasurer. Fourcroy, who had worked so hard to facilitate the plan, had too much of a revolutionary past to be put in charge. He was consoled with the title of count, but nevertheless died of disappointment in December 1809. Those who ran Napoleon's University must think like him, so that those whose help was coopted tended to be imperial officials – Councillors of State or inspectors – or political clerics.

From 1 January 1809 the University was the only body in France that had the right to public teaching, and any school or college that was not authorized by its grand master ceased to exist. That year lycées were obliged to follow a new syllabus. In 1810 the University council, at the grand master's bidding, promulgated the statutes of the faculties of letters and sciences, of the Ecole Normale that trained *professeurs* and of the *agrégation* that ensured a high standard among them. In spite of Napoleon's quarrel with the Pope, he conceded that in every department there could be one Church secondary school, but a decree of 1811 made clear that all institutions, whether a state secondary school (or college), or a private secondary school (day or boarding, lay or ecclesiastical), were ruled by the University. The decree also gave the academic body its rank in society, below a town council and above a chamber of commerce. Napoleon wished to give his teachers their place in his well-ordered society.

'My University in the way that I conceived it was a masterpiece of organization,' he was to declare in 1815. Whether or not he was justified in saying so, the organization he set up had a lasting effect on France.

By the decree of 17 March 1808 the kinds of educational institutions recognized by the University were reduced to six: faculties; Lycées, which had replaced the central schools of the Revolution; colleges or state secondary schools; private secondary schools; private schools run by particular *instituteurs* along the lines of the colleges or boarding schools that were less demanding; and small schools or elementary schools where children learned to read, write and calculate. A seventh type, the Church secondary school, was added in 1811. Those attending one of the five faculties – of theology, law, medicine, science and literature – could gain one of three levels of qualification: the baccalaureate, the licence and the doctorate. For the best part of two centuries the Napoleonic reforms have given Frenchmen a yen for paper qualifications that was unknown to those of earlier generations. The University also had jurisdiction over teachers. They were to obey their superiors and respect the rules, to leave the University only when authorized to do so (permission was normally granted at the third time of asking every two months), to take no other post without permission and to denounce abuses. It was the first obligation that was uniquely important. Even during holidays, the members of the University were subject to it. All initiative in French education came from above.

The salaries of the University officials were good. In the new system, the number of bureaucrats soon grew and grew and grew. In the Paris region alone there were more than eighty of them. There were rectors, inspectors, bursars, councillors, lawyers and, at the top, men who rejoiced in titles like 'the under principal in the general secretariat of the bureaux'. Napoleon, ever anxious to spend as little as possible, sought to reduce the financial contributions of the State. In Paris, two-thirds of the budget of the University was spent on administration (in 1812). These expenses were met by two sorts of taxes: those levied on the heads of institutions, and those levied on pupils.

A strict syllabus of subjects was followed throughout the nine years of a lycéen's schooling, to which an order of the University council added in 1810 a compulsory course in philosophy after the traditional course in literature. As only the candidates for the Ecole Polytechnique took advanced mathematics, lycéens were divided into students of literature who studied philosophy and those who specialized in science. Latin rather than French became the basis of literary pursuits, as it had been the case in the colleges of the pre-revolutionary university. There was equal prestige for *professeurs*, whose gowns had hoods lined in either amaranth (for the sciences) or orange (for the classics), but in any assembly of teachers there were more hoods lined in orange. By setting so high a standard in mathematics, the University willy-nilly kept the well educated in France more familiar with the humanities than the sciences.

When the University regime came into operation, there were 697 day or boarding schools, 273 colleges and 35 lycées. In the last academic year of the Imperial period (1813), the figures were respectively 1,001, 346 and 36. Though the number of students had risen from just over 50,000 to almost 70,000, very few more parents of these children had chosen state instead of private schools. It was to be only in the long term that the University had the remarkable effects that Napoleon hoped for. In the short term the University concerned itself with little apart from secondary education; it was undemocratic; it served the interests only of the middle and upper classes. The lycées were institutions that opened a career for all the talents of the sons of the Napoleonic notables, both military or civilian, not for all the people. In the last century a poor peasant boy from Auvergne could win a scholarship to the Ecole Normale, qualify as an *agrégé*, become a *professeur* at the Lycée Henri IV, a political adviser to General de Gaulle, Prime Minister and at the end of his life President of the Fifth Republic. A century earlier, such a curriculum vitae would have been impossible even for a child as able as Georges Pompidou.

Napoleon's bureaucrats had little success in their attempts to organize a viable system of higher education, except in Paris. The University's forty-one academies contained just nineteen faculties of science and thirty-one faculties of the humanities, most attached to the Lycées, many more preoccupied with collating grades than with teaching. Often the teachers and even the pupils were identical in both lycée and faculty. At Pau in the south-west, Abbé Eliçagaray's positions make him sound like a Pooh-Bah of academics, as Rector of the Academy, President of the Academic Council, Dean of the Faculty of Letters, Professor of Philosophy in the Faculty, Bursar of the Lycée and finally Professor of Philosophy in the Lycée. In Paris, however, there was a need for higher education, with able *professeurs* to provide it and able students to enjoy it. Public lectures in the humanities were attended by large audiences – it was the age when public lectures began – and the Ecole Normale was sanctioned in 1808 to receive three hundred pupils who were to be 'formed in the art of teaching letters and sciences'. The school was located in the Lycée Impérial, originally with just forty-three pupils, among whom were the future philosopher Victor Cousin and the future historian Augustin Thierry. As with the Ecole Polytechnique, an inauspicious start marked the birth of one of the great institutions of modern France.

Girls and small children were outside the University's remit. 'I do not think,' the Emperor told the Council of State, 'that we must concern ourselves with the way in which young girls are taught. They cannot be better taught than by their mothers.' Girls' boarding schools and convents continued to look after their charges in whatever way they thought fit. And so it was that the real Aurore Dupin, born in 1805 into the landed gentry, was in the charge of nuns, so that she learned to enjoy reading novels, writing letters and playing the piano – without her strength of mind she would never have become George Sand – and a little later the fictional Emma Bovary, a young bourgeoise, gained from her upbringing with the sisters a love for pious feelings and beautiful fabrics and romantic fiction that led her to emotional childishness, bankruptcy, adultery and suicide.

Napoleon was also robust in his view of primary education. In 1802 a law ordered that schoolmasters, chosen by mayors and town councils, should use buildings given them by the commune and receive fees paid by the parents according to a scale laid down by the council. The next year, when the admirable Fourcroy enquired about what had been done, he found that nothing had been done. While French villages had to wait for the arrival of the devoted *instituteur*, the only teacher who was available had to be the devoted *curé*. 'I prefer,' Napoleon said, 'to see the children of the village in the hands of a monk who knows nothing beyond his catechism and whose beliefs I know than in those of a half-learned man who has no basis for his morality and no fixed ideas . . . An ignorant brother will do for the man of the people.' A radical change, however, was put forward. The University henceforth would have charge of the training of *instituteurs* and a little money was put aside for the purpose. It was assumed that primary schools would be religious schools. The long battle for the control of the souls of the young children between *Monsieur l'Abbé* and *Monsieur l'Instituteur*, between a clerical Catholic and a lay secular education, lay far ahead.

Of all Napoleon's educational inventions, the one that has been the most admired is the lycée. Matthew Arnold, as a Schools Inspector, was to write of 'the French Eton' at a time when Eton probably offered a much less impressive academic education. It was also the first of the new teaching institutions to come into being, established by a law in 1802.

In 1800 Lucien Bonaparte, then Minister of the Interior, had addressed a typically passionate letter to the consuls:

> Since the suppression of the teaching bodies, teaching is almost non-existent in France. It is not that there do not exist both in Paris and in the departments several clever *professeurs* who are enthusiastic, but so widely dispersed that . . . they are like so many sparks that, because they do not act together, give out only a feeble . . . light . . . A great people, with settled institutions, should have a national education in harmony with those institutions.

He added the thought that there was 'in the midst of the ruins one last refuge open for public instruction', by which he meant the

Prytanée français. Brother Napoleon, though he shortly afterwards quarrelled with Lucien and dismissed him, took note.

The Prytanée français, named after the Prytaneum of ancient Athens, had an extraordinary history. Formerly the Jesuit College of Louis-le-Grand, it had survived the suppression of the Jesuits in the 1760s, as the small colleges of the old university of Paris were also abolished and their scholarships reassigned to it. In the Revolution, the university itself was suppressed, along with all other colleges, and the professors and students became members of a new body, the Institute of Equality. In 1800, in response to Lucien Bonaparte's report, the Prytaneum was split into four sections – at Fontainebleau, Versailles, St-Germain as well as at its Paris home – then at three more, in Brussels, Compiègne and Lyon. But only in Paris and at Compiègne were there any pupils. There was also a military Prytaneum, having a school of cavalry at St-Germain and a military school at Fontainebleau, that was transferred in 1808 to St-Cyr.

The First Consul preferred to give scholarships to the sons of officers, and he prescribed military dress for the boys and he insisted that twice a *décadi* they perform military exercises (the revolutionary calendar was still in force and the Christian week had not yet returned). As early as 1801 Lucien's successor Chaptal persuaded Napoleon that, at twelve, boys should choose between arts and sciences; and in 1802 all the Prytaneum colleges got a chapel. Whereas the revolutionary central schools of each department had been conceded liberty, the new institution was rigidly controlled, with its boarders, its uniforms, its military ambience, its religious practice and its devotion to Latin. Later, in 1802, France got a Ministry of Education (or public instruction) that had as its function the direction of 'minds by the mind', as one civil servant put it.

A result of this ordinance was that between October 1802 and

October 1803 forty-three Lycées were set up in principle, of which two-thirds did not begin to operate for another three years. As often with Napoleonic reforms, the administrators were the first people to be employed; so that they could not be celibate priests, they must be married, widowed or divorced, but no women could live in a lycée. For every single administrator there were just two or three *professeurs*, whose salaries were about three-fifths that of their bureaucratic colleagues; and all were appointed by the First Consul. The *professeurs*, however, were drawn from many classes of academic – ex-employees of the central schools, ex-directors of extinct colleges, ex-priests, ex-religious – and they were often mediocre, except in Paris, and were not loved in the areas where the new lycées were imposed.

The way of life in the lycées was regimental in its precision. In each library there was the same number of books – exactly 1,500 – and each followed the same syllabus. In Rouen, no student of the humanities knew a word of Corneille and only exams to enter the celebrated Ecole Polytechnique made classes in higher mathematics viable. The Lycée Impérial, recently known as the Prytanée, retained many of the failings of the Jesuit schooling that had been offered when the buildings had been called the Collège de Louis-le-Grand. A classical education, which had been exciting in the reign of Louis XIV, was too narrow for the age of Napoleon. Though with drums to beat the changes in timetables and their military uniforms the lycées seemed well adapted to creating a class to run the Empire, Napoleon had had to abandon his dream of a widespread scientific schooling. That lay in the future. There were to be many distinguished French scientists in the nineteenth century, but it was only since the shock of defeat in 1940 that France has been transformed into a nation of technocrats.

The Napoleonic lycées already bore some of the marks of the lycées that have been the butt of Anglo-Saxon jokes, for they were subject to a Minister of Education who may have liked to think that he knew what any lycéen was about at any moment of the day. For all their failings, they were institutions that opened a career to all the talents of the sons of Napoleonic notables, both military and civilian. To that extent they were meritocratic. The most vivid account of life in a lycée appears in the memoirs of Alfred de Vigny, *Servitude et Grandeur militaires*:

Towards the end of the Empire I was a schoolboy preoccupied with matters outside school. The war was the first thing we thought about; the sound of the drums drowned the voices of my teachers, and the mysterious words of our books spoke to us in a frigid, pedantic tone. The only point of logarithms and figures of speech was to be the means of aspiring to the star of the Legion of Honour, the brightest star in the heavens, as far as we children were concerned.

No subject of meditation could hold our attention for any length of time when our heads were turned by cannon-fire and bells pealing out the Te Deum. Whenever an elder brother, who had left the collège a few months ago, reappeared in Hussar's uniform, with his arm in a sling, we blushed at the thought of our books and hurtled them at our masters. The masters themselves kept on reading us the communiqués of the Grand Army, and our shouts of 'Long live the Emperor' stopped all talk of Tacitus and Plato. Our masters were like heraldic kings-of-arms, our classrooms were like barracks, our recreation periods turned into manoeuvres and our examinations into military reviews.

War so clearly seemed to us the natural state of our country that when we had escaped from the classroom we hastened to join up . . . This idea remained with us throughout the Restoration. Every year brought renewed hope of war, and we dared not give up our swords in case the day we resigned might prove the day before a campaign. In this way the days dragged by and we lost precious years, dreaming about battles as we drilled in the Champ-de-Mars, wasting away in military shows and duels our strong but pointless reserves of energy.[7]

Alfred de Vigny was but one of a remarkable group of gifted artists and writers educated in the time of the Empire. Like unusual boys at any time, many had unhappy memories of their schooldays. Vigny himself, born in 1797 at Loches, moved to Paris as an infant and was at the pension Hix before moving on to the prestigious Lycée Bonaparte, where he specialized in mathematics in order to be able to enter the Ecole Polytechnique. The fall of the Empire came too soon for him to serve the Empire and, as a member of a royalist family who recalled having been taunted for the 'de' in his name, he was glad to rely on influence to join the Mousquetaires Rouges under Louis XVIII. Despite his politics, he felt keenly his generation's nostalgia for Imperial glory.

His ambivalence is matched by that of Théodore Géricault, who was six years older and felt a similar attachment to military life, in his case to the cavalry. Born into a well-to-do Norman family, Géricault also arrived in Paris as a small child and he also went eventually to a smart lycée, the Lycée Impérial, where the only lessons he enjoyed were drawing lessons. Though he learned to read Latin fluently he disliked classical studies and read little French for pleasure; he lived for the circus and for riding. He was at the lycée for only two years, as an undistinguished pupil, and was relieved to become a full-time painter, luckily one with sufficient private means to be free of the necessity of selling his pictures. He became prominent as an equestrian artist in 1812 and so longed to go to war as a cavalryman that in 1814 he fought for Louis XVIII. It was an episode of which he became embarrassed, for he was essentially a Bonapartist.

More obviously Bonapartist was a younger artist, who was at the same Lycée for much longer. Eugène Delacroix, born in 1798 the youngest son of a former Foreign Minister who became a Napoleonic prefect, came to Paris on his father's death. At the Lycée Impérial, Delacroix was a good student of the humanities and excelled in the drawing class. It was only the death of his mother that forced him to choose an artistic career, for money had run out. As the most literary of painters who had benefited from an old-fashioned education, he had the ability, just not the money, to have a less risky vocation. His earliest surviving drawings indicate that his political reaction to the restored Bourbons was that of a convinced Bonapartist.

Honoré de Balzac and Victor Hugo had the unhappy childhoods that may have been obligatory for them to be the two grandest French novelists of the middle years of the nineteenth century. For six years Balzac endured the bleak form of education offered by the Collège de Vendôme, some thirty-five miles from his birthplace at Tours. The ex-Oratorian college still boasted seven ex-Oratorians on its staff of sixteen, but had tactfully replaced the fleur-de-lys on the school buttons with the words 'Arts and Sciences' and used a catechism that called Napoleon 'He whom God has summoned in difficult times' . . . to 'defend the State with his powerful arm'. There Balzac, who may never have gone home as the school did not hold with holidays in summer, suffered from chilblains every winter and was sent to 'prison' for at least a hundred times. 'Prison' was a form of detention that was, in his case, punishment for not producing work on time. As the habit persisted into adulthood, 'imprisonment' did him no good. By way of contrast, Hugo's schooldays were only too unsettled, as his progressively estranged parents moved from one garrison town, such as Besançon, where he was born, to Madrid, where he acquired a taste for the exotic. Like Balzac, he was taught by an unfrocked priest, one Abbé Rivière, at the former convent of the Feuillantines in Paris, but his mind was never shackled by disciplined learning.

Of that generation, only perhaps Prosper Mérimée was a well-adjusted pupil. His father was professor of drawing at the Ecole Polytechnique in 1803, the year of his birth. Between 1805 and 1816 the family lived in the quartier of the Panthéon. From two English ladies, friends as well as neighbours he learned English, which was to become fashionable when Napoleon fell. As his father became professor of drawing at the Lycée Napoléon (now the Lycée Henri IV), he was enrolled there, and he quickly became a member of a remarkable group of contemporaries. They included Armand Bertin, future editor of the *Journal des Débats*, Isidore Geoffroy Saint-Hilaire, son of the great naturalist, Jean-Jacques Ampère, son of the physicist, and Montalivet, a future Minister of the Interior. Mérimée, even more than Delacroix, was on the edge of the ruling class, and his social position would clear the way for him to be a government archaeologist as well as a writer of fiction.

Napoleon had not loved his own schools. The physical privations and emotional buffetings that these young Romantics suffered would have left him unmoved. He would have been more interested to know that his educational system would produce an elite, for that was its point.

For Napoleon the word 'elite' was no insult. A man distinguished for achievements in the arts and sciences could strive for election to The Institut. An ordinance of January 1803 divided the Institut into four classes that re-established the academies of Louis XIV. The class of physical science and mathematics, Napoleon's class, corresponded to the old Royal Academy of Sciences, the class of French language and literature to the Académie Française, the class of history and ancient literature to the Academy of Inscriptions and Belles-Lettres, that of the Beaux-Arts to those of painting, sculpture and architecture; and there the musicians, whose predecessors had been in the Academy of Music, found their section. The class of moral and political sciences set up in the 1790s had proved troublesome, so it was suppressed and its members dispersed among the other classes. The Institut that was reconstituted in 1803 found its natural home in a building dating from the reign of Louis XIV, but the occupants knew that, as meritocrats who had their just reward, they belonged to the modern Imperial France. In joining the Institut, they had joined the elite of the elite.

10

NAPOLEON'S FRANCE

Not all French paintings of this period are concerned with battles and triumphs and handsome men dressed to kill. Under the Consulate and Empire, as in the years of the Revolution and the Directory, Louis-Léopold Boilly continued to paint light-hearted scenes of everyday life. Born in 1761 and trained in French Flanders, he had come to Paris in 1785, the year when David's *Oath of the Horatii* caused a sensation at the Salon with its stark celebration of masculine patriotism. Boilly lacked the force and the single-mindedness to be a painter like David. By nature he had a sunny disposition that he retained throughout the vicissitudes of a career pursued in unstable times. He arrived in the capital just in time to gain customers for charming scenes of sexual intrigue. *The Mockery* or *The Jealous Lover* suggest that his artistic sympathies lay with young, beautiful and resourceful people who were unscrupulous in the art of outwitting rich, ugly, middle-aged men bent on frustrating their amorous plans. By 1793 this proved to be a dangerous way of making a living. The doyen of painters of this kind, Fragonard, fled to his native town of Grasse, where he painted for the cathedral a picture in the severest neoclassical style. Boilly, who stayed in the capital, was publicly denounced by his fellow artist Wicar for pandering to immoral taste. He was quick to appease his critics by producing works that could serve as revolutionary propaganda: first of the singer Chenard dressed up as an heroic member of the Parisian working class, the *sansculottes*, then *The Triumph of Marat*, a picture dating from 1794, the year after Marat's murder, that focused on a crowd of supporters delighted at the news that the notorious journalist has been acquitted of political charges by a revolutionary tribunal. In this painting Boilly stayed cleverly within the category of art he had made his own, the depiction of scenes of modern life. His Marat is nothing like the noble martyr butchered in his bath that had been depicted by David. Rather, Marat's moment of glory is an excuse for showing a group of people in the act of enjoying themselves while they lionize their pin-up. They could have been cheering anyone exulting in any kind of victory. It was easier for Boilly to adapt to the less earnest mores of the Directory, and he was soon painting a very different crowd, this time of raffish speculators outside the Palais-Royal, where various individuals barter forks, sell newspapers, jingle coins, kneel down to examine a sheet of paper against the light, flirt or pick pockets. When he pictured the galleries of the Palais-Royal during the time of the Empire (in 1809), Boilly chose as his subject a group of prostitutes touting for business. It was not perhaps the view of France that the Emperor would like to remember.

Boilly managed to survive all the changes of regime without altering his perspective on events. His pictures show how very many Frenchmen had an interest in heroes only as distant figures. In another painting of a Paris street, a man, women and children tiptoe gingerly across a plank to miss the puddles; in yet another a group loiters outside the gate of the Turkish garden café. Other scenes are set indoors. In a café, emancipated girls play billiards while men look on, in a home *The Reading of the Bulletin of the Grande Armée* shows how military affairs affect bourgeois family life, though the children and a dog play on unaware of adult interests, and in the Louvre a fashionable crowd stares at David's huge *Le Sacre de Joséphine.* Another work was to show subjects petitioning the Emperor, but for some reason it was left unfinished. Boilly enjoyed working with a large cast of characters, but his instinct was to concentrate on typical, not extraordinary events. When in two companion pieces the industrialist Oberkampf, his wife, sons and daughters pose nonchalantly by a stream, Boilly is intent on their private relationships, involving a memorial to the heir who died and the role of a mother in a family of the *haute bourgeoisie.* He ignores Oberkampf's importance in the country's economy – there is in his oeuvre nothing like his friend Isabey's sketch of Napoleon visiting a textile factory in Rouen. Boilly's point of view was firmly civilian and apolitical. The Empire brought his patrons security and peace. Not until 1814 did the sound of foreign cannons disrupt their comfortable routines.

It requires an exercise of imagination to understand that in Napoleon's France most people, even most men, were civilians. In 1802, after the conclusion of the Peace of Amiens, droves of rich and fashionable English men and women, who for ten long years had been deprived of the pleasures of the Grand Tour, converged on Paris by packet boat, *diligence* and *berline,* where they were amazed at the numbers of the soldiers strutting round the city in flamboyant uniforms. England prided itself on being able to recruit its armies by devices no more systematic than pressing the king's shilling into the hands of a drunken wretch in a dingy tavern and its navies by means of the press gangs. France, like its Continental rivals, relied on conscription. Its economy, in the eyes of Napoleon, was geared to war. But many Frenchmen shared the views of the temporary tourists: the heart of the nation was found in its capital, where pleasure ruled.

No contemporary painter in France could compete with Boilly's sense of the panorama of the nation's life; and yet having made his home or rather homes in Paris, for he was often on the move, his comments on Napoleon's France involve just that one place. Paris was easily the most lively city in the country, much the biggest, and thanks to the Emperor's projects the builders were continually busy there, laying out streets, erecting arches and columns to the army, temples to religion and to commerce, digging foundations for one palace (the palace of the King of Rome), redeveloping others (the Louvre and the Tuileries), siting markets for the growing population and yet always struggling to catch up, for the number of inhabitants topped over half a million, possibly 650,000, at the end of the Empire, having at last regained the figures of 1789. Apart from the few who made it a sign of their provincial loyalty that they would stick by Lyon or Marseille, under Napoleon the most ambitious Frenchmen made their way to Paris.

A government career, as a Senator, a Tribune, a *chef de bureau*, a clerk, a copyist, gave to the dedicated a secure income – and the jobs of a prefect, subprefect or *maire* were best secured through connections in Paris. It was only in Paris, too, that there was a community devoted to making money large enough to create a style of life recognizable as distinctively upper middle class. In 1800 six partners formed a company in the Hôtel de Longueville to manufacture tobacco. One, Pierre Antoine Robillard, lived in a house valued at 145,000 francs in Place Vendôme; another, his nephew Jacques-Florent, also a Robillard, soon bought a house in the Chaussée d'Antin for 130,000 francs and then for 290,000 further francs four other properties in Paris, a farm near Orbais and hectares of woodland at St-Martin d'Ablois. A third partner, Bernard-Jean Etienne Delaître, came from a landowning family whose members had been in the army, the law and finance. With such entrepreneurs in charge the business prospered, so that in 1807–08 it paid 600,000 francs for buildings between Rue Grange-Batelière and Boulevard Montmartre that became its new centre of operations. Meanwhile, Jacques-Florent became a regent and later a *censeur* of the Bank of France and in 1810 a baron of the Empire, so joining the small coterie of bankers who had achieved this rank.

It was during this period that Protestant financiers and industrialists resumed the place in French commercial life they had lost in 1685, the year when Louis XIV revoked the edict that had permitted to Huguenots a strictly limited form of toleration. The Says from Nîmes had fled to Amsterdam and Geneva, from where Jean-Etienne tentatively returned to Lyon, where he dealt in silks, then to Paris, where he took to working in foreign exchange. His son, Jean-Baptiste, ran a cotton mill in the Pas-de-Calais from 1804 to 1813, but his heart lay in writing and in 1803 he published the first edition of his *Treatise on Political Economy*. A second brother, Horace, who died young at the Siege of Acre, trained at the Ecole Polytechnique and married a Delaroche, a doctor's daughter from Geneva (her oldest brother, as a partner to a Delessert, was to be a notable businessman in Le Havre), while the third brother, Louis, went from Abbeville, as a calico manufacturer, to Nantes, where, in association with another Delessert, he ran a sugar beet factory until he settled in Paris, still a sugar refiner. From Louis descended the dynasty of the Says, which became enormously rich and married into princely families all over Europe. Their story lasts far beyond the time of Napoleon, but it was under Napoleon that they had the chance to be accepted into the society of the wealthy. Careers were now open to Protestants with the necessary talents, and they took their chance.

The success of the Napoleonic marshals proved to be more

ephemeral. In the Faubourg St-Germain, the old nobility, many of whom had kept their lands as well as their heads, lived side by side with the brash and vulgar dukes and counts who owed everything to the Corsican upstart. One way of keeping them loyal to himself was to give them titles and property outside France – if he lost, they lost too – but they betrayed their *nouveau riche* instincts by buying huge estates outside Paris. In the latter days of the Empire, the visitor to the Île-de-France could find the Duke of Rovigo at Nainville, the Duke of Massa at Plessis-Piquet, the Duke of Otranto at Pontcarré and the Duke of Auerstädt at Savigny. Old nobles survived, especially in the west, the centre and the south, provided that they had returned from exile before the sales of appropriated land had gone through, but they found that under Napoleon it was best to be discreet. If they finally rallied to him when he married into the Habsburg family, they had to wait until he fell to try to resume that key role in national affairs that had been theirs in the previous century. In the days of the Restoration (1814–30), many would emerge from obscurity, but some had begun that retreat into a private world that is now the French norm for large sections of the ancient aristocracy, whose members find it hard enough to hold on to their estates in spite of Napoleonic inheritance laws to be too concerned about the fate of a government or even a regime. After the Revolution of 1830 made the bourgeois king Louis-Philippe King of the French, his first two Prime Ministers were his own banker, Laffitte, and Casimir Périer, both of them men of the *haute bourgeoisie*, and a later Prime Minister was the former Marshal Soult, who survived defeat at the Battle of Waterloo to become an elder statesman. The new men had begun to arrive in the time of Napoleon, and at least until the collapse of the Second Empire in 1870 it was they who directed the course French politics should take. Under Napoleon they had little desire or chance to influence events; their role was to co-operate. At his factory at Jouy, Boilly's Oberkampf had modernized the process of printed textiles, but his aim, as the double family portrait makes clear, was to found a dynasty of gentlemen.

If the grander *haute bourgeoisie* longed for a tranquil life devoted to the amassing of riches, they could not entirely escape the effect of warfare on a militaristic regime. Nobody could miss news of a relative or acquaintance dead on a distant field, their wives regretted the loss of muslin (from India) and mahogany (from Central America) and sugar (from the islands of the Caribbean), and even the richest industrialist might suffer from the effects of trade war (in 1811 some had to seek the Emperor's help). The good fortune of Nantes and Bordeaux had ended with the closure of long-distant trade routes across the sea (a similar fate hit many towns in the Netherlands and north Germany), but cross-Continental traders did well (the problems of the Lyon silk trade came only in the 1830s). The war economy that Napoleon forced on all areas he controlled implied the value of a common market stretching far beyond the borders of France; and yet by instinct he inherited the views of Colbert (and Louis XIV) that the economic good fortune of one country must be won at the expense of another. The British had started to follow the ideas of Adam Smith, and, as they captured one colony after another and so were on the way to being the one worldwide power (the Spaniards and Portuguese would soon lose their American possessions), the more universal trade became, the better it suited them. If Britain was in Napoleon's phrase a nation of shopkeepers, then France was a land of *rentiers*. The British chose commercial enterprise, the French financial security.

The contrast between the countrysides of the two countries could not have been sharper. While the general Act of Enclosure (1801) had speeded up the ending of medieval strip farming in Britain, in

France most peasants were determined to keep the land that they had grabbed in 1789, even if the poorest of them remained poor because they were left with strips that were uneconomic to run. The agricultural revolution across the Channel, fanning out from the East Midlands and East Anglia, was slowly spreading to the rest of England. In France, the process of change was slower, for France would be a land of peasant farmers at least until 1950.

In remote parts of the country there was little sign of change. In 1806 the prefect of Haute-Vienne complained to the Minister of the Interior:

> Agriculture is still in its childhood in this department; run by routine and ignorance it makes little progress. In vain have some individuals wanted to introduce new methods or improve the old ones . . . the mass of growers . . . stick invincibly to their antique ways and look on any kind of change as dangerous.[1]

What he failed to note is that, if the harvest was too plentiful, the price of corn went down and farmers failed to recoup their costs. In these circumstances, with no adequate marketing organization to help them, there was no incentive to do better. While peasants were divided over whether to use a sickle or a scythe to cut the corn, there was little likelihood that farm machinery would be modernized. As the harvest involved entire villages, it was the special concern of *maires*, who gave orders that every able-bodied person should take part and who, if necessary, would arrange for extra help from other areas; and, similarly, gleaning became more and more regimented as a communal activity.

If bread was one necessity of life, drink was the other, and in certain parts of the country viticulture was a lucrative pursuit – that is, where wine was exported to other parts of France or abroad. The proceeds went chiefly to the owner of the vineyards, so that there were many rich growers in Beaune in Burgundy, and the proprietor of Moët et Chandon had the good fortune to have studied with Napoleon at Brienne and so came to supply the Empress Joséphine with champagne. By contrast, the châteaux of Bordeaux suffered from the restriction placed on trade with the English, the traditional lovers of claret, and even *grands crus* like Château Margaux and Château Lafite changed hands. There was work for a whole peasant family in the weeks while the grapes were harvested, began to ferment and were stored in barrels. But precisely because the wine industry at its best was so efficient, employment was erratic. Some of Napoleon's agricultural ventures, designed to make up for the loss of British goods, such as the development of sugar beet and the cultivation of crops from which indigo could be extracted, were of little use to master or man. The prefect of the Tarn grumbled that the trouble with indigo production was that nobody knew how much profit would be made on sales. Attempts to set up a monopoly for tobacco growers were resented in the countryside and Napoleon's insistence that there should be more mulberries for the silk trade was criticized by those, such as a writer in the *Annuaire* for the department of the Drôme, who realized that not all soils were equally appropriate for the task. Like many other dictators before and since, Napoleon wanted to be an innovator in rural areas, while most of the peasants hated the very thought of change. A peasant needed dung for his crops and so needed to keep livestock. He was perturbed when horses were taken away to suit the cavalry and he had to make do with oxen, or when there were outbreaks in 1807 and 1811 of swine fever or in 1814 of cattle sickness or when his flocks were threatened by wolves. In coping with this last threat the Imperial government proved useful. Between 1805 and 1815 more than 15,000 wolves were killed. The woods were not yet free of them, but at least it was now government policy to make forested alpine regions safer for country folk to walk in.

Over such regions, as indeed in much of rural France, Imperial edicts had less authority than the Emperor liked to imagine. As a general rule, the further a district was from Paris, the less it was affected by the dictats of the centralized administration. In every department the prefect was supposed to be lodged, but a zealous official in the Landes, one Méchin, was soon complaining to the Minister of the Interior that in the town of Mont-de-Marsan he could not find anywhere to live; and subprefects were even more vulnerable to the truculent moods of the local inhabitants, as when one St-Geniès, appointed subprefect of Villeneuve d'Agen, soon found that his Parisian ways involved him in a duel with a local ruffian, which quickly brought his term of office to an end. A *maire*, unless he was *maire* of a large town, did not yet count for much in local affairs. The subprefect of Annecy reported that three-quarters of his *maires* could scarcely sign their names.

Napoleon was well aware that he needed to educate his countrymen if they were to become modern French men, but he made only a beginning to the task of making them literate and numerate. The *maires* were supposed to set up primary schools, but a prefect of the Côtes-du-Nord was only too typical in his frustrated reaction to the lack of effort by communes, which either did not establish schools or could not find the *instituteurs* to man them. In 1808 the prefects hopefully announced that everyone in France understood French and blamed the survival of *patois* on the clergy, but in many parts of the country *patois* was the normal means of communication even in schools; and in Brittany large sections of the population spoke Breton and in Alsace the advance of French at the expense of German was slow. It was also a struggle to impose metric weights and measures on an uncomprehending people.

In one respect, however, the government had an ever increasing effect on country life. The demands of Napoleon's war machine meant that news of what was happening in the outside world began to penetrate every area, and those who were behind the times soon had to learn to cope with the present reality of requisitioning and conscription. It was above all the call to serve the Emperor, especially towards the end of his reign, that caused the most offence. Early on, Napoleon's battles had appealed to young bachelors in search of adventure, but in 1813 it was a different matter for the father of three children who was asked to leave his farm at the age of forty. While the rich bourgeois managed to secure exemption for his sons, the poor ignorant peasant had no way of protecting himself except by flight or by just not answering the call to arms. In 1809, after the end of the brief war against Austria, as many as 100,000 men were pardoned for failing to take part in the campaign. From 1812 on, more and more men deserted, and when the Empire collapsed, first in 1814, then in 1815, there were far too many men in the countryside who had just enough military training to settle scores with their enemies or to take to brigandage.

Two hundred years after Napoleon came to power, it may seem clear that in the early nineteenth century the future lay with the minority of French men and women who worked in industry. Since the reign of Louis XIV France had been noted for its luxury trades and its one large industry, textiles. During the revolutionary years of the early 1790s, luxury trades had suffered because austere souls disapproved of items of luxury and because mobs had destroyed them. Under Napoleon they revived, and rich men filled their châteaux and hôtels with Empire furniture and furnishings, and their wives and daughters dressed in the latest fashions. Expensive habits, as they returned, did not help the development of a mass textile market. Oberkampf at Jouy and the drapers of Louviers and

Elbeuf demanded high prices for quality goods; and if the cotton printers welcomed the temporary resumption of trade with England in 1802–03, since it made imported cotton cheaper, this was not good news for French spinners, who worked from home, or the merchant manufacturers, who controlled the domestic weavers. Even before Napoleon imposed a blockade against Britain, the protectionists had got their way when a decree in February 1806 forbade the import of cotton cloth and muslin – much of this came from India – and placed high duties on raw cotton and yarn. This law, in keeping with much of Napoleon's economic policy, was true to the ideas of Colbert in the time of Louis XIV. Napoleon, like Colbert, wished to dictate the patterns of trade and, as Colbert had seen the free-trading Dutch as his chief enemy, so Napoleon took a similar view of the British. His attitude appealed to many entrepreneurs, like the Sevène brothers, whose factory he had visited in 1802, the visit recorded in Isabey's picture that announced his involvement in the creation of the nation's wealth (ironically the picture was never finished). Steadily, a native cotton industry took root. Around St-Quentin there was a large concentration of linen workers before 1789. As their production rate fell from 1807, so that of the local cotton workers took off. Cotton cloth had the advantage of costing half the price of linen cloth. If in St-Quentin modern industry was in its birth pangs, then it was born in Rouen, Lille and Mulhouse.

The impetus came first from close contact with England. A 1786 free-trade treaty with England had driven many firms into bankruptcy, and yet, by copying the English, French manufacturers introduced spinning jennies and mules into their factories – and later when the contact was cut, closure of seaborne trade led to an opening up of transcontinental trade. The lack of adequate supplies of raw cotton stifled growth, but the simultaneous lack of English competition enabled local firms to modernize their methods, so that after 1815 the newly equipped textile firms flourished. Because it was needed for bleaching, starching and dyeing textiles, the chemical industry also progressed. In the textile trade amateurs who loved tinkering with machines had made technical advances. By contrast, trained scientists had most to contribute by altering chemical processes, and France had excellent chemists who were fascinated by the practical implications of their discoveries. In pre-revolutionary days the great Lavoisier controlled the manufacture of gunpowder. And now one of Napoleon's Ministers of the Interior, Chaptal, who as long ago as 1782 had set up a firm to produce sulphuric and chloric acids, in partnership with one of Napoleon's two chief Egyptian *savants*, the chemist Berthollet, added factories at Neuilly, Fos (in the south) and Nanterre. The difficulty of acquiring Spanish natural soda for the soap makers of Marseille led Napoleon to order the use of artificial soda, a decision that further enriched chemical businesses in the area. Iron merchants, on the other hand, were reluctant to use modern knowledge to improve the technology of their forges. Many refused to replace scarce wood with charcoal, so that they flourished in areas where iron ore deposits were close to forests. For a long time the British, with much less available wood, had sited their foundries close to coal mines; and it was the Walloon Belgians rather than the French who were the first on the Continent to take on the new techniques.

During the 1790s the revolutionaries had abolished the guilds, and the passing on of manual skills by a system of apprenticeship had become harder to enforce, but artisans and industrial workers had gained little freedom from the changes. The ending of the distinction in furniture making between an *ébéniste* and a *menuisier* enabled the firm of Jacob Frères, later Jacob-Desmalter, to dominate the trade in the Empire style, but this did not help carpenters. Paris and Lyon remained the homes of craftsmen, who worked long hours for low pay. Elsewhere, in mills, mines and factories, conditions were often worse. The law sided with the owner and the entrepreneur, and a trade union movement had yet to begin. Napoleon's France was uneasily poised between an old-fashioned and a modern economy, and all too many Frenchmen had the worst of both worlds. Napoleon gave France an illusion of prosperity because it was the countries that he defeated that suffered most during his reign. In the end France had its Waterloo – and found out that war did not pay. But, as in Britain, the changeover from a wartime to a peacetime economy caused new traumas, so that in the years after 1815 social tensions seemed worse than during the time of the Empire.

Meanwhile, more French men had learned more about other inhabitants of the Continent than any generation of French men before them. Lyon and Strasbourg flourished because they were open to countries well beyond the borders even of the France of 1792. No city had benefited so much from Napoleon's rule as Paris, from which, as once from Rome, all roads radiated to the major cities of France and the Grand Empire. Paris was the centre of the banking system, of much modern industry as well as of most traditional crafts, of the law, of education, of the new bureaucracy. Paris ran France, just as France ran Europe.

Of life in Napoleon's capital city the best visual witness is Boilly. He lacked the moral and social convictions that give power to the pictures of Daumier, Courbet and Millet in the middle years of the century – he never showed how unjust or miserable human existence can be; indeed he treated the vagaries of his world as an excuse for whimsical delight in the whirligig of the *comédie humaine*. In Napoleon's France it was good that there was one artist who made a profit from knowing how to smile.

11

NAPOLEON'S EUROPE

In the revolutionary period, French cartoonists of any political persuasion or none had enjoyed ridiculing the supposed sexual promiscuity of the 'Austrian whore' Marie-Antoinette, the shameless measuring up of a naked 'France' by the Financial Minister Necker, a plump Louis XVI being recaptured after his flight to Varennes (with the inscription 'fat birds fly slowly': '*les gros oiseaux ont le vol lent*'), a young couple marrying *au naturel* on a boat in accord with republican rites while a *sansculotte* makes off with their clothes, Robespierre guillotining the executioner after he has had all other French men guillotined. Once he was in power Napoleon never allowed such shameless attacks. It was left to English caricaturists to make fun of him. In England, there was a long tradition of political satire, which stretched back to the time of Hogarth and Swift and which would reach forward to the days of Cruikshank and Dickens; and at the start of the nineteenth century its master, in art, was Gillray and, in literature, would be Byron. In English politics, Gillray had subjects enough for laughter: the red-faced

King George and his scraggy queen, the gross Prince Regent, a Voluptuary under the horrors of Indigestion, a scrawny Pitt, a ballooning Fox, the drunken Sheridan, the prissy Burke. But with the coming of the French Revolution, war and the rise of Napoleon he had a grander topic. There were national stereotypes to call on – the plump, beef-eating John Bull or Britannia, the tall, thin, deceitful, lustful Frenchman, but Gillray never bothered to check that his 'Boney' was like the original. Napoleon thus became a figment of his imagination, a slender Belshazzar beside a bulging Joséphine, a madman in a fit, a would-be crowned apple floating downstream amid republican turds, a Gulliver sailing on a tiny boat in a miniature basin under the concentrated gaze of the King of Brobdingnag, who has the unmistakeable features of King George. In February 1805 he produced his masterpiece. *The Plumb-Pudding in Danger*, subtitled 'State Epicures Taking un Petit Souper', seems to anticipate by months the results of the Battles of Trafalgar and Austerlitz and by two years the situation that developed when one of the diners, Pitt, was dead, for by the time of the peace of Tilsit with the Tsar, it seemed as if Napoleon was in control of the Continent, as Britain already had grabbed for itself mastery over the ocean. A quotation – ' "The great Globe itself, and all which it inherit", is too small to satisfy such insatiable appetite' – shows how intuitively Gillray grasped that the world was not enough for the greedy French and English.

The French revolutionary and Napoleonic wars continued and concluded a struggle for supremacy between France and Britain that had already been going on, on and off, for a period of a hundred years. In every major European war between 1689 and 1789 there had been one constant: the French and the British had been on opposite sides. William of Orange had come to England in 1688 not so much to promote civil liberties or the Protestant cause – he was a good ally, after all, of the Catholic Holy Roman

Emperor – as to add British resources to those of Holland in his obsessive fight against Louis xiv; and after his sudden death in 1702 his policy was continued during the War of the Spanish succession by the governments of his sister-in-law, Queen Anne. For a generation after the Treaty of Utrecht (1713), the wise rule of Sir Robert Walpole in Britain and of Cardinal Fleury in France had pursued an ideal of prosperity at the price of peace, until the cost of good neighbourliness seemed too high when the young Habsburg princess Maria Theresa, Britain's natural ally and France's natural foe, was determined to win the right to succeed in Austria for herself. In mid-century, while a diplomatic revolution temporarily changed France and Austria into allies, Britain and France remained consistent in their rivalry throughout a fresh bout of hostility on the subcontinent involving the East India Company and the Compagnie des Indes, the nine-year French and Indian war in North America and the concomitant European Seven Years War. As in all three contests France was humiliated, it might seem only fair that in the American war of Independence France's intervention on the side of the colonists should prove decisive and that in 1783, when a treaty at Versailles ended the contest, France's prestige had been restored. The restoration did not last long. Two events, one the previous year, the other the following year, pointed to a future that no one could have expected then. In 1782 Admiral Rodney, by winning the Battle of the Saints with new tactics, not only secured for Britain its West Indian colonies but did wonders for the reputation of the British navy. In 1784 George iii took the bravest political gamble of his reign by appointing the youthful younger William Pitt to be Prime Minister. Rodney was the mentor of the commanders of the age of Nelson, and in every major sea battle between Britain and France from 1793 to 1815 the men who looked back to Rodney were victorious. Similarly, Pitt had a remarkable impact on British government finances, so that, whereas between 1783 and 1792, when France went back to war, the ministers of Louis XVI lurched from one scheme to another to fight off bankruptcy, during the period 1784 to 1793 Pitt made an insolvent exchequer rich. By the time that Britain joined the first coalition against France, its attitude towards European warfare seemed based on assumptions that were drawn from common sense. It would use its naval power to dominate the ocean and the seas of Europe and its seemingly bottomless wealth to subsidize Continental friends to produce the armies to defeat France on land. In 1805, when Gillray drew his witty cartoon, this policy had proved only partially successful. Britannia indeed ruled the Atlantic waves, but despite British gold it looked as if nothing could check Napoleon from carving out for himself the landmass of Europe. Neither power could do much to hurt the other. Britain by following its traditional habit of blockading enemy ports, stifled the colonial trade of seafaring nations like the Netherlands, Spain or France itself and brought disaster to Amsterdam, Cadiz, Nantes and Bordeaux. Napoleon felt compelled to devise a riposte. One scheme would prevent British commerce from trading with the Continent; another would integrate Europe under the suzerainty of France.

The most important result of Austerlitz may have been the death of Pitt, for it was a dispirited and exhausted man who died in January 1806, his latest attempt to beat Napoleon an obvious failure. Had he lived through the year, he would have become still more dejected. With Prussia as well as Austria crushed, only Russia could halt Napoleon, who could now decide the fate of Germany and restore the Empire of Charlemagne.

Up until the treaty of Amiens in 1802, which brought about a truce rather than a peace in the twenty-odd-year struggle between Britain and France, the French, even at their most revolutionary, adopted strategies in the conduct of international relations that derived from seventeenth-century attitudes.

By the time that Louis XIV came of age in 1661, Cardinals Richelieu and Mazarin had broken the ring of Habsburg encirclement that had tightened around France when Charles V had been King of Castile and Aragon, duke of the Netherlands, Holy Roman Emperor and the dominant power in Italy. None of his successors owned all his European possessions, but Habsburgs in Madrid and Vienna saw value in the family firm cooperating, so that it was only when the chains of the alliance were broken that France was free to react. Having taken Catalonia on the north side of the Pyrenees from Spain, Louis felt able to advance on his eastern borders. He made gains in the north-east in French Flanders, in the south-east in Savoy but above all in the east, where he grabbed Franche Comté and Alsace. To protect these acquisitions, the foremost engineer of the day, Vauban, built a line of forts, often two deep. France, it seemed, was almost secure because it had found 'natural' frontiers: at the Pyrenees, at the Alps and along the banks of the Rhine. Overreaching himself in the north-east, Louis XIV had to restore some enclaves and to let the Dutch protect themselves by installing garrisons in some Belgian towns, but in the eighteenth century his indolent great-grandson, Louis XV, pursued a similar line, so that, after he won Lorraine peacefully, he freed his successors to concentrate on the area where France was most vulnerable to attack: on its north-eastern borders.

Even the weakness of Louis XV could not disguise the fundamental truth of European politics: that France was inherently the most powerful nation on the Continent. After Russia, it was the largest country. Without exception, it was the most populous. Unlike two of its neighbours, Italy and Germany, it was unified. Unlike a third, Spain, unified as recently as 1714, it had a long history of progressive unification. Whereas Madrid had become the

capital of Spain simply because Philip II realized that one insignificant village, as Madrid had been in 1560, was conveniently in the
centre of his Iberian kingdoms, Paris was a capital around which
France had been created. Although the French kings had recognized
that the newer provinces should have some institutions that
acknowledged their recent status, so that Besançon (in Franche-
Comté), Strasbourg (in Alsace) and Nancy (in Lorraine) had their
own law courts, the preponderance of the centre over the periphery
seemed the norm in French politics. The more power Paris had, the
more efficient the government of France, and the more effectively
France dictated to other countries how they should run their affairs.
At the end of his life, Louis XV realized this, but died before he
could enforce it. His grandson, Louis XVI, was too indecisive, too
nice, to be ruthless, and his rule collapsed because he was unable
to rule. The story of revolutionary power politics ended with the
triumph of a despot, but even before Napoleon was First Consul,
the federalists or Girondins, so called because many of them came
from the area of the city of Bordeaux (capital of the new department named after the Gironde), had been outmanoeuvred. If
France was to count, the people must be given their head. A
committee, even if Robespierre was prominent on it, did not give
an adequate sense of direction, still less the inaptly named Directory, but, though many Frenchmen hated to admit it, there was no
alternative to Paris as the capital and an absolute monarch installed
there.

From the time of Louis XIV France enjoyed unequalled cultural
prestige. Not only had French replaced Latin as the lingua franca
of diplomacy, but French had become the tongue of the European
ruling class. From Madrid to St Petersburg, sophisticated men and
women communicated in French. Learned men – Leibniz and
Newton or Samuel Johnson and the French monks he encountered
on his travels – might still read, write and talk to each other in

Latin, but the *beau monde* had long since abandoned it. While Frederick II, King of Prussia, wrote political treatises in French and corresponded with and offered friendship to Voltaire, until he was repaid with ridicule, Catherine II, the Tsarina, courted Diderot and invited him to visit her in Russia. A generation later, Metternich, Austrian Foreign Minister, by choice expressed himself in French. As late as the mid-nineteenth century, when Tolstoy wished to give *War and Peace* a sense of the Napoleonic age, he retained enough of the culture of the period to be able to start his epic in French. By contrast, in England, whose first four Georges were electors of Hanover (and later its Kings), only one among the leading Whigs, Carteret, talked easily in German, and his unique ability to converse with his sovereign made him a man inherently untrustworthy.

With the French language went the arts of civilized living. French terms were normal in ballet and fencing, because the rules had been fixed at the French court; and French *cuisine* and French *couturiers* were already on the way to the fame that was taken for granted in the nineteenth century. Louis XIV's France was admired as the centre of the luxury trades, a position maintained by Louis XV, whose most tasteful *maîtresse en titre*, the Marquise de Pompadour, patronized the ceramics of Sèvres, and willy-nilly by Louis XVI, whose wife spent a fortune on the furniture of France's distinguished *ébénistes*.

Voltaire was cruel when he mocked German princelings for their tiny armies that could scarcely fit on to the stage at Vicenza, their ridiculous obsession with the quarterings in their coats of arms and their anxiety to ape the King of France by keeping a mistress. The consequences of the self-importance of petty princes have been happy. Typically, Brunswick and Cassel boast excellent art galleries, Frankfurt and Stuttgart fine opera companies; and many may prefer the light, airy rococo style of a German schloss, as in Tiepolo's staircase ceiling at the Residenz in Würzburg, or of the secluded pilgrimage church Die Wies, to the pompous baroque manner encouraged by Versailles. To Voltaire and his fellow countrymen, however, German achievements were too provincial to be taken seriously. Even if in the visual arts Catholic Germans drew inspiration from contacts with Italy and music drew on a culture that meant there could be a Bach in almost any wealthy Protestant town or court, in politics most German electors, dukes, margraves, counts and councillors of the free cities looked nervously to France. France traditionally manipulated Germans by its policy of divide and rule. It was virtually impossible for the Holy Roman Emperor to be sure that all his subjects would stay loyal, at least not since the crisis of 1683 when the Turks camped outside the gates of Vienna. To destabilize Austria, France had only to look to Bavaria or Baden or Cologne or Saxony. Once, after 1740, Prussia had emerged as Austria's rival, the French had a problem they failed to solve as long as the great Frederick was king, but the logic of the new situation was to apply methods against the Hohenzollerns that had been devised to deal with the Habsburgs. The revolutionaries demonstrated that Prussia, like Austria, could be defeated. Napoleon showed that both could be crushed.

France had other spheres of influence: the Netherlands, Switzerland, Italy, Spain and Poland. Until 1648, in international law the United Provinces (the northern Netherlands) and Switzerland had been parts of the Empire, but in fact both had long ceased to acknowledge the authority of either the Emperor or that of any Habsburg cousins. What mattered more were the divisions, mainly linguistic and religious, within both the Netherlands and Switzerland. Parts of each spoke French, parts of each some kind of German or Germanic tongue, some Swiss spoke Italian or Romansch, parts of each were Calvinist, some Swiss Protestants were Waldensians (of a sect then with medieval origins), some

Dutch Protestants were Lutherans or Mennonites or Anabaptists or Amish, most Belgians, many Swiss and some Dutch were Catholics, and lots of Jews lived in Amsterdam. Towards these peoples France took no firm line of principle. At the risk of making the English anxious, they would like the southern, Austrian Netherlands (Belgium) and the northern, independent Netherlands to be client states; they also hoped that the Swiss would understand their interest in Geneva, keep the 'Spanish' road (or roads) through their lands closed to Habsburg troops, provide the French King, like the Pope, with devoted guards, but, though the French tried to conquer the Belgians and the Dutch, they never set out to divert massive armies into the mountains of Switzerland. All Belgium and several provinces of the United Provinces lay west and south of the estuaries of the Rhine, but Bâle, or Basel, was the only major Swiss city on the river. The fate of both parts of the Netherlands mattered to Britain, Prussia and Austria as well as to France. Nobody fretted over the Swiss, until France had a revolution.

Italy, like Germany, was a patchwork of small states, several of which had important international links and none of which was more than of a local consequence. Spanish Bourbons ruled in Sicily and Naples; Austria was the power in Milan. The Papal States were supposed to give the Pope freedom from the pressures that Catholic princes could exert, but in the late eighteenth century one Pope after another did what Austria or Spain or Portugal or France or all four told him to do. Venice had been a republic for a thousand years, but the city was appreciated not so much for its glorious past as for the delights it offered foreign tourists who rode in gondolas, dressed up for Carnival or applauded the girl violinists who played Vivaldi and the players with commedia dell'arte training who acted Goldoni. In Florence the line of the Medici had died out, and the once-faithful ally of France was rejuvenated by the Habsburg heir, the Archduke Leopold, who showed there that he was the most enlightened ruler of the late eighteenth century. French kings had long looked with envious eyes on Italy: it was to be their republican successors who conquered it.

Spain could have become a junior partner of France when the Bourbon Philip v succeeded a Habsburg with the help of his grandfather Louis xiv, but a partnership was forbidden by international treaty; and not until 1762 was there a Family Compact between the two senior Bourbon kings (the King of the Two Sicilies was the junior, the third). Both Louis xv and Louis xvi allied with Charles iii against Britain, and the alliance distracted Britain from the attempt to subdue the Americans, but the Spaniards could not snatch back Gibraltar. When the fool Charles iv succeeded his father, he shillyshallied between defying the French republic and abjectly appeasing it. Spain, the French tended to assume, would follow where France led. The ablest politicians, writers and administrators in Spain were the *afrancesados*. A French observer could be forgiven for thinking that Spain was a natural counterweight to Portugal, which called itself Britain's oldest ally. No one could have predicted that a few years later Spain and Portugal would be on the same side, with Britain, against France.

The most forlorn of France's allies was Poland, sadly too far to the east for France to support it. In the War of the Polish succession in the 1730s, the candidate of France, Stanislas Leczynski, Louis xv's father-in-law, was the loser, but he was happy to be consoled with the Duchy of Lorraine (and so a Lorrainer called Chopin went to Warsaw, married a Polish girl and had a musical son whose career flourished in Paris). If Louis xv could not decide who should rule Poland, still less could he stop the first partition of the country in 1771. In the 1790s French armies drove back the armies of Austria and Prussia, but, even had it wished to do so, the republic of France failed to stop those countries, instigated by the Tsarina Catherine, from dismembering and destroying Poland in 1793 and 1795.

Only if France defeated Austria and Prussia in Germany and pushed the Russians eastwards would France revive Polish aspirations, and these circumstances did not arise before 1807.

It was the French republic that laid the foundations on which Napoleon could build an Empire that extended far beyond the borders of France, as one after another countries within France's sphere of influence became the subjects or the satellites of France.

At the turn of the year 1792–3, the republican Convention declared that it offered 'fraternity and aid to all peoples who want to recover their liberty', and it told its generals to grant freedom to govern itself to any territory that they overran. The revolutionaries saw their cause as embattled: it was the reactionary rulers of Austria and Prussia who had provoked war, the land of France that had been first invaded. Avignon and the Comtat Venaissin (papal enclaves), Nice and Savoy (in the Kingdom of Sardinia) freely voted to join France. Other lands were given no choice. By the end of March 1793, the Convention had announced that Belgium and much of the land on the left bank of the Rhine were now parts of La Grande Nation, further annexations in 1795 and 1798 gave France its 'natural' north-eastern border and in 1799 France also took over Piedmont, leaving its King only the island of Sardinia; the neighbouring island of Corsica had no choice but to be French. Such an enlarged France was just the core of France's Europe. The great nation was soon ringed by a series of sister republics with names redolent of the classical past: the northern, Batavian Republic (the Netherlands), the Helvetic Republic (Switzerland) in the centre and then a group that straddled the Italian peninsula, from the Ligurian (around Genoa), via the Cisalpine (in the north-east) and the Roman (a band across central Italy) to the Parthenopean in

the south. Venice, its proud republican story curtailed by Napoleon, had been given, along with the Venetian *terra firma*, to
Austria, but elsewhere Habsburgs were cruelly treated. They were
stripped of Modena and the Grand Duchy of Tuscany, while for a
time Napoleon courted the Spanish house of Bourbon Parma. The
King of the Two Sicilies, one of which was Naples, had been left
with only his island thanks to the British navy. In 1801 he got the
mainland back. Another member of the family was still Duke of
Parma, and to his son was bequeathed a kingdom of Etruria.
Napoleon also got rid of the Roman republic, so that even before
he had negotiated the concordat with the Pope, the Pope was back
again in the Papal States. But he was not satisfied to leave things
as they were. After he signed the Treaty of Amiens with Britain in
March 1802, he annexed Piedmont, Elba and Piombino and
occupied Parma. He had made clear that the shape of the political
map of Italy would be fashioned by him, just as he felt free to bully
the Germans or the Spaniards into making whatever concessions he
decided were appropriate.

Being First Consul of a republic, from 1802 for life, officially
Napoleon stood for republicanism. In the eighteenth century the
most incompetent of European regimes – those that governed the
Dutch, the Swiss and the Venetians – had been republics. The one
kingdom that managed its affairs even worse was Poland, where
important decisions in parliament, the Diet, had to be unanimous.
Only the French saw virtue in ridding themselves of absolutist
rulers, but once Louis XVI's head had been chopped off their
republican values became contagious. Ancient Rome had been a
great power long before Julius Caesar, and in 1800 there were
educated men queuing up to be Catos or Brutuses or Gracchi. At
first the French found local notables who combined idealism with
attention to their own careers – Count Melzi d'Eril in Lombardy,
Durazzo the last doge of Genoa, Rutger Jan Schimmelpennick,

who became Grand Pensionary of Holland – but, as it became clearer that French intervention was usually on French terms, the task of recruiting others proved hard. Those willing to serve were often despised or envied by their neighbours. Increasingly gaps in the new administrations were filled by French administrators. German-speakers from Alsace saw opportunities for advancement grow as more and more of Germany came under direct or indirect French rule. Some men became experts at the creation of new departments on the French model. There were still others who devoted themselves to the looting of art collections, a practice that went back to the removal of van Eyck and Rubens altarpieces from Belgium as early as 1795 and received a boost from the overwhelming success of Napoleon's first Italian campaign, when one by one the treasures of Parma, Modena, Milan and Bologna and, most spectacularly of all, sculptures, panel paintings and canvases from Rome were removed to the Louvre in Paris. It was also obvious that the French had no intention of paying for their conquests. Napoleon was obsessed with sound finance. To avoid any repetition of the disastrous inflation of the 1790s, he founded the Bank of France in 1800. To keep down the charges on government finance for his expeditions, he made his defeated enemies pay.

In 1802 both France and Britain were exhausted from their efforts and so signed the Peace Treaty of Amiens. As relations between them deteriorated, for neither side wished to leave things as they were, Napoleon, while angry that the British would not evacuate Malta, became ambitious to exercise control of more and more of the Continent. By renaming the Cisalpine Republic 'Italian', he seemed to be bent on irritating Francis II, the Holy Roman Emperor, one of whose traditional titles was King of Italy; and he created yet more offence by inviting the Pope to be present in Notre-Dame while he crowned himself the Emperor of the French, for such a papal trip had been made before only to recognize Pepin as King of the Franks, an event that was a preparation for the coronation in Rome of Charlemagne, Pepin's son, first of the Holy Roman Emperors. By using Carolingian symbolism, Napoleon made a claim to be the monarch of Western Europe. He demonstrated on the field of Austerlitz in 1805 that he had made good his claim; after victories at Jena and Auerstädt in 1806 and at Friedland in 1807 he was able to dictate what shape the new Carolingian Empire would take.

There were no republics left. Napoleon was Emperor of the French, with an empire extending from north of Antwerp to south of Parma, he was the protector of the Helvetic Confederation and the King of Italy (restricted to Lombardy, Emilia, Venetia and Istria). He gave his brothers kingdoms – Joseph Naples, Louis the Netherlands, Jérôme Westphalia and his brother-in-law Murat the grand Duchy of Berg (Lucien, with whom he had fallen out, got nothing) – and sixteen south German princes were forced into the unit known as the Confederation of the Rhine. Together, these states almost exactly re-created the Empire of Charlemagne. Austria, once the eastern mark of the Holy Roman Empire, had to make do with becoming a new Empire east of Germany. Prussia, which had never been part of that empire, retained little that had been in it, other than Brandenburg and Silesia.

In 1808, while at peace with Austria, Prussia and Russia, Napoleon's need to damage Britain led him to make the first of a series of fatal errors: he sent troops into the Iberian Peninsula. In Portugal, from which the royal family fled to the colony of Brazil, General Junot lost the Battle of Vimiero to an obscure former East India Company general named Wellesley, but in Spain Napoleon ejected the most important of the Bourbon-Parmas – he had already dethroned all members of the family in Italy – and sent his brother Joseph to be king (and so Murat was made Joachim I of Naples). Every year the limits to his empire-building were pushed back. When the Austrians defied him in 1809, and were beaten, Napoleon took Illyria and Carniola. In 1809, too, he gave his sister Elisa nominal authority over Etruria – as a woman she was incapable of ruling and her husband was a nonentity – and he stripped the Pope of his lands, on the ground that what Charlemagne had conceded he could take back. In this way the country of Italy was divided into just three parts: Imperial Italy (to the west), the Kingdom of Italy (to the east) and Naples (in the south). In the following year he deprived the Tsar's brother-in-law of the Duchy of Oldenburg. In 1811 from the borders of Portugal, where even Masséna could not oust British troops directed by Wellesley, to those of Russia, the whole Continent was controlled by Napoleon, divided into Imperial France, satellite kingdoms and duchies, the dependencies – the Helvetic Confederation, the enlarged Confederation of the Rhine and the new Grand Duchy of Warsaw – and the allies, insignificant like Baden or grand like Denmark, Austria and Prussia. He ruled more of Europe than had been in Charlemagne's and Charles v's dominions combined. Undefeated, but consigned to the periphery, were Russia and Britain and the areas linked with them – Sweden, Portugal, Sardinia, Sicily, Malta and the Ionian Islands. At the centre of the continent was France.

It suited Napoleon's purposes to stand for the integration of Europe, for in his mind that benefited France, and Europe too.

To bring Europeans closer together, Napoleon had to make it easier for them to communicate with one another. As the British had closed the sea routes, the subjects of the Empire had to travel by land. Sadly, many of the rivers, including the all-important Rhine, ran north and south rather than east and west, so to make them more useful for his purposes Napoleon envisaged building canals to connect the Baltic to the North Sea, the Rhine to the

Rhône, Amsterdam to Paris, the Channel to the Atlantic, but the money and the technology he needed were lacking. As with the Romans, his Empire must be built on roads. For over two centuries France had boasted of its inspectorate of *Ponts et Chaussées*, Bridges and Highways, and it was to this body of men that the Emperor's grand designs were entrusted. In 1811 he reminded his Minister of Finance:

> What matters now . . . is road works. The highway from Amsterdam to Antwerp will bring the first town to within twenty-hour hours of Paris, one from Hamburg to Wesel will bring Hamburg to within four days of Paris. That will ensure and strengthen the links of these areas to the Empire . . .

Shortly after, he reiterated an earlier suggestion that Paris should be at the centre of a network of twenty-seven radiating principal roads, either first or second class, that were the responsibility of the Imperial Treasury. Two hundred and two third-class roads, which ran between important towns, being more of local than of national importance, should be paid for partly by the departments through which they passed. Lower-class roads, radiating out from these towns, were to be in principle the responsibility of the department.

Though many of the workmen who built the roads were prisoners of war, Napoleon wanted those who directed the construction works to be treated with respect. Under the director-general of the *Ponts et Chaussées* there were 5 inspectors-general, 15 divisional inspectors, 134 chief engineers and 306 ordinary engineers. They wore special uniforms, a mark of the Emperor's approval. The roads that they made were seldom beyond the capacity of their eighteenth-century predecessors, but they achieved much more, notably in the passes they made in the Alps, such as at Mont Cenis. The crossing that Napoleon had made by way of the St Bernard in 1800 became less hazardous. Napoleon was determined that it would be simpler to move troops from France to Italy or from France to Spain, but he spent most money on the road that went from Paris via Soissons, Namur, Liège, Wesel and Münster to Hamburg. The modern motorist who tootles round the quieter parts of France still enjoys the benefits of Napoleon's vision, such as the trees that line the roads because once they may have shaded the heads of marching soldiers from the sun. Outside France, too, his influence is still felt, not just because on the Continent cars drive on the right. Napoleon provided Italy with a predecessor to the *autostrada del sole*, leading down from the north to Naples, and he made a road to Trieste that encouraged trade with Salonica. Along all these routes sped droves of Imperial postmen.

The director-general of the post was Lavalette, and Lavalette, who married into the Beauharnais family, was subject to the Minister of Finance. Every department had its principal sections and secondary sections and sections with the duty of distribution, all under the control of inspectors; there was also a distinct group entrusted with official mail, drawn in Piedmont, Belgium and the Rhineland from the local population. Lavalette aimed to keep mail circulating daily from Paris to Naples and Milan, to the bay of Cattaro (now Kotor in Montenegro), to Madrid and Lisbon; and once a week the Emperor received replies to his letters from Milan, once a fortnight from Naples. The cost of the post was determined according to a scale set by the distance from Paris, and this scale was divided into eleven zones. The system, first applied in France, was gradually extended to occupied territory, and, as territories were given independent status, so postal links with France were regulated by treaty. In Germany, the Prince of Taxis, who had organized the mail of the Holy Roman Empire, was in charge of

French Imperial mail. There was one postal service to Constantinople via Italy and Illyria, another to St Petersburg via Westphalia and Saxony. Side by side with this admirable system was a less reputable service whose purpose was to intercept other countries' diplomatic correspondence, with main centres in Turin, Genoa, Florence, Rome, Amsterdam and Hamburg. Some of France's enemies had more direct ways of checking up on the mail. Spanish guerillas were so effective at eliminating postmen that it is said that at the height of the Peninsular War four hundred men were needed to get a letter safely from Paris to Madrid. Once again, Paris was at the hub of the communications wheel, with spokes reaching out via Lille and Antwerp to Amsterdam, and via Lyon, Mont Cenis, Turin and Milan to Venice, but there was no similar spoke from Bordeaux via Toulouse and Marseille to Genoa. Everything in the Empire flowed to and from the capital.

Increasingly from 1806 the roads and the post were used by the armies of Le Grand Empire. Late in that year a Polish legion was given to Prince Poniatowski, and defeated Prussians were invited to join the regiment of La Tour d'Auvergne as mercenaries and Germans from the north of the Main that of Isembourg. Conscripts were recruited from the Kingdom of Italy, there was a Dalmatian legion, there were Dutch, Swiss and even Spanish soldiers. In 1808, when Napoleon raised conscripts in Italy, he got 5,500 Poles, 8,000 Saxons, 30,000 Bavarians, 15,000 from Württemberg, 6,000 from Baden. In the following year, at Wagram, only two-thirds of the army were from France. While Poles in white and red fought in Spain, Spaniards in scarlet and gold fought by the shores of the Baltic. When Napoleon invaded Russia in 1812, less than a third of the Grande Armée was French. His campaigns may have stirred up anti-French feeling all over Europe, but, just as thousands of French men, and some women, lived with memories of their journeys over many parts of Europe, so many other

Europeans had nostalgic feelings stirred by recollections of their campaigns on behalf of the Emperor. In 1837 Niklas Müller published his *Livre des chants pour les vétérans qui servirent dans la Grande Armée de Napoléon*, confident that it would be cherished by German veterans over twenty years after the Battle of Waterloo.

Old soldiers die, but bureaucracy goes on for ever. For a century before 1789, French ways of running a country had been fashionable, and the new Napoleonic version of these ideas turned out to be eminently exportable. Being authoritarian and modern, they were easy to apply.

Of his achievements, none in Napoleon's eyes equalled the *Code Napoléon*, and he made clear that it was a blessing for countries other than France. He told Joseph, when he went to take over his first kingdom: 'Establish the civil code in Naples. Everything not connected to you will wither away in a few years and what you would like to preserve will flourish – that is the great advantage of the civil code.' Months later he was insisting that 'Germany is adopting it, Spain will not delay to adopt it', and he was pressing Champagny to tell his former secretary Bourrienne to introduce it in the Hanseatic cities of north Germany. 'Please also write to M. Otto in Munich, to my chargé d'affaires at the court of the Prince Primate [the former Archbishop of Mainz] and the Grand Dukes of Hesse-Darmstadt and Baden to introduce the civil code surreptitiously as the law of their states . . .' He even bothered General Junot, who had pressing military matters to attend to, to demand if there was any reason why the civil code could not be introduced into Portugal.

Napoleon was too sanguine. Many defeated enemies were slow to abandon their ancient legal customs just because he recommended that they should. In Germany, the faculties of jurisprudence discussed the Code always with passion and sometimes with perspicacity. On the left bank of the Rhine it was accepted; indeed, it was said that peasants knew its clauses better than the verses of the Bible. In Westphalia, the model Napoleonic state where Jérôme Bonaparte was King, as feudal rights had been already abolished, Napoleon saw no reason why, in spite of noble opposition, the code should not be introduced in its entirety, and the official translator, one Leist, was not allowed to modify any of its terms – it came into operation between 1808 and 1810, followed by a similar process involving criminal procedure. In nearby Berg, Beugnot, who was in charge of the administration, was careful first to abolish serfdom and feudal privileges before then bringing the code into force. In Bavaria and Württemberg, staunch allies though they were, there was lively debate and the radical philosopher Feuerbach praised the way in which the code was one means by which lesser states in the Napoleonic system could be like the principal state, France. In Italy there was a like divergence of opinion and practice. As early as 1 January 1806, the code had the force of law in the Kingdom of Italy, was translated into Latin and Italian and was resisted by the aristocracy in matters of inheritance and by the clergy in the matter of divorce. In Naples Murat allowed the population one year to get used to the idea of divorce but made no concessions over changes to the law of inheritance. In Rome, even after the Pope had been spirited away, it was judged inopportune to laicize the state, and similar concessions were made in Catholic Poland, so that in the Grand Duchy of Warsaw the clergy retained authority over matrimonial cases; and in this fiercely anti-Semitic country Jews, who had been emancipated in Western Europe, were not permitted to acquire land without permission. On the Continent the Code did not quite become the norm.

What won much more enthusiastic support from civil servants everywhere was the French method of governing. The territories that were annexed in Italy, the Netherlands or Germany acted as intermediaries between the French and other nations. Once some

Italians, Dutchmen and Germans were ruled by prefects and sub-prefects and mayors, fellow countrymen found it easy to follow their example. Between 1807 and 1809 the Poles in the Grand Duchy of Warsaw found themselves adapting to the presence of prefects, as had happened before in the Grand Duchy of Berg and the Kingdom of Westphalia, where French local councils and French courts of law were copied; and Joseph had hardly become King of Spain before he, easy-going and moderate though he was, set about the job of reorganizing Spain according to French principles. In Tuscany, which as the home of Dante and Petrarch still regarded itself as the best-educated part of Italy, there was a scheme to reproduce the teaching methods of the Napoleonic University. What had worked in France must be made to work in other European countries for their own good.

Napoleon stood for breaking down ancient barriers that divided peoples. The most obvious ones were those that blocked trade. But France's traditions, as established by Colbert, Minister of Finance, Commerce and the Navy under Louis XIV, were protectionist. There was therefore at the heart of the Empire's economic policies a logical contradiction, for freeing up trade was in the interests of the Empire as a whole, but might not be in the interests of France as Napoleon perceived them. In that case, over and over again, the needs of France were treated as paramount.

In one obvious way Napoleon continued one of the favourite practices of Louis XIV's age in trade warfare: he encouraged privateering. Americans, who had their own troubles with the species, estimated that between 1793 and 1800 French and Barbary corsairs had captured some 3,000 British ships in the Mediterranean and, especially after Trafalgar, only corsairs enabled the French to strike back against British traders.

Napoleon had a warlike attitude to trade as such. According to Chaptal, who after 1810 was a permanent member of the board for commerce and manufacture, 'he presumed to manoeuvre it like a battalion and demanded that trade submit as passively'.[1] Before the official imposition of a Continental blockade in 1806, Napoleon, like revolutionary rulers before him, intended to banish the British from areas the French controlled, so that France would replace Britain as the economic powerhouse of Europe. Saved for a time from British technical superiority, so the argument ran, French industry would become foremost in Europe. In fairness to those who held this opinion, the freeing up of trade introduced in 1786 by the treaty negotiated between Pitt (for Britain) and Vergennes (for France) had not made France prosperous, and nobody influential in France after 1789 onwards found Adam Smith's beliefs congenial. It paid the French to make the Rhine a more important trade route than the Channel or the North Sea, so in 1804 France organized a convention with the cities along the river bank to reduce their restrictive tariffs. Germany inevitably became France's leading trade partner. It was the crossroads between Northern and Southern Europe, between East and West; its fairs at Leipzig and Frankfurt had won international prestige, and it became the recipient or conduit of most of France's agricultural exports. Italy was a subordinate market, useful for supplying raw materials, such as hides, oil, wool, cotton and above all silk, but Italians were not treated fairly, so that the silk manufacturers of Piedmont suffered in the interests of those of Lyon. By comparison, Spain, Portugal and the Netherlands were valued chiefly for the contacts that could be made with their colonies and, as progressively these contacts were cut by the British, so these more peripheral regions of Napoleon's Europe, like the French ports on the Atlantic seaboard, had to endure a downturn in their trade.

What Napoleon had not realized was that, despite all the disruption he caused, under his all-embracing protectionist regime new transcontinental patterns of trade developed. It suited the cotton and iron producers of Belgium, Luxembourg and Alsace to have to operate within one market. The creation of the Grand Duchy of Berg brought together the coal and iron industries of Mark and Berg, the addition of the Black Forest area to Baden provided Baden's businessmen with a larger labour force, a larger Bavaria was good for Munich beer producers, the Kingdom of Italy helped Lombard textiles, the Confederation of the Rhine expanded the market for Baden cotton, and the link between the Grand Duchy of Warsaw and Saxony that for Saxon cotton. There was also a Napoleonic military-industrial complex. War encouraged mining and metallurgy in the valleys of the Ruhr, the Rhine (by Strasbourg), Aosta and Brescia, and soldiers needed hides (for their shoes) and textiles (for their uniforms). War distorts economies, but much survived the downfall of the Grand Empire. After 1815, first Belgium, then Germany became modern industrial nations. Politically, Belgium had been part of a greater French nation since 1795, and under Napoleon it was drawn into a new industrial region that stretched from Liège and Verviers to Aix-la-Chapelle and Cologne, so that industrialists in Walloon Belgium, at the centre of this area, were much less provincial than in the 1780s, when the country rose in revolt against the reforming Holy Roman Empire because Joseph II had wanted change. Similarly, Germans had learned the advantages of working and trading within larger units, so that the creation of a customs union (or *Zollverein*) within the German confederation was again a direct consequence of the country's experience under Napoleonic rule.

In Napoleon's time the industrial revolution on the Continent had scarcely begun; indeed, politically the Emperor was a Luddite, favouring economic advance only if it benefited his Empire. Gillray was right: late in 1805 Napoleon had to concede Britain the ocean and the seas around Europe, just as Britain had to leave him in control of the land. To beat Britain, he must make a Continent conquer the offshore island it could not reach. His vision of Europe entailed the exclusion of Britain from Europe.

Ever since he came to power by the coup d'état of Brumaire 1799, he had set about impeding the flow of British goods to the Continent. Each time he made peace with a cowed or a defeated country, with Naples, Spain, Portugal, Russia, Turkey or the republic, later Kingdom, of Italy, he demanded that French exports should be given preferential treatment. In the circumstances that resulted from his military victories in 1805 and 1806 Napoleon felt strong enough to be more ruthless. The collapse of colonial trade made it urgent for French businessmen to find new markets within Europe. After Russia had made peace at Tilsit and Portugal had been invaded, the prospects for French merchants seemed glorious, for, as a metal dealer Deloche wrote in 1807, 'political and friendly relations have turned Germany, Holland, Spain and Italy into vast fairs where France will always find a certain sale for her surplus industrial products'.[2] But while British cotton consumption accelerated at a much faster rate than that of France, while British cotton yarn and sewing yarn remained cheaper than French, there was an incentive for those with access to British markets to buy from Britain, so that smuggling became a necessity of life for respectable merchants in Hamburg or Amsterdam. Meanwhile, protectionist action against Britain favoured German, Prussian and Austrian textile producers to compete successfully against the French. Besides, when France used protectionist measures against her staunchest ally, Bavaria, the Bavarians responded in kind. Other allies suffered more. The faithful Poles relied on exporting foodstuffs to Britain, so that wheat exports collapsed, noble landowners got further in debt and their peasants deserted the land. Highhanded though the British were in their treatment of shipping, including that of neutral powers like the USA, the immediate cause of their economic troubles seemed to many Continental entrepreneurs the state of commercial warfare to which the Empire's laws condemned them. The British controlled islands put a ring around the continent – Heligoland, the Channel Islands, Sicily, Malta, Corfu and Vis – and from 1808 they also had access to the ports of Portugal. It was because he knew how disastrous the blockade was for his adopted trading nation that Louis Bonaparte protested against its harmful effects and so was deprived of the Dutch throne by his bullying brother. As the French made life harder for the Netherlands, so the British shifted their attention to the east, to Tönning in Denmark, to Oldenburg just south of Jutland, to Altona beside Hamburg. When the North Sea and the Baltic became too hot for them, British merchants moved to the Balkans and the Adriatic. The effect of Napoleon's attempt to issue ever more stringent regulations to favour France was to move trade towards the south-east; the Rhine, it was feared, might be replaced by the Danube as Europe's primary artery for the flow of trade. Men, meanwhile, grew rich by bending the system to their wills. The Rothschilds got permission to trade from the French and from the British, as from their initial base in Frankfurt they moved to Paris and London. At a humbler level, smugglers along the Rhine earned up to ten or twenty times at night what a peasant gained in the day, and it was much more profitable to cross the Pyrenees with contraband than to till the soil in Roussillon.

The climax of the blockade came when decrees were issued in 1810 at the palaces close to Paris, at St-Cloud, Trianon and Fontainebleau. By a licence system, the French government hoped to reduce the popularity of smuggling – for years the former Empress Joséphine had been buying her roses from Kew – and yet by permitting the sale of prizes seized by French corsairs and colonial goods impounded in the Netherlands, Napoleon was not helping hard-pressed French manufacturers. The attempt to restrict trade soon had adverse effects on the principal belligerents. As Britain imported more and yet more coffee, sugar, raw cotton, wool, flax and raw silk, British merchants found it harder to export. Some had hoped to make a fortune in South America, but found that the South Americans could not pay them. Others found that commercial relations with the North Americans had grown less friendly – in 1812 ill feeling turned into hostility – and at home one result of technical modernization was growing unemployment, which some workers in the Midlands blamed on new machines and so the 'Luddites', followers of the mythical Ludd, destroyed them. As Napoleon had hoped, British gold reserves declined. What he could not prevent, however, was the ingenuity of the British government in raising loans – it was able to go on financing Wellington's army in the Iberian Peninsula and to find the credit to help any Continental government that was willing to take on Napoleon. Besides, the effect on France was even worse.

On the Continent established trade routes were disrupted, supposedly to help the French, but in reality to the disadvantage of all, for as Sismondi, the secretary to the Geneva Chamber of Commerce, complained, 'the financial laws of France and all the countries subjected to it have lacked all stability'.[3] As it became more difficult to discover outlets for trade, interest rates were raised, more businessmen and speculators in the major cities from Hamburg to Basel went bankrupt and resentment against French actions grew. Customs men have never been popular, but, as France lost its hold on other countries, they and the gendarmes became as hated as the soldiers who rampaged through villages in search of loot and sex; and they were much more vulnerable to popular attack.

In the end, Napoleon's obsessive pursuit of a Continental blockade was militarily disastrous. In seeking to make the Continent watertight against seaborne trade with Britain, Napoleon made fatal errors. To his mind, he had to invade Spain and Portugal, he had to deprive the Tsar's brother-in-law of the Duchy of Oldenburg, finally he had to invade Russia itself. That expedition he saw as a war of Europe against a country he named as 'the Colossus of the barbarian north'. If Alexander wanted victories, he said, 'let him fight the Persians, and not interfere in Europe. Civilization rejects these northerners. Europe can manage its affairs without them.'[4] By the end of 1812 he was proved wrong. The Tsar's armies proved that Europe could not manage without Russians – indeed, they helped other European nations to recover self-respect – and soon French defeat in Spain showed that France was also unable to keep Britain from playing a Continental role.

The idea of a Continental European economy did have a future, but in the nineteenth century Germany rather than France came to dominate it. In the short term Russia rather than France was the dominant continental power. But France had gained some advantages from their Napoleonic experience. More Frenchmen knew the rest of the Continent than had ever been the case before, just as more of the rest of the continent had come into contact with the French. In European history, the period made a break with the past – after Napoleon nothing was the same again. Outside Europe, Britain, the only world power, was dominant economically until surpassed by Germany and America – Britannia, as Gillray saw, ruled the seas. What was harder to grasp was that the seas and the land were both parts of the same plum pudding.

EPILOGUE

12

THE LEGEND

In his last testament Napoleon wrote: 'I desire that my ashes rest on the banks of the Seine, in the midst of the French people whom I have loved so dearly.' The word 'ashes' was a product of his classical education – he never intended that his remains should be cremated – and he was careful to receive the last rites of the Catholic Church and expected that his bones would be buried. For almost twenty years they lay, as he asked, in a quiet stone tomb in the remote Geranium Valley on the island of St Helena. Not until 1840 was there a request to the British to honour his will. The Prime Minister, Adolphe Thiers, took a nationalistic view of European affairs that attracted him to the glamour of the Bonapartist cause. In 1833 he had argued that the Emperor should be replaced on top of the Vendôme column. In 1836, as head of the administration, he oversaw the completion of the Arc de Triomphe as a memorial to revolutionary and Napoleonic victories. When he met Jérôme Bonaparte in Florence in 1837, he told the prince: 'I am one of the Frenchmen of the present age who are most attached to the glorious memory of Napoleon.' As a journalist with scholarly ambitions, he was currently preparing a twenty-volume history of the Consulate and Empire that was to appear between 1845 and 1862. In 1840 his ministry struck a Napoleonic attitude in the Levant by urging the khedive of Egypt, Muhammed Ali, to wrest Syria from the Sultan; and the anti-Napoleonic alliance of 1813–15 was re-formed, as Russia, Austria and Prussia, led by Britain, prepared to settle the quarrel with no reference to France. Luckily for French prestige Thiers had already suggested the return of the 'ashes' to the banks of the Seine. In this he had shown a masterly sense of timing. He first approached the heir to the throne, the Duc d'Orléans, who was favourable, then the King, Louis-Philippe, who was less enthusiastic but was keen on posing as guardian of the nation's past – he had just turned Versailles into a museum – and knew that his attempt to satisfy imperialistic longings by conquering Algeria had done little for French international prestige. The British gave their consent; and the Prince de Joinville, the sailor son of the King, and Bertrand, who had been in the island, and his son, who had been born there, and Emmanuel des Las Cases, son of the Emperor's principal memorialist, were sent aboard the *Belle-Poule* to collect the body.

While they were on their return journey, the Near Eastern crisis revealed the miscalculations of Thiers's foreign policy. Joinville, expecting that Britain and France would soon be at war, decided that, if he were attacked, he would perish at sea, along with Napoleon's bones. Before he came home, however, the crisis had passed. Thiers, who was aware of the inadequate defences of Paris in 1814, had built a wall around Paris (known today from the gates that stand at the end of the Metro lines) to defend it against the enemies he anticipated, but, when he tried to conscript 150,000 men for the forthcoming struggle, the King, who had no love of melodrama, would not agree and he forced Thiers to resign.

National honour was restored in the depth of a freezing winter. On 30 November the *Belle-Poule* had docked in Cherbourg, from where the boat-catafalque made its way to Rouen. All the bridges along the Seine were dressed with flags, as crowds flocked to the banks. The mayor of Meulan resigned from his post because the cortège had not slowed down as it passed through his commune. At Malmaison, ladies in mourning lined the windows, Soult, who had a comfortable career as a minister of Louis-Philippe as previously of Louis XVIII, was seen to cry as he knelt beside the coffin, veterans of the grenadiers, the lancers, the dragoons, the light infantry and riflemen converged on Neuilly and Courbevoie to salute their Emperor as he passed. On 14 December it was eight degrees below zero, while the old men rested on the ground, warmed only by their mantles. Next morning a great procession made its way slowly through the icy mist from the Place de l'Etoile, where the Arc de Triomphe was temporarily topped with a plaster statue of the Emperor, past pillars draped in tricolours and crowned with Napoleonic eagles, down the Champs-Elysées to the Place de la Concorde, then across the river to the military hospital of Les Invalides, where Napoleon's body was laid to rest.

Napoleon's tomb is placed under one of the most beautiful domes in Paris, the gilded semicircular structure over Hardouin-Mansart's Greek cross royal chapel behind the main church of St-Louis. Today, the focus of attention inside is Napoleon's hefty tomb, carved out of dark red Finnish porphyry set on a green Vosges granite pedestal. Against the walls, ten bas-reliefs represent the benefits Napoleon had brought to France, while facing the sarcophagus are twelve figures symbolizing his greatest victories, between which are six flags won at Austerlitz. The purist may note that the cumbersome, sombre tomb spoils the architecture of Louis

XIV's beautiful Invalides chapel, and yet it serves to remind the people of France that the Emperor's work survives.

The change in Napoleon's reputation that had occurred since 1814 was perhaps the most remarkable of the Emperor's achievements. In 1814 the greatest prose pamphleteer in France, René de Chateaubriand, had denounced him in *De Buonaparte, Des Bourbons* as a usurper, impious and cruel. Chateaubriand's title insisted that Napoleon was a foreigner, for it spelled his surname in its original, Corsican form, not in its later, French form. Chateaubriand viewed the Revolution with contempt: 'in the name of the laws people turned religion and morals upside down, they renounced the experience and customs of our fathers.' After the many disasters that followed people despaired of finding among Frenchmen someone who would dare assume the crown of Louis XVI. There was no one. 'A foreigner' presented himself and was chosen. 'Buonaparte' concealed his aims. Republicans believed him 'the popular head of a free state', monarchists saw in him a man who would play the role of Monk, who restored the Stuart Charles II to the English throne; everyone believed in him. But he was intoxicated with his own success, and soon his tendency to evil became apparent. He arrested the young Duc d'Enghien on foreign soil and had him imprisoned for the hereditary crime of being the great-grandson of the great Condé, Louis XIV's distinguished general and cousin. Parisians then began to ask 'what right a Corsican had to spill the finest as well as the purest blood in France'. We French are not a nation devoted to treachery and ingratitude. 'The murder of the Duc d'Enghien . . . the war in Spain, the imprisonment of the Pope betray in Buonaparte a character not truly French.' France became an 'empire of lies' where newspapers, pamphlets and speeches all hid the truth. Conscription became an article of faith in the catechism, and in the arts there was the same kind of slavery. Napoleon has been praised for his administration, but 'if the best administration is one that leaves the people in peace', clearly 'Buonaparte's government was the worst of governments'. His exactions put France to the sack, so that property was never safe and civil liberty even less secure.

His economic policy had appalling effects. Not only did the Continental system lead to war in Spain and Russia, but it also closed Mediterranean and Baltic ports to trade; and Buonaparte had to go on and on, seeking to close the ports of Greece, Constantinople, Syria and North Africa, in short to conquer the world. How, then, had this foreigner seduced the French? By military glory. 'A Frenchman's pen should refuse to paint the horror of his battlefields; to Buonaparte a wounded man became a burden; it would be better if he died so as to get rid of him.' Now the war has reached us. Buonaparte, Chateaubriand affirms, is 'a false great man'.

Even great writers have their rhetorical problems, and it required all the talent of France's finest man of letters to glamorize the cause of Louis XVIII, so fat, so cautious, so unmagnetic. His attack on 'Buonaparte' was published in April 1814. Two months later, Louis XVIII granted his subjects a constitutional charter that guaranteed many fundamental freedoms; and Chateaubriand was soon able to recommend *Monarchy according to the Charter*. When, therefore, Napoleon returned to the Tuileries in 1815, he was obliged to appear a liberal too. Once the arch-liberal Benjamin Constant had drafted for him an Acte Additionel to be added to the Imperial Constitution, he claimed to rule only in accord with the freely expressed wishes of the citizens of France. As within a hundred days he had left office for good, his conciliatory intentions had never been thoroughly tested, but on St Helena he could assure the world that the final version of Napoleon was the true one. His defeat relieved him of the need to prove that he would be as good as his word; and for the rest of his life he devoted himself to reinventing himself.

The final stage of Napoleon's life, from October 1815 to May 1821, was passed on a remote island in the southern Atlantic.

At first he almost enjoyed himself. He took time off to flirt with Betsy Balcombe, the pretty daughter of the East India Company agent, and there was a period when he took to gardening. In the early days of captivity, he was resilient. Having become used to reverential treatment from subordinates who found him terrifying, on the journey out he had adapted well to the cramped quarters on board ship and he passed many evenings quietly playing cards with Admiral Cockburn and his fellow officers. He had even tried to learn English, but languages were not his forte and he had to rely on the common perception that the lingua franca of European polite society was French. After staying for a short time in James-town, the island's capital, he was soon transferred to Longwood, the summer seat of the lieutenant-governor of the island, situated five miles inland on a plateau. It was when installed there that he noticed The Briars and arranged to settle in a pavilion in its grounds until his own house was ready for him. So began his relationship with the younger daughter of the main house. Betsy was learning French and made rapid progress by showing off her new knowledge to her distinguished neighbour, who was delighted to reveal that he was not the ogre his critics saw in him; and even after he left for Longwood, he often invited the Balcombes to visit him, until they disappeared from the island in 1818. By then he was feeling morose. For a time, as on Elba, he had had grand schemes. Just before leaving the environs of Paris to try his luck on the coast, he visited Malmaison for the last time and marvelled at the wonderful gardens Joséphine had constructed. Once the Bal-combes had gone, in 1819 he took to transforming his new estate into a little garden worthy of an ex-Emperor. He rose at 5.30 a.m., roused his companions and set to work digging, weeding, planting oaks and having Chinese labourers plant orange and peach trees, and laying out pools with fountains he could turn on with a tap. The exercise did him good, but it was the last time he showed himself so energetic. More and more, Napoleon took to staying indoors, grumbling with good reason at the petty vexations caused him by the governor, Hudson Lowe, ageing rapidly until he died when only fifty-one. Some historians think his life may have been cut short as a result of arsenic poisoning.

Throughout most of his last six years he was sustained by a conviction that he had work to do. Monologues, to which he was prone, became a means to create a legend. The gospel of Napoleon, according to Jean Tulard, had four evangelists: Las Cases, Gourgaud, Montholon and Bertrand. There were also other texts, by his Irish doctor O'Meara, a British spy, and by his valet, Marchand. Of all these writings none was to equal the effect of the publication of Las Cases's *Le Mémorial de Ste-Hélène*. Napoleon's lengthy accounts of his campaigns could be dull. When he declaimed speeches from Racine or Corneille he often got the emphasis wrong. But, when he talked of his mission in the words of Las Cases, he became riveting, a prophet, if not a messiah. The elegant words of Las Cases gave the most convincing account of what Napoleon liked to think he had been and could have been. *Le Mémorial de Ste-Hélène* is a memorial to a great man.

If there was a general thesis that Napoleon outlined to the members of his tiny circle over a period of six years, then the core of the message had been worked out by the time Las Cases left the island in December 1816. Las Cases's skill as an apologist lies not alone in his ability to chronicle every petty incident of the captivity, but in the way he combines a narrative of the events he witnessed over eighteen months with his master's rambling reminiscences and prophetic utterances. Las Cases was a little older than his hero, born in 1766, the son of a marquis, and was destined to be a sailor. When the Revolution broke out, he was a fervent royalist who soon found himself an exile, first serving with other emigrés in the Austrian army, then making his way to England, where he became tutor in an English family and devoted his spare time to cartography. In 1799 he slipped quietly into Brittany to marry his girlfriend secretly and hurried back to England, leaving her pregnant. Once he knew he had a son, he had good reason to wish to return to France, so he took Napoleon's offer of amnesty and, back in Paris, published his atlas. In 1806 he was one of the old nobles who joined the new Imperial court, and he was rewarded by receiving the title of Baron of the Empire early in 1809. He became a Councillor of State, a count, a man who could be trusted on occasional missions, as when he was sent to report on the state of Illyria, the recently acquired province on the Dalmatian coast, but as yet he was unknown to Napoleon. By 1814 he was a loyal Bonapartist, who turned down a request that he should remain in the Council – rather than serve a Bourbon again, he took himself off to England. He came back for the last phase of Napoleon's rule and was confirmed in his offices, but he became close to the Emperor only when he volunteered to go into exile with him. For the rest of his life, until he died in 1842, he was a devoted Bonapartist. Emmanuel, his first child and older son, became Napoleon's page and secretary on St Helena, and in 1840, when his father was old and blind, he was of the party that went to St Helena to collect the Emperor's body.

It was on the journey out to St Helena that Las Cases senior began to make notes, and he continued to write assiduously as long as he was in Napoleon's presence every day. His labours were halted abruptly in 1821, after he wrote to Lucien Bonaparte to protest against the cruel way in which Hudson Lowe, the governor, was treating his captive. At once Las Cases was sent to the Cape, his papers were confiscated and on his return to Europe he was forbidden to live in France. It was only after Napoleon's death, which Talleyrand dismissed as merely news, not an event, that Las Cases was allowed back to France and allowed back his manuscript. The first edition was published in 1823. There were to be further editions in 1824, 1830–32, 1835 and 1840, in response to later events. Only after the 1830 Revolution could he dare to drop his elusive manner, but as the cult of the Emperor spread he was tempted to alter his words to suit the mood of the moment. Even before his son returned to St Helena, his book was itself a cultic object.

What gives the *Mémorial* its wonderful fluency is the skill with which Las Cases gives the reader the impression of reading a copious diary, so that he can hear the Emperor speak, feel for his woes, be stirred to anger at his sufferings. He can follow the Emperor's life day by day as he darted from one subject to another, lingering on his triumphs, in Italy in 1796–7, in Egypt in 1798–9, while Las Cases noticed that like a good bourgeois he had addressed Joséphine as 'tu' and his second wife as 'ma bonne Louise'. In one aside he says that the Imperial post did not open many letters but only those that might be dangerous. When at his toilette, he would show the large hole in his left thigh. Napoleon was curious about Las Cases's experience of emigration and mused that he might have gone to India, in which case he would not have ended up on St Helena. Then he decided that he must learn English, which was not a success, and within days – it was January 1816 – he was expatiating on his first campaign in Italy and retailing the words of his famous speech, probably penned for the first time nineteen years after the events he was describing: 'Soldiers, you are naked, you are ill fed; we are owed much, nobody can give us anything . . .

I take you to the most fertile plains in the world. Rich provinces, large cities will be in our power . . .' And he was off on a tale of one victory after another, until he had got his troops to the river Po, and it was a new month. His English lesson was to read the article on the Nile in the *Encyclopedia Britannica*; and he was fascinated by the idea of the Portuguese explorer Albuquerque, who had suggested that the river could be diverted into the Red Sea, so that Egypt would become a desert. A few days later, he was bitter about the Bourbons, who are, he remarked, the allies of our enemies. Europe has annihilated France, but France will rise up again when there is an explosion of the peoples against their rulers. Early in March a Chinese fleet arrived in Jamestown, and Napoleon began to explain how he would have conquered England. With the army of Austerlitz he could have reached London in four days. If only England and France had worked together, they could have regenerated Europe. Soon it was early April, and he told anecdotes about the Persian and the Turkish ambassadors. In June he was defending the liberty of the press.

The man living under house arrest at Longwood on a forlorn island presents himself as essentially a man of peace, whom his enemies had driven to fight. He wished to bring back to France respect for religion and family life that the Revolution had shattered, he had dreamed of uniting Italy and Germany as nations (had he not helped by drastically reducing the number of the political units in both countries?), he had longed to restore Polish independence and to liberate the Irish from England. If his methods had been autocratic, it had been by necessity – instinctively, he loved freedom, he had been reluctant to imprison his opponents (how few prisoners there had been!), he had shown good faith by giving the press its head in 1815. He had been strict because in 1804 only four per cent of Frenchmen could read. After Las Cases had gone, in 1820 the Emperor drew up a constitution

that revealed how clement would be the government of Napoleon
II – and how indebted to the wisdom of Napoleon I – but the belief
in his own future as a statesmen kept him talking and talking day
after day, until fatigue and illness forced him to rest; and he only
stopped when he was close to death. No defeated ruler has ever
been so clever at reinventing himself as the ruler he would like to
be.

While Napoleon was dictating his view of the past and the future,
his eaglet heir, Napoleon II, the Duc of Reichstadt, was virtually the
prisoner of his Austrian grandfather and his wife was enjoying a
liaison in the tiny court of Parma – not without irony to be the
setting of Stendhal's most Napoleonic of romances. In Europe,
literary men and artists kept the legend alive. Hazlitt wrote a
biography (so did Scott, from the opposing point of view), while
younger radicals – Byron and Shelley – concentrated on satirizing
his Tory enemies, whether Castlereagh or Wordsworth or Southey
or Coleridge. On the Continent outside France, some Poles and
some Italians remained sympathetic, but in France the dullness of
the Bourbons, the pride of the old nobility and the narrow-minded
conservatism of many of the clergy did wonders for Napoleon's
reputation. In 1815 it was romantic to be a royalist, but by 1823,
when Frenchmen could read the *Mémorial* it was Bonapartism that
attracted the young. The ogre of 1815 had been transformed into
a Promethean figure chained to a distant rock, whose will was to be
buried among the French people he loved so dearly. The popular
verses of Béranger, like the vivid paintings of Horace Vernet, called
to mind the dazzling glamour of Napoleon that the restored
Bourbons lacked. Since 1815, too many civil servants had lost their
posts, too many new nobles had been snubbed, too many army
veterans left with nothing to do.

The turning point came in 1830, when the restored regime went the way of the *ancien régime* and a Bonapartist revival seemed possible. Many of the street fighters brought out their pistols or their swords to set about the royal soldiers led by Marmont, who had betrayed Napoleon in 1814; and though there was to be neither a Bonapartist government nor a republic, the ageing republican Lafayette embraced the portly Duc d'Orléans and so sanctioned a bourgeois monarchy, which had to employ Napoleonic bureaucrats and found allies in Napoleonic nobles who longed to be rich. As the Restoration came to an end, Stendhal was penning its epitaph in *Le Rouge et le Noir*, whose tragic hero, Julien Sorel, had no dearer aim than to be like the Napoleon of the *Mémorial*, a man of infinite aspirations.

In the time of Louis-Philippe, the King of the French the tricolour had replaced the fleur-de-lys, so it seemed only natural that a royal prince was dispatched to bring Napoleon home. As Louis-Philippe hoped to unite Frenchmen around his throne, he was prepared to risk a flirtation with Bonapartism. By doing so, unwittingly he helped to prepare the way for the return of a Bonaparte to take his place.

The Napoleonic legend had just been restated in a pamphlet, *Les Idées Napoléoniennes* written in 1839 by Prince Louis-Napoleon, the only surviving son of Louis Bonaparte and Hortense de Beauharnais and since the death of 'Napoleon II', the great Napoleon's heir. The pamphlet said little about his foreign policy, which it argued was largely defensive – the main aggressor was England – and it expatiated on his inventive home policy. Above all, it argued that Napoleon I stood for a united Europe, a European Court of Justice, a European currency. *Les Idées Napoléoniennes* became a commercial success, selling maybe 500,000 copies before it was followed up by an attempted coup d'état by the young prince. The coup was a disaster but his subsequent trial gave Louis-Napoleon the chance to repeat his case in court. In 1840 he escaped from gaol in a workman's uniform. The sudden fall of Louis-Philippe in February 1848 gave him the chance to put his case to the nation. The introduction of universal suffrage by the new republic gave all French men the chance to vote for their president. On the ballot papers there was just one name most of them knew well, Bonaparte, and so before the end of the year Prince Louis-Napoleon Bonaparte was overwhelmingly elected President of the Second Republic. The plebiscite, a technique blessed by Napoleon I, was shown to be the perfect means by which his nephew could reinforce his power. A coup on 2 December 1851, the anniversary of Austerlitz, was blessed by a fresh plebiscite that made him President for ten years and then, after yet another plebiscite, on 2 December 1852 the Second Empire succeeded the Second Republic as Prince-President Louis-Napoleon was proclaimed the Emperor Napoleon III. The Napoleonic legend had made possible the elevation to supreme authority of Louis-Napoleon, a man with almost no military and little political experience, for the legend depended just on a magical name.

The beginnings of the modern world lie in Napoleon's achievement, in war and in peace. His conquests forced his world to attend to him, so that he had the opportunity to start reshaping France and much of Europe. As a soldier, however, after some sixty-odd victories he was eventually defeated in each of his last campaigns. What has survived him has been his civilian work, and it has been this rather than his style of warfare that by force has done so peacefully, by providing a model of how a country can be well run.

NOTES

Chapter 1: On Top of the Mountains

1 E. J. Delécluze, *Louis David, son école et son temps* (Paris, 1855; 1983 reprint), pp. 203, 204.
2 Owen Connelly, *Blundering to Glory: Napoleon's Military Campaigns* (Wilmington, revised edn, 1999), p. 13.
3 J. E. Howard, *Letters and Documents of Napoleon*, vol. 1 (London, 1961), p. 169.
4 Vincent Cronin, *Napoleon* (London, 1971), pp. 117–18.
5 J. E. Howard, op cit., p. 175.
6 Las Cases, *Le Mémorial de St-Hélène*, vol. 1 (Paris, 1983), pp. 387–8.
7 Las Cases, op. cit., p. 169.

Chapter 2: On the Plains of Europe

1 Felix Markham, *Napoleon* (London, 1963), p. 98.
2 Owen Connolly, op. cit., pp. 90–91.
3 David Chandler, *The Campaigns of Napoleon* (London, 1967), p. 550. Cf. Jean-Paul Kauffman, *La chambre noire de Longwood* (Paris, 1997), pp. 208–10.

Chapter 3: The Route to the East and Back Again

1 Felix Markham, op. cit., p. 174.
2 David Chandler, op. cit., p. 746.
3 These figures are taken from David Chandler, op. cit., p. 756. Owen Connolly, op. cit., p. 159, gives slightly different figures.
4 *Memoirs of Sergeant Bourgoyne, 1812–1813*, with an introduction by Richard Partridge (London, 1995), p. 12.
5 Henry Kissinger, *A World Restored: Metternich, Castlereagh and the Problems of Peace 1812–1822* (London, 1957), *passim*.
6 Felix Markham, op. cit., pp. 188–92.

Chapter 4: Waterloo and Vienna

1 Henry Kissinger, op. cit., p. 170.

Chapter 5: Describing Egypt

1 Yves Laissus, *L'Egypte, un aventure savante 1798–1801* (Paris, 1998), p. 24.
2 J. Christopher Herold, *Bonaparte in Egypt* (London, 1963), pp. 220–21, 265.
3 Ibid., p. 187.
4 Ibid., p. 303.
5 Ibid., p. 313.
6 Ibid., p. 230.
7 See Robert Anderson and Ibrahim Fawzy, *Egypt in 1800* (London, 1987), and *Description de l'Egypte, passim*.
8 Yves Laissus, op. cit., pp. 210, 211, 252–4.

Chapter 6: Ancient Rome Restored

1 Norman Hampson, *A Social History of the French Revolution* (London, 1963), pp. 112–13.
2 William Doyle, *The Oxford History of the French Revolution* (Oxford, 1989), p. 127.
3 Jean Tulard, *Napoléon et la noblesse d'Empire* (Paris, 1979), p. 42.
4 Anita Brookner, *David* (London, 1980), pp. 171–2.

Chapter 7: The Coronation

1 E. J. Delécluze, *Louis David, son école et son temps* (Paris, 1855; 1983 reprint), p. 313.
2 Ibid., pp. 247–9.
3 William Doyle, op. cit., pp. 136–141.
4 Margaret M. O'Dwyer, *The Papacy in the Age of Napoleon and the Restoration, Pius VII, 1800–1823* (London, 1985), p. 25.
5 Adrien Dansette, *Histoire religieuse de la France contemporaine* (Paris, 1965), p. 153.
6 Anita Brookner, op. cit., pp. 159–60.

Chapter 8: The Man of Law

1 T. Crow, *Emulation: Making Artists for Revolutionary France*, pp. 227–8.
2 Pierre Villeneuve de Janti, *Bonaparte et le Code Civil* (Paris, 1934), *passim*.

Chapter 9: The Man of Learning

1 David Maland, *Culture and Society in Seventeenth-Century France* (London, 1970), pp. 244–5.
2 Yves Laissus, op. cit., p. 27.
3 Adrien Dansette, op. cit., p. 107.
4 Georges Lefebvre, *The French Revolution, vol. 2: From 1793 to 1799* (London and New York, 1964), pp. 287–92.
5 Georges Lefebvre, *Napoléon* (Paris, 1965), p. 399.
6 Ernest Lavisse, *Historie de la France contemporaine*, t. 3, G. Pariset, *Le Consulat et l'Empire* (Paris, 1921), p. 335.
7 Timothy Wilson-Smith, *Delacroix: A Life* (London, 1992), p. 39.

Chapter 10: Napoleon's France

1 Jean Tulard, *La vie quotidienne des Français sous Napoléon* (Paris, 1978), p. 29.

Chapter 11: Napoleon's Europe

1 S. J. Woolf, *Napoleon's Integration of Europe* (London, 1991), p. 140.
2 Ibid., p. 145.
3 Ibid., p. 153.
4 J. M. Thompson, *Napoleon Bonaparte, His Rise and Fall* (Oxford, 1963), p. 324.

SELECT BIBLIOGRAPHY

Adkins, Lesley and Roy, *The keys to Egypt: The Race to Read the Hieroglyphs* (London, 2000)

Agulhon, Maurice, *1848 ou l'apprentissage de la république 1848–1852* (Paris, 1973)

Anderson, Robert and Fawzy, Ibrahim, *Egypt in 1800* (London, 1987)

Ardagh, John, *France in the New Century* (London, 1999)

Athanassoglou-Kallmyer, Nina, *Eugène Delacroix: Prints, Politics and Satire 1814–1822* (New Haven, 1991)

Bann, Stephen, *Paul Delaroche: History Painted* (London, 1997)

Barnett, Corelli, *Bonaparte* (New York, 1978)

Bergeron, Louis, *Banquiers, négotiants et manufacturiers du Directoire à l'Empire* (Paris, 1978)

Bergeron, Louis, *France under Napoleon* (Princeton, 1981)

Biver, M. L., *Le Paris de Napoléon* (Paris, 1963)

Boime, Albert, *Social History of Modern Art, 2: Art in an Age of Bonapartism, 1800–1815* (Chicago and London, 1990)

Bourgogne, Sergeant, *Memoirs of Sergeant Bourgogne, 1812–1813*, with an introduction by Richard Partridge (London, 1995)

Brogan, D. W., *The French Nation from Napoleon to Pétain 1814–1940* (London, 1961)

Brookner, Anita, *David* (London, 1980)

Bury, J. P. T., *France 1814–1940* (London, 1949)

Carr, Raymond, *Spain: 1808–1975* (Oxford, 2nd edition, 1982)

Chandler, David, *The Campaigns of Napoleon* (London, 1967)

Chateaubriand, François-René, Vicomte de, *Mémoires d'Outre-tombe* (Paris, 1849)

Chateaubriand, François-René, Vicomte de, *De la Vendée; De Buonaparte, Des Bourbons* (Rennes, reprinted 1998)

Cobban, Alfred, *A History of Modern France*, 3 vols. (London, 1957–65)

Connelly, Owen, *Blundering to glory: Napoleon's military campaigns* (Wilmington, revised edition 1999)

Connelly, Owen, *Napoleon's Satellite Kingdoms* (New York, 1965)

Cronin, Vincent, *Napoleon* (London, 1971)

Crouzet, F., *L'Economie britannique et le blocus continental, 1806–1813*, 2 vols (Paris, 1958)

Crow, Thomas, *Emulation: Making Artists for Revolutionary France* (Yale University Press, 1994)

Dansette, Adrien, *Histoire religieuse de la France contemporaine* (Paris, 1965)

Delécluze, Etienne, *Louis David , son école et son temps* (Paris, 1855; 1983 reprint)

Denon, Vivant, *Voyage dans la Basse et la Haute Egypte* (Paris, 1802)

Doyle, William, *The Oxford History of the French Revolution* (Oxford, 1989)

Elting, John R., *Swords around the Throne: Napoleon's Grand Army* (New York and London, 1988)

Esposito, Vincent J. and Elting, John R., *A Military History and Atlas of the Napoleonic Wars* (New York, 1964)

Fisher, H. A. L., *Bonapartism* (London, 1908)

Furet, François, *Revolutionary France, 1770–1880* (Oxford, 1992)

Garlick, Kenneth, *Sir Thomas Lawrence* (Oxford, 1989)

Geyl, Pieter, *Napoleon, For and Against* (London, 1949)

Godechot, Jacques, *La Contre-Révolution* (Paris, 1961)

Guerrini, Maurice, *Napoleon and Paris* (London, 1970)

Hales, E. E. Y., *Napoleon and the Pope* (London, 1962)

Hales, E. E. Y., *Revolution and Papacy, 1769–1846* (London, 1960)

Hampson, Norman, *A Social History of the French Revolution* (London, 1963)

Hart, Liddell, *The Ghost of Napoleon* (London, 1933)

Herold, J. Christopher, *Bonaparte in Egypt* (London, 1963)

Holtman, Robert, *Napoleonic Propaganda* (Baton Rouge, 1950)

Holtman, Robert, *The Napoleonic Revolution* (Philadelphia, 1967)

Horne, Alistair, *How Far from Austerlitz? Napoleon 1805–1815* (London, 1996)

Howard, John Eldred (ed. and trans.), *Letters and Documents of Napoleon* (London, 1961–80)

Ingamells, John, *The Wallace Collection: Catalogue of Pictures, vol. II: French Nineteenth Century* (London, 1986)

Jardin, A. and Tudesq, A. J., *La France des notables, 1815–1848*, 2 vols (Paris, 1973)

Kauffman, Jean-Paul, *La chambre noire de Longwood* (Paris, 1997)

Kissinger, Henry, *A World Restored: Metternich, Castlereagh and the Problems of Peace, 1812–1822* (London, 1957)

Lacouture, Jean, *Champollion, une vie de lumières* (Paris, 1988)

Laissus, Yves, *L'Egypte, une aventure savante 1798–1801* (Paris, 1998)

Las Cases, Emmanuel De, *Les Mémorial de St-Hélène*, 2 vols (Paris, 1983)

Lavisse, Ernest (ed.), *Histoire de la France contemporaine*, t. 3, G. Pariset, *Le Consulat et l'Empire* (Paris, 1921).

Lefebvre, Georges, *Napoléon* (Paris, 1965)

Lefebvre, Georges, *The French Revolution*, 2 vols, trans. John Hall Stewart and James Friguglietti (London and New York, 1962 and 1964)

Louis-Napoleon, *Napoleonic Ideas* (New York, 1967)

Lucas-Dubreton, J., *Le Culte de Napoléon 1815–1848* (Paris, 1960)

Lucas-Dubreton, J., *La France de Napoléon* (Paris, 1981)

Lyons, Martyn, *Napoleon Bonaparte and the Legacy of the French Revolution* (New York, 1994)

Magraw, Roger, *France 1815–1914: The Bourgeois Century* (London, 1983)

Maland, David, *Culture and Society in Seventeenth-Century France* (London, 1970)

Mansel, Philip, *Paris between Empires, 1814–1852* (London, 2001)

Markham, Felix, *Napoleon* (London, 1963)

McLynn, Frank, *Napoleon* (London, 1998)

Millar, Sir Oliver, *Later Georgian Pictures in the Collection of Her Majesty the Queen*, 2 vols (London, 1969)

O'Dwyer, Margaret M., *The Papacy in the Age of Napoleon and the Restoration: Pius VII, 1800–1823* (London, 1985)

Paret, Peter (ed.), *The Makers of Modern Strategy: From Machiavelli to the Nuclear Age* (Princeton, 1986)

Prendergast, Christopher, *Napoleon and History Painting: Antoine Jean Gros' La Bataille d'Eylau* (Oxford, 1997)

Roberts, Warren, *David and the Revolution* (Chapel Hill, NC, 1989)

Rochette, Jean-Claude, and Poche, François, *Le Dôme des Invalides* (Paris, 1995)

Schama, Simon, *Citizens: A Chronicle of the French Revolution* (London, 1989)

Schama, Simon, *Patriots and Liberators: Revolution in the Netherlands (1780–1813)* (London, 1977)

Schroeder, Paul W., *The Transformation of Europe* (London, 1994)

Siegfried, Susan L., *The Art of Louis-Léopold Boilly: Modern Life in Napoleonic France* (New Haven and London, 1995)

Sutherland, D. M. G., *France 1789–1815: Revolution and Counter-Revolution* (London, 1985)

Thompson, J.M., *Napoleon Bonaparte, His Rise and Fall* (Oxford, 1963)

Thomson, David, *Europe since Napoleon* (London, 1957)

Thuillier, Guy, and Tulard, Jean, *Histoire de l'administration française* (Paris, 1984)

Thuillier, Guy, and Tulard, Jean, *Les écoles historiques* (Paris, 1990)

Tocqueville, Alexis de, *L'ancien régime* (Oxford, 1904)

Tomlinson, Janis A., *Francisco Goya y Lucientes* (London, 1994)

Tulard, Jean, *Dictionnaire Napoléon* (Paris, 1987)

Tulard, Jean, *La vie quotidienne des Français sous Napoléon* (Paris, 1978)

Tulard, Jean, *Procès-verbal de la cérémonie du Sacre et du Couronnement de Napoléon* (Paris, 1993)

Tulard, Jean, *Le Grand Empire* (Paris, 1982)

Tulard, Jean, *Napoleon: The Myth of the Saviour* (London, 1984)

Tulard, Jean, *Napoléon et la noblesse de l'Empire* (Paris, 1979)

Tulard, Jean, Fierro, Alfred, and Léri, Jean-Marc, *Napoléon et la peinture* (Paris, 1991)

Viennet, O., *Napoléon et l'industrie française* (Paris, 1947)

Villeneuve de Janti, Pierre, *Bonaparte et le Code Civil* (Paris, 1934)

Wilson-Smith, Timothy, *Delacroix: A Life* (London, 1992)

Wilson-Smith, Timothy, *Napoleon and His Artists* (London, 1996)

Woolf, S. J., *Napoleon's Integration of Europe* (London, 1991)

Zeldin, Theodore, *France 1848–1945, vol. I, Ambition, Love and Politics* (Oxford, 1973)

INDEX